# UNLEASH YOUR LIFE

## 166 Truths to Unlock Your Inner Peace, Freedom & Success

Bernadette Logue

Brought to you by:

**www.PinchMeLiving.com**

First Edition published in 2014 by Pinch Me Publishing

Cover image by iStockphoto.com

Cover design by Teddi Black

Edited by Caroline Webster

## Also by the Author:

*Pinch Me*

*Going Out on a Limb*

978-0-473-29721-3 (Paperback)

978-0-473-29722-0 (eBook)

A copy of this publication is available from the National Library of New Zealand.

# Contents

**INTRODUCTION**    7
Wake Up and Stand Up—Your Soul Needs You    7
Wake Up and Stand Up—Society Needs You    8
The Old World Model of Success    9
The New World Model of Success    10
Transitioning    11
Intrigue and Discomfort Go Hand-in-Hand    12
Avoidance Is Not the Answer    13
The Shift Starts Within    15
Cracks Start to Form    17
Courage Is Required    18
The Purpose of This Book    19

**YOUR JOURNEY**    21
Your Soul    22
Your Birth    23
Your Conditioning    23
Your Life Inside the Fog    25
Your Reality    27
Your Full Potential    29
Your Choice    30
Resistance and Judgment    31
Staying in the Fog    31
Dispel the Fog    32
Be a Leader    34
How I Unleashed My Life    34
Are You Ready to Unleash Your Life?    36

**PART I—SEE THE TRUTH**       **39**

Truth       39
Tuning into Your Soul       40
Never Hold Hard and Fast to Anything       41
166 Truths—A Solid Foundation for Thriving in
the New World       42
     Energy       43
     Love       61
     Humanity       70
     Soul       76
     Conscious Creating       104
     Reality       123
     Challenges       131
     Inner Peace       141
     Freedom       151
     Success       157
     Relationships       185

**PART II—CLEAR THE FOG**       **203**

Declaration       204
Letter of Commitment       204
Letting Go—Practical Exercises       206
Let Go of Hurt, Guilt, Regret and Resentment       207
Let Go of Resistance       211
Let Go of Painful Reactions       213
Let Go of Validating Yourself Externally       216
Let Go of Muting Yourself       219
Let Go of Excuses       223
Let Go of Limiting Beliefs       227
     400 Positive Affirmations to Support Inner
     Peace & Sense of Freedom       236
     300 Power Affirmations to Support Career &
     Professional Success       255
     166 Truths as Affirmations to Embed Your
     Unleashed Paradigm       272

**PART III—CREATE & BLOSSOM**     **283**
Your Purpose     284
Your Clean Slate     285
Your Soul Speaks to You     285
Soul Language Guides You in Every Aspect
of Your Life     286
Transforming Current Circumstances
and Navigating Forward     286
Giving Expression to Your Passion     286
Acting Upon Your Inspirations     291
Following Your Intuition     296
Creating Your Personal *Unleash Your Life*
Action Plan     299
Defining Your Values     300
Defining Your Life Anchors     302
9 Recommended Holistic Well-being Rituals     308
Your Life Map—The Life You Want to Live     322
Gap Identification     339
Chart Your Actions to Close the Gaps     340
Prioritizing and Effectively Managing Your Energy     341
Remain Completely Open to how Life May Unfold     343
7 Strategies for Slippage     344

**CONCLUSION**     **351**
About the Author     353

# INTRODUCTION

*"Three things cannot be long hidden:
the sun, the moon and the truth."*

— Buddha

**Wake Up and Stand Up—Your Soul Needs You**

How do you know when something needs fixing?

The answer is, "It's not working."

First, something has to be functioning below optimal level for you to notice it and question what is wrong. Then, with that awareness, you have a choice to make about whether to resolve it. Next, you investigate options for resolution, make decisions and take action accordingly.

If your life is balanced, peaceful, expressive and you feel fulfilled, it is unlikely that you are reading this book. Instead, assuming you are here looking for answers, it is likely that your search is driven by a sense that something within you or in your life is broken in some way, or you sense you are missing something—either inherently missing something in who you are or that you are missing a piece of the jigsaw puzzle in making sense of life. Alternatively, you may sense some greater possibility available to you beyond how you are currently being and what you are doing in your life right now.

This inner sense sits deep down inside of you, below the noise of your mind, and below the clamor and busy-ness of daily life. This inner sense has the potential to call out to you with a vein of excitement and possibility, as a motivating force inside to bring about transformation, guiding you to unleash yourself. But left unanswered, that positive energy turns dark and sits festering inside. It becomes unease. Sometimes it lies dormant, almost forgotten. Or, it quietly niggles at you, like an itch that never quite goes away. Other times it roars loudly and you can barely escape it. That unease is an inner call for answers. It is your intuition saying to you ... you do not have the full picture.

The longer you ignore this call from within, the louder it becomes. You are destined to eventually turn your attention onto this unease, to quench your thirst for answers.

Attending to the unease pushes you to seek out and absorb truth—truth about who you really are, what you are truly capable of and what is available to you in this life—and to then make choices about how to apply that truth. It is this process of learning and living from truth that allows you to set yourself free.

But first you must willingly wake up and stand up for yourself, to come to this point of your own freewill. No one can force awakening on you, just as you cannot force it on another. It is often when the inner call bellows so thunderously and the void can no longer be ignored that the process of awakening into full conscious living begins.

## Wake Up and Stand Up—Society Needs You

Our world is in disarray. Political systems, economic systems, financial systems, health systems, social systems, ecological systems, businesses, families and communities— imbalance is felt everywhere and by everyone. The systems that support and govern how we live our lives, which are meant to lift up humanity, are breaking down and not meeting the needs they were intended to serve.

It's easy to fall into a helpless and passive position, imagining the societal macrosystems we live within as giant, complex and faceless organisms, which no one has control over. Yet, these "systems" evolved from groups of people applying their knowledge and skills collectively. As groups of people, we created these systems, and we created all the issues arising out of these systems. The issues, of course, were not necessarily by design, but rather they came into existence by accident because of human unconsciousness in the way the systems were predicated and operated.

Collectively, we do have the power to create new systems, with new designs, as solutions to the issues we face. But here is one of the major blocks we face: Individually and collectively, we are trying hard to find solutions to problems by using the same type of approach and thinking that caused the problems in the first place. Unconsciousness creates issues and that same unconsciousness cannot resolve them.

Intelligent but controlling minds, without heart, without conscious awareness and without respect for age-old wisdom is what got us into this state of affairs, the imbalance we face in modern society. It is not anyone's fault. It is simply the outcome of unconsciousness, and part of our journey here in life, as we evolve as human beings, is to become more and more conscious, and to use that consciousness for the benefit of ourselves and all those around us. We are being asked to wake up and stand up collectively, to focus on a more collaborative and sustainable way of living together on the planet.

It is time to consider—what could be possible if we set the problems aside, in order to start over afresh?

We have the opportunity to make conscious awareness the space from which we create solutions and to draw upon age-old wisdom to inform those solutions. Not to fix old ways of operating, but to give rise to brand new ways of operating, to be led and nourished under a New World model of success, making the Old World model obsolete.

## The Old World Model of Success

The Old World model of success, which we are well overdue for a departure from, is characterized by unconsciousness, ego, force, dominance, quantity and productivity, competition, lack and limitation mind-set, painful reaction, perfectionism, status, image, a perception of everything and everyone as separate and the belief that when someone wins someone else loses.

This Old World model has seen our planet populated by people thinking, "What can I get?" as they operated from an "every man for himself" approach, under the sad illusion that external success would somehow be the primary solution for creating sustainable inner peace, freedom and happiness.

Thankfully, the number of people who still subscribe to this notion is diminishing, yet few individuals are translating that knowledge into action. Many people may feel their souls rising up and screaming out for a transition from this Old World model of success into a New World model of success, yet as a collective we somehow sleepily accept the old and deflect, avoid, despair and follow the crowd like sheep to the slaughter.

It no longer has to be this way. There is another way—a new model of what success looks like for both individual human beings, and for society as a collective.

## The New World Model of Success

The New World model sees the planet populated by people thinking, "What can I give?" while operating from an approach of "we're all in this together," and knowing with deep faith that inner peace and a sense of personal freedom are the engine room behind both sustainable external success and happiness.

This New World model of success is based upon consciousness, authenticity, integrity, collaboration, quality, balance, presence, intuition, well-being, peaceful response, allowing, true self-expression, abundant and limitless mind-set, heart-led behavior and decisions, the perception of everything and everyone as integrally linked energetically, and the knowledge that if one person authentically thrives then everyone benefits.

## Transitioning

It is time to think unconventionally in a conditioned and conventional world. It is time to be radical with what we imagine to be possible and to be courageous in our willingness to give 100 percent of ourselves to bring our visions into reality. It is time to stop numbing our conscience in order to follow the crowd. It is time to let the sense of possibility overwhelm the notion of giving up and accepting the status quo.

And here is where you come in. As much as this is true for the collective, and critically needed if we are to be a sustainably functioning humanity for generations to come, it is even more important for you personally in your own life right now, in the microsystems that make up the tapestry of your day-to-day experiences—from friends and family networks, to the work you do, your workplace and colleagues; from your financial situation to your physical, mental and emotional health. These are your personal "systems," which also need to be designed and operated from the New World model of success. If every person did this at the microlevel, imagine the impact on the collective.

People have become numb to the suffering created in the Old World way of being, living and working; they think it's normal and that it's "just how life is." There is an old saying that if you place a frog in boiling water, it will jump right out. Smart frog. That same anecdote suggests that if you place a frog in cold water and slowly bring the water to a simmer, then to a boiling point, the frog will get used to the incremental temperature change and be numb to the pain being inflicted upon it, eventually dying in that pot of boiling water.

You are the frog. If you stepped onto this planet right now for the first time, with no previous experience as a human being, and you observed your current way of life, you might well be shocked and want to jump right out! You might think it crazy what you have come to accept and consider as normal over your lifetime. You might wonder how anyone could bear to live that way, even with all the current successes and blessings you have—they mean very little if you do not have inner peace and you do not feel free.

You have slowly been brought to a boil since the day you were born, along with all the other frogs in the water with you. You are numb to, or resigned to, the various degrees of suffering in the ways you are being, living and working. You don't necessarily know there is another way to be and live. It's not your fault. No other frogs appear to be jumping out of the pot, at least not that you can see. So you stay there. And your staying there, in the boiling pot of water (the Old World model of success) will suffocate your soul. Your life and soul are just too precious for that, so it's time to make a choice ...

Humanity is slowly but surely splitting into two models of reality—the Old World and the New World. The split becomes more marked the more time passes. But do not mistake the word "split" for literal division. This is not about separation. Simply it means that people are seeing reality in two fundamentally different ways. The interpreted experiences of life that occur in both models are vastly different. You have to choose which world you want to belong to, and then proactively align your paradigm (your model of reality) and resulting actions with that. This process of shifting your paradigm holds the key to your inner peace, freedom and success. If you don't consciously choose, your non-choice is by default actually selecting to remain in the Old World.

## Intrigue and Discomfort Go Hand-in-Hand

It is understandable if you or other people in your life find this type of dialogue uncomfortable. It can be intriguing and confusing at the same time. It can be inspiring, uplifting and confronting all at once. It can seem clear and accessible in many ways, and yet bewildering in other ways.

Right now you might feel that it is idealistic to even consider that there could be a new way of living and operating in our world, a way that could give rise to better outcomes and have any level of positive impact in the face of rising tides of unrest. To that, I encourage you to leave your pessimism behind and to receive this book with an open mind—the only way new possibilities can become available to you. And, I encourage you to remember that you do not need to change the world in order to change the world. You can simply change yourself from the inside out. By doing so, you instantly change the world in which you live.

This is true in more ways than one. Firstly, when you transform from the inside out by shifting your perspective, then you view the world around you in brand new ways. Your reality has, in fact, changed. Secondly, when you create powerful transformation from the inside out, your personal change has a tangible impact upon the world in which you live. Your actions in this world will be different, thus creating change, even on a small scale. Your relationships will be different, thus creating change in other people, who then go on to create different outcomes themselves, impacting upon the world via a ripple effect. Thirdly, your personal energy vibration becomes different once you view the world through new eyes, and because our world is a living and breathing energy field of which you are an integral part, your energy sparks and lifts the overall vibration of the collective energy.

## Avoidance Is Not the Answer

There is a reason many people avoid this kind of discussion or path of awakening altogether. They are too afraid to look at anything that they don't like, don't understand or don't know how to fix, as they fear seeing the full extent of an issue and feeling helpless and disillusioned in the face of it.

Nowhere is this avoidance more evident than at an individual level when it comes to inner peace and happiness. If you feel a pervading sense of unease inside of yourself, like something needs to change, but you don't know what it is, it's natural to try to avoid that discomfort by not looking too closely at it. If you can't name the unease and the root cause of it, then it takes on a mysterious and scary quality. And how can you powerfully transform something if you don't even know what it is?

Society conditions us to believe that having all the answers is an incredibly important thing, like it is somehow weak to feel uneasy and to not know why, or to not know what to do. Often people err on the side of caution and decide that pretending the uneasy feeling doesn't exist is the safest and smartest course of action, and they hope that ignorance will be bliss.

Imagine for yourself how painful it might be if you went through a process of introspection to discover what questions you had about yourself, your life and the world, and to discover why you feel uneasy within, only to then reveal a gaping void within yourself that you couldn't understand and didn't know how to fill. It would be deeply unsettling to experience that. Your mind would avoid that happening at all costs. In self-protection, your mind would attempt to ignore feelings of uneasiness whenever they rose up, and it would ignore your intuition, which was telling you that there was something out of place, something missing or something more to be revealed. Instead, your mind would be obedient to what it has been conditioned to respect and align with your entire life: limiting beliefs, expectations, fear and societal conditioning—all of which warp your perception and tell you to put your head down and get on with it, to not elevate your intuition above your rational and logical mind and, most definitely, to ensure you toe the line in the way everyone else seems to be doing.

The message your mind sells you is this, "Please simply adhere to what is familiar and acceptable. This is your safest bet."

Your mind loves this approach. It wants the easy road. It wants to believe that what you perceive and experience as reality right now is the truth. It doesn't want to know there is any illusion or warped perception occurring. However, your mind may be ignorant to the fact that the "easy road" of downplaying or ignoring the uneasiness within actually comes at great cost to you—emotional pain and a feeling of soullessness, which echo in your daily life.

And yet still, in the face of that pain, your mind tells you to stop being weak. It tells you that everyone else has it together and that you should just get on with it. Your mind tells you that you're being ridiculous to expect that there is something more to life; it just is what it is. Your mind tells you to ride the mainstream—don't rock the boat, don't ask the big questions, don't go outside of the norm, don't risk what you have, don't let people see into your void; plaster a smile on your face, and everything will get better one day.

Your mind does this because it has been conditioned into a paradigm that does not serve you. Your mind convinces you to Band-Aid straight over the top of your symptomatic uneasy feeling, to cover the gaping void inside with anything that will distract you or give you a hit of pleasure to get you through.

But this is not a solution. It is a recipe for recurring pain and continuing default unconsciousness, which breeds and grows the more it is left unchecked. Ignorance, in this case, is not bliss.

## The Shift Starts Within

If you experience pain and dissatisfaction at any level, it is easy to point to external reasons as the cause, be it people, things, situations or circumstances. You may then go about changing those external factors in your life as the primary method for transforming your inner pain and dissatisfaction. However, the answer is not solely to shift your external experiences. The outer world alone is not causing your pain.

What is causing your pain?

It is your interpretation of everything and everyone, through the filter of your unique beliefs, thoughts and feelings, which causes your pain. This paradigm you live from, like a pair of colored lenses through which you see the world, either limits or unleashes you.

Of course you can remove yourself from what and who you do not like, you can craft what you do, how you do it and the environment within which you live, and yes these are important components of a happy life. That is called setting yourself up for success and being conscious about the life you design and live. But these external changes alone are never going to give you *sustainable* inner peace and sense of freedom. Why? Because no matter what you change outside of yourself, no matter where you go or what you do, you take your paradigm with you—you drag along your beliefs, thoughts and feelings just as they have always been, and you use them to interpret whatever new people, things, situations or circumstances you create and encounter.

When it comes to having inner peace, freedom and success, all of the external changes available to you are secondary to the primary focus.

What is the primary focus? You.

Few people realize they are held prisoner by their own paradigm. Even fewer realize they hold the key that unlocks the cell door.

If you can address the root cause of all your unease, pain and dissatisfaction, then you can stand in the face of *anything* in life and be at peace. That inner peace is your ultimate freedom, and it will drive your success in all areas of your life. Inner peace is energetically one of the most powerful states you can hold as a human being.

If your mind is trying to logically rationalize how an internal shift could be more important and exponentially more powerful than a shift in your external experience, then consider this ... as you stare into a mirror and see a sad face, you do not reach out to wipe the mirror and draw a new smiling face over it. Instead, you recognize that the reflection mirrors your inner state of being.

Unleashing your life is exactly the same. It is about looking within yourself to pull back the illusionary veil you have been living behind and seeing what is true about yourself for the first time. It is about rising out of the warped, illusionary paradigm you have been living within mentally and emotionally, and going beyond limiting beliefs, expectations, fear and societal conditioning—to wake up, live consciously and see reality as it actually is.

If, from that awakened and empowered state, you desire to make changes in your outer world, then embrace the urge and take targeted action to facilitate the transformations you long for.

## Cracks Start to Form

You have been shackled by a limiting paradigm for as long as you can remember. The irony is that most people who are shackled have no idea that they are shackled! It is unconsciousness that keeps you stuck, and unconsciousness by its very nature has no awareness of itself. It is a vicious cycle.

The uneasy feeling of the void within is one of the main mechanisms that can trigger your awakening. It can break through the unconsciousness to start the transformative process, alongside equally powerful triggers such as intense loss, challenge, pain and suffering, or a complete breakdown of self or circumstances—all of which can create cracks in the illusionary veil you have been living behind. This is when pain of any nature serves a powerful and illuminating purpose.

In the face of the uneasy feeling, it is your willingness to stare into that void within and hear all your deeply held questions without having answers or any guarantee of resolution that actually allows solutions to manifest seemingly out of nowhere. To get answers, you have to be willing to allow space for answers to come to you. You have to open your eyes and ears to receive them. It is your capacity to courageously open your mind up to entirely new ways of perceiving that is key to setting you free.

This you can do. This is entirely possible. It is your choice. If you are not willing, you are simply not ready and that is completely fine. People unshackle and come into their power at the moment that is best for them. That point often comes when the uneasiness, void, pain or suffering becomes so intolerable that there is no option left but to surrender and fling open your arms, heart and mind to the possibility of a better way, a more truthful way of perceiving, being and living. That is the awakening—the light of your consciousness begins to emerge when cracks form in the illusion you previously accepted as "reality," bringing into question the only way in which you previously viewed the world.

The change starts from within, always, and emanates outwards. It is like a lighthouse switches on inside of you in the dead of a dark night, illuminating the previously disorienting pitch-black landscape you had been trying hard to navigate through.

## Courage Is Required

Even when you awaken, unleashing your life still takes courage; to fully unleash yourself, you must first strip down to your core and allow yourself to be vulnerable, existing without attachment to anything you have previously been, done, experienced or believed.

Why must awakening involve such dramatic detachment from all that has gone before? Why must it involve such vulnerability?

Because this book is not called, *How to Make Your Life a Little Bit Better than Bad.*

And it is not about how to live your life with a little less drama and pain.

And it is equally not about how to be successful while avoiding your blocks.

This book is about how to unleash your life. It is about playing a big game, not playing small. It is about showing up fully in your life, not mucking around thinking there's plenty of time to figure it out later in the hope that you will find a cushier and easier way to get around your questions, challenges and issues. It is about taking ownership of your "stuff," not hiding away and hoping someone will ride in to save the day.

To unleash yourself is to build a brand new foundation of truths to stand upon, recognizing all the untruths that you have previously believed in and built your life upon and letting go of all that has limited you in the past that does not align with your new foundation of truths. All of this so that you might finally see yourself and your life through fully conscious and informed eyes, allowing you to navigate forward powerfully.

## The Purpose of This Book

This book has been designed to

- trigger within you transformational shifts in your consciousness and paradigm—to help you see your world as it truly is and form a New World model of reality;
- echo age-old wisdom that your soul knows but your mind may not;
- give rise to an emotionally charged sense of massive possibility for yourself and your life;
- offer you motivation;
- tap the courage within you to be who you authentically are, which allows you to do what you love with passion— indeed ... to live your life unleashed;
- provide you with practical exercises and tools to do just that, so that you can develop your own unique *Unleash Your Life* action plan for implementation going forward.

The format of this book is based upon the 3-Step *Unleash Your Life* method for unlocking your inner peace, freedom and success:

Part I—See the Truth: Reconnect to age-old wisdom and build a solid new foundation of understanding.

Part II—Clear the Fog: Apply the truth to let go and break free of your limiting paradigm.

Part III—Create & Blossom: Redefine your life to live with clear vision and inspired actions.

# YOUR JOURNEY

*"Make no mistake about it—enlightenment is a destructive process. It has nothing to do with becoming better or being happier. Enlightenment is the crumbling away of untruth. It's seeing through the facade of pretense. It's the complete eradication of everything we imagined to be true."*

— Adyashanti

What if what you believe to be true about yourself, about other people, about life and about this world you live in, isn't true?

What if it is an illusion created by your mind?

What if the illusion keeps you from living the life you were destined for?

What if there is more than one version of reality happening right now, and the version you are living within—by choice or by accident—is completely limiting you?

What if the illusion you live within keeps you playing it safe, uninspired and unfulfilled? What if it is keeping you small, fearful and blocked from living on purpose and with passion?

What if you were to learn age-old truths that so many have strayed from or forgotten, truths that would establish a brand new powerful paradigm for you, setting you free from illusion and literally allowing you to step into a whole new reality, indeed a whole new world, as a new you?

What if you were here in life on a journey, and that journey involved coming to know these truths for yourself, in a way that set you free from limitation, unleashing your life from the inside out?

What if that journey was the very purpose for your being here—for learning, for evolution, for you to discover that you actually have the inherent power within you to either limit yourself or unleash yourself?

What if right now you are exactly where you are meant to be in that journey of awakening?

What does this journey look like? Let's examine it ...

## Your Soul

Your soul is the essence of who you are. It is your spirit. It is a unique energy, with a distinctive imprint of experiences, wisdom and gifts, having travelled a specific journey of lifetimes to this point, walking a path now that no one else will ever walk.

Your soul goes beyond who you know yourself to be. You are more than the body and mind you find yourself living within in this lifetime. You are more than the name and personality you accept as "you." You are more than the face you see in the mirror staring back at you.

Your soul is not bound by the constructs that define and rule life in our tangible world; it exists beyond location, time and physical laws.

Your soul has lived before and may live again. It has chosen to be here at this time for a purpose. It breathes life into every part of your physical form for that exact reason.

When it chose to be here, that choice was crucial. Whether willingly or reluctantly, your soul knew that lessons were to be learnt and contributions were to be made in this physical existence of life—for the betterment of your soul evolution and for the betterment of all.

Your lifetime is about remembering who you really are and what you are here for, and for mustering the courage to live those truths wholeheartedly.

## Your Birth

When you first arrived here, in your soul's chosen place and time, you were a bright and vibrant energy. Your mind and body connection to the soul part of yourself was fresh and strong.

You came imprinted with, and connected to, universal wisdom (as all souls are), as well as carrying your unique soul knowledge accumulated from past lifetime experiences.

Birth was the time when you were actually more nonphysical than you were physical. You were more spirit and essence than body. Your soul was naturally at the forefront, and your mind was a quiet little sponge, dwelling in the background, ready to awaken and absorb.

## Your Conditioning

And then the conditioning began. You observed the world around you—situations, people, expressions, emotions, challenges, outcomes, labels, stories, words ... and you absorbed it all. Your mind, a tool that you were blessed with, took on the busy and necessary job of processing everything you saw and heard in order to make sense of life.

No matter how loving and enlightened your upbringing was, your mind formed beliefs about who you are—your value, worthiness, capability, safety, security, wants and needs, and not all of those beliefs were positive. You formed perspectives of what the world is about, how to "get by" in this world and what it means to be good and successful.

You formed expectations of *how* you should be, and indeed *who* you should be, based on those beliefs, and based on the overt and covert expectations of your family, friends, peers and society, which bombarded you every waking moment of every day. A look here, an opinion there, advice on tap, a well-crafted maze of marketing and advertising everywhere— all leading you to believe that there is some *way* that you need to be other than how you naturally are, and all leading you to believe there is *someone* you need to be, other than who you already are.

Fear set in, perhaps not consciously, but at a deeper level. Cautiousness. A sense of needing to change yourself. A sense of needing to self-protect and be on guard. A sense that all was not safe. An uneasiness in your personal and professional endeavors, driving your actions or lack of action. In many cases, clearly defined fears began to emerge. Fear of not being enough. Fear of not doing enough. Fear of other people. Fear of the future. Fear of the past repeating. Fear of failure. Fear of things. Fear of situations that your mind deemed to be unsafe. Alongside your limiting beliefs and the weight of expectations, fear became the crippling straw that broke the camel's back.

This conditioning formed like a metaphorical fog that shrouded you, grey and heavy as it closed in on you. This fog was the paradigm through which you perceived everything in life, including yourself. It colored your entire experience of life, whether you were aware of it or not. It became your version of reality.

This fog created a sense of separation between you and the outer world and, worse yet, a gaping chasm between your soul and your physical self, to the point where you no longer resonated with yourself (in thought and feeling) as a soul first and foremost. You came to operate primarily as a physical human being run by your mind, unaware of your true soul nature.

The more time passed, the further the fog thickened and trapped you. You started to believe you were your mind, that everything that went on in your head was who you actually were. Your mind came to dominate the driver's seat position in your life, as you obeyed what it believed was best (as observed from the cloudy and warped perspective of your fog of limiting beliefs, expectations, fear and societal conditioning), and your soul was relinquished to a quiet and dark corner somewhere far behind.

There your soul lay buried ... for a time.

## Your Life Inside the Fog

With a fully loaded set of beliefs, some helpful but many limiting, and conditioned by your upbringing and interactions "out there" in the world, you were formed into who you think you are today. Every new experience is viewed through those beliefs.

Unconsciously looking for evidence to support your existing view of the world, you soak up anything that aligns to your paradigm and use it as fuel to back your beliefs about yourself and life, more deeply embedding what you assume to be true. This, combined with the expectations you bear weightily upon your shoulders (your own expectations of yourself and of life, and the expectations other people have of you), means that you find yourself unwittingly living as a conditioned human being within a version of reality that limits you, rather than as the bright soul full of wisdom and gifts that you really are, unlimited and unleashed.

Life inside the fog is confusing. You know what doesn't work for you and what habits keep you down, but you can't seem to rise beyond these. It may appear that you sabotage yourself, but not consciously, and you have no idea why it keeps happening, or why the same negative patterns repeat over and over. You feel imbalanced, with obvious impacts upon your physical, mental and emotional well-being. You feel like you have to force things to happen, and you regularly resist how life is going for you.

As you walk through life living within your fog, you have completely forgotten who you really are—the astonishing miracle that you are, and you have forgotten the fundamental truths upon which our world is based, which feed your ability to thrive as a soul. But listen closely ...

It is not your fault, and the perfect time to stand up and wake up is right now.

There are many people in the world who would rather you didn't wake up and remember the truth. There are people in our world that rely upon you being unconscious and conditioned in order to fit their preferred model of reality.

The well-being, sanity and peace of mankind depends on every single one of us being willing to wake up. If we are to thrive, and our children are to thrive, and their children are to thrive, then we need as many people as possible stepping up to explore who they really are and how our universe fundamentally operates, in order to start living conscious, loving, fully unleashed lives. Anything less, founded upon foggy illusion, is cheating ourselves, and we will continue to witness the negative effects of this in all areas of our lives—in our relationships, in our health, in our careers and businesses, in our communities, in the macrosystems that run and support our countries and in the delicate natural systems of this beautiful planet that supports human life.

The absurdity is that life inside the fog is like living inside an illusion with no idea that there is any illusion. It is like looking into a distorted circus mirror and believing that what you see reflected is true, and then living your life in alignment with the distortion. The fog, like the circus mirror, warps your view of reality.

The fog is entirely created by, and based upon the contents and operation of, your mind and your mind's perception of absolutely *everything*. Your mind creates what you see, what you hear, what you know, what you believe, what you think, what you feel and what you do.

Your mind did the best it could. It absorbed and tried to make sense of everything you experienced and witnessed. Your mind soaked up the well-meaning advice and opinions from all those that had gone before you. The problem is that those who went before you were also conditioned and living within the fog, with few exceptions.

Wouldn't it be just a little more than ironic if those exceptions—the people who were seen throughout the centuries as odd outliers, heretics, crazy mystics or dreamers—were actually living in the center, and the conditioned masses were, in fact, the ones outlying the truth?

## Your Reality

Every person on this planet is unique. The molding of each individual's mind is, to a certain extent, also unique. We all perceive life and the world around us through our own paradigm. As a result, there is no single accepted version of "reality." The majority of people live within their own fog-based reality, however dense and dark it is. Imagine that ... over seven billion people, over seven billion unique perceptions of life and the world; thus, over seven billion different realities occurring at the same time. It's little wonder that people make vastly different choices and experience vastly different results; essentially we could all be living on completely different planets based on how we experience the world.

The powerful point is this: You can perceive life in any way you choose. When you shift your perceptions, your life changes dramatically. You literally shift into a whole new world, a whole new reality, as a whole new you, because you decided to. Your consciously chosen paradigm is what takes you there. No one can stop you. No one.

The more you clear the foggy, limiting paradigm, the less there is to cloud you from expressing out into this world as the real you, as the unleashed you.

Your foggy mind is a breeding ground for inner pain. Your free mind, clear of the fog, is a breeding ground for inner peace. Your life is either a fortress of illusions controlled by your mind, or it is an open landscape of truths overseen by your soul. You make the choice of whether you live in the fortress or in the open landscape. Your choice will create either pain or peace.

Let's say that you choose to live in the fortress controlled by the mind. You need to accept that your experiences and the quality of your life will be entirely defined by that choice.

For example, if your perspective from within the fog is that things go wrong because life isn't fair, you are in pain. If another person's perspective, from a life unleashed, is that things "go wrong" in order to clear a path for greater, more soul-aligned opportunities, then they are at peace.

If your perspective from within the fog is that love has to be earned and love from others is necessary in order to feel whole and complete or to validate who you are, then you will experience pain. If another person's perspective, from a life unleashed, is that we are all rooted in love, that we are all valid, valued, whole and complete no matter what, then they are at peace.

If your perspective from within the fog is that the world is a challenging place and opportunities are limited, you will perceive each day through this paradigm and easily find evidence to support your view, and you will experience pain. If another person's perspective, from a life unleashed, is that the world is a supportive place designed for us to awaken and thrive, and opportunities are abundant for those that welcome them, they will perceive each day through this paradigm and easily find evidence to support this view; they will experience peace, excitement, inspiration and joy.

All human experience derives meaning from the mind. With your mind, you perceive what happens around you. You align what you observe with your beliefs, processing thoughts that arise from that belief programing, and living with the resulting feelings. All suffering is based in perception. Without your mind giving you the ability to perceive and process, there is no way pain can exist. There is also no way that peace can exist. It is a double-edged sword, with your experience entirely dependent upon whether you are inside the fog or free of it.

Many people have forgotten that they are souls having a human being experience, with the ability to use the mind as a tool to navigate and fulfill their soul journeys, and instead have become lost in the fog, being used by their minds, and experiencing pain as they resist, push, question, fight and force.

## Your Full Potential

Your soul, imprinted with its unique set of wisdom and gifts, is here to make a contribution to this world (your service to others), and to learn lessons for your evolution along the way (your service to yourself). That full contribution is achieved, and those lessons are fully learnt, by being the true expression of who you really are, beyond your conditioned mind.

This full expression means living your life uninhibited, choosing to be exactly who you naturally are, unapologetically, without being blocked by, or adapting yourself to fit within, limiting beliefs, expectations, fear and societal conditioning.

What does it mean to live as the full expression of who you really are? This statement is touted often in personal growth materials, but what do you actually do to turn it into practical reality in your life?

To be the full expression of who you are means tuning into and honoring your instincts—playing out your passions, acting upon inspirations and following your intuition. It means paying close attention to your feeling guidance system. All of these are ways in which your soul communicates with you. This is how the divine realm, the plane of higher consciousness from where your soul energy stems, channels through you to co-create with you in this life, to give expression into the physical world.

It is by living from this true essence, unleashed, and using your mind as a navigation tool (as a servant, *not* a master), that you live in the way your soul intended.

If you wish to bring your soul essence from the intangible realm into the physical world—to share all that you have to offer and to learn all that you can on your journey—then you begin the process now with a choice.

## Your Choice

Every person on this planet, including you, has to consciously and willingly make a choice. The choice is to see the mind-made fog of limiting perception for what it is (an illusion, which holds no power unless you give it such power), and rediscover the fundamental age-old truths that will set you free—the reality of how life on earth really works and the process by which you can grow into the fullness of what was intended for you in this life. These age-old truths are universal wisdom; they belong to no one and everyone at the same time.

Until this choice for awakening is made, the fog will continue to suppress your ability to be fully expressed, blocking your soul wisdom, gifts, passions, inspiration and intuition from freely making their way from your soul essence through you (as the channel) out into the world.

Once you decide to inform yourself with universal wisdom and see the fog for the giant, painful illusion that it is, you can never go back. Once you pull back the veil and resonate with the fundamental truths of life, you will never again be the same. Your paradigm will shift, and you will be ready to live moment by moment in a whole new world, as a whole new you.

This doesn't mean that you become an untouchable Zen being in a constant state of peaceful bliss. It also doesn't mean that you won't have challenges. All the factors in the external world around you that led to your original conditioning will still exist, but it is your new awareness of them and your conscious choices that allow you to remain clear of the fog, anchored in truth, rather than being sucked back in as your mind witnesses all the stimuli that trigger old conditioning.

The truths and your conscious awareness, partnered together, are your pathway toward inner peace, true freedom and success from the inside out.

## Resistance and Judgment

The fog has, at some point in time, had all of us stuck. Even if you have had great success and happiness based on external experiences, as long as you live within the limitations of harmful mind conditioning and are, thus, blinded by the fog, you will continue to be blocked from your *fullest* potential and subject to bouts of inner pain and suffering to various degrees.

Considering this concept of the fog and how it has limited you, you might be feeling the urge to label it as bad or to declare that it shouldn't be that way. You may want to look for someone to blame for your fog. Any upsetting feelings in relation to the fog are due to your foggy perspective. That is the fog playing out in relation to how you perceive the fog! This is ironic, amusing and frustrating all at the same time. Rest assured that there is nothing negative, upsetting or wrong about being stuck in the fog. It just is. All interpretation about it is just that, interpretation.

## Staying in the Fog

There are people in our world right now, and possibly people in your own networks, who prefer to remain stuck. They like the comfort of what they believe to be true, even if it is an illusion and the cause of some pain. They resist anything that threatens to crack open reality as they know it.

Some people cling for dear life to what they know and fight hard to hold and protect their position and version of reality. They are unwilling to give up anything in order to meet the truth, not their limiting beliefs and habitual negative thought patterns, nor their sense of security, image or ego. Instead of choosing life unleashed, full possibility and soaring to the greatest heights as their soul intended (even beyond what current success and happiness they may have experienced), they choose to remain in the fog.

It might seem insane. Why would anyone choose to live in an illusion over meeting the truth? The answer is this ... because it appears familiar and therefore safe, regardless of how uncomfortable or painful that illusion might be from time to time. The comfort zone that some operate from has an electric high voltage perimeter fence, which they obediently stay within. Fear runs that fence and so, for those living within that comfort zone, fear runs their lives.

There are also people living in the fog who do not sense anything amiss. They are completely addicted to the fog. Perhaps they will not wake up in this lifetime at all. They are not yet able to help themselves because they identify so completely with their minds and view their perspective as being the only reality available to them. No one has the right to say there is anything wrong with that or with them. There isn't. Awakening occurs differently for each soul.

The paradox is that the seemingly safe and comfortable fog, which appears as such due to its level of familiarity, is the cause of every ounce of pain and suffering that mankind has ever experienced, or will ever experience. The fog dims our uniqueness that we were put on this planet to express, keeping us trapped in unhelpful ways of thinking, feeling and behaving, and it leads us to participate in utterly unnecessary conflict with others, operating as though we are separate from one another, rather than part of an energetically, integrally linked collective humanity.

Where is the heart of humanity? Where is the ability for each of us to see our own likeness in those surrounding us? Where is compassion not just for those we love, but also for every person?

The heart of humanity is represented in the soul of every single person walking this earth; for every person in the fog; that slice of humanity is suffocated.

## Dispel the Fog

While there are people who may not wake up, you are not one of them! The fact that you chose to read about how to unleash your life means you are already part of the emerging consciousness that continues to grow and gain momentum, boosting the New World.

You may feel confusion or a sense of resistance as you read on, but you are still reading, so somewhere within you your soul is stirring and calling out to reclaim its position in the driver's seat of your life, and you are connecting to that feeling rising within.

As you read the one hundred and sixty six truths in Part I, you may notice yourself resonating with what seems to your mind like new information or perspectives well beyond your currently accepted view of reality, but, at the same time, they may also *feel* familiar and/or true as they pierce to the core of you. The reason the truths resonate is because they are the wisdom of the ages, which your soul knows, and the resonance you feel is soul-level recognition vibrating through your being. That inner knowing is nothing that your mind can reason or explain. And the beauty of awakening to truth in this way is this ... not even the most resistant and conditioned foggy mind can stop a stirring soul. Truth has the power to dispel the fog.

And when it dispels, what is left is a clear channel through which your soul can finally shine out into the world beyond, with you powerfully living out your full unique expression, sending all of your creative energy in the direction of all you desire, with nothing to suppress, block or dilute you.

The one vital thing you can do right now for yourself, for all those you love, for society and for this planet, is to make your own self-awareness and conscious living your highest priority. To live your life in alignment with truth. This is the key to cultivating inner peace, creating true freedom and generating success from the inside out. It is natural. It is your birthright. It is what is intended for you. And it is magnetic, because, as the light of your unleashed consciousness shines brighter, you in turn illuminate the way for others to see what is possible for them as well.

## Be a Leader

If you have your own precious children or are around young people in any capacity, please, for the love of all things, own your personal passage out of the fog. For their sake, shine bright like a full moon in the deep of night.

Children are like sponges for the words they hear. But, more importantly, they are like the all-seeing eye. They witness how you behave (not just toward them, but generally), and they are formed by what they see. They miss nothing.

Each of us has a responsibility to not only clear our own fog, but to do what is within our capacity to help the young people in our lives stay clear of the fog in the first place. Imagine how your present life would be if someone else had done that for you.

When we see children's limiting beliefs begin to form and play out, we can offer new perspectives and help them remember their own true nature. When we desire to express our love for them, we can remember that love is all they need, not expectations. When we see their fear, we can help them understand what fear really is and how to walk through it. And when we educate them at school and at home, and send them out into the world, we can do so in a way that puts the emphasis on awareness, presence, conscious living and freedom to be, do and express just as they are. We can support them to embrace their own uniqueness, not force them to meet a societally accepted version of what "normal" looks like and lives like.

This evolution can happen all at once if our generation makes conscious living our top priority, if we embrace the New World.

## How I Unleashed My Life

I wrote this book for you because I know what it feels like to live a limited life—to be restricted by negative beliefs, to feel the weight of expectations, to be afraid and to have life decisions unwittingly influenced by societal conditioning.

I also know what it feels like to radically unleash one's life. I did that for myself and I want that for you. I personally drew upon the age-old wisdom shared in this book, and I know what a transformational impact it has when you awaken to, and live from, such truths.

Remembering back to the years before I unleashed, I felt like my life was missing true meaning. I felt a sense of emptiness within. While I had external success in various areas, I had other dreams for my life but wasn't living them. No matter how hard I worked, how busy I kept myself, how much money I earned, how many possessions I accumulated, how much recognition I strived for, where I went or what I did, none of it changed the core of my underlying thoughts and feelings. Inside I was experiencing low-level fear and anxiety. I was a worrywart about everything and carried that level of tension both physically and emotionally. I was extremely conservative and avoided risk at all cost. I did my best to hide all of this from everyone, by looking and acting completely "together" on the outside and focusing on being grateful for what I had. Over the years, I managed as well as I could to process whatever life "threw at me," from loss and grief, to unexpected health issues and career challenges. All the while, I tried to control whatever I could in order to feel at peace.

Then, I woke up. There came a point when the unease within me hit an all-time high and I finally answered the call when it screamed too loudly for me to ignore.

I began to drastically alter my inner paradigm and completely change my outer circumstances. This happened over several years, when I started to pay attention to, and align with, my soul and its intuitive nudges. I redesigned my life— starting again from a blank slate, saying no to anything within myself or outside of myself that did not serve me, and saying yes to everything that did. I began living consciously.

Through various phases, my career changed beyond recognition. I discovered my deepest passions and built a business around it. My health improved remarkably. My network of relationships expanded and deepened. I travelled the world. I put myself in the face of my major fears in order to show myself that those fears could not stop me from living a life unleashed. I systematically worked on identifying my limiting beliefs and transformed them to empowering new beliefs. I defined my own values and vision to live by, to replace the societal norms that had not worked for me. I chose a lifestyle that I intuitively knew was best for my mind, body and spirit. The full story of how I changed my life, with the highs and lows of that journey, is shared in my earlier books— *Pinch Me* and *Going Out on a Limb*.

Irrespective of the extent of positive external changes I created in my life, the most profound change, for which I am forever grateful, was the shift in my paradigm. My journey of discovering the truths shared in this book, and living those truths in my daily life, led me to my true nature. And, when you live from your true nature, you come to know firsthand what it feels like to experience inner peace, freedom and success.

## Are You Ready to Unleash Your Life?

Rather than consider that there is anything to fix about yourself in order to live your life unleashed, please recognize that it is merely that the light of your wondrous true nature has been hidden below layers and layers of mind conditioning. All you need to do is shed the layers for the light to appear, so that it may grow and shine brighter and brighter.

You are a powerful creator, a wise and loving soul and a perfectly imperfect human being (as we all are, by design), who knows at a deep level all that you need to know in order to be at peace and thrive in this world.

To live the life you desire, you must simply be willing to let go of all that you no longer need. So the question begs, what are you personally willing to let go of in order to break free from the fog and live as the bright and vibrant soul that you were born as?

You came into this world with nothing. You will leave with nothing. There is no need to cling onto anything—not your beliefs, your thoughts, your feelings, your expectations, your fear, your past, your future, your relationships, your material belongings, your titles, your labels, your societally dictated identities, your reputation, your status, nor your ego. The tighter you grip on, the more white knuckled you are, the more pain you will experience.

Please, release your grip. You have a window of time here on earth, as your soul continues to breathe life through you. It is a small and fleeting window in relation to the eternity of all that is. What you fill your time with from birth to death is your unique message to the world.

What will that message be?

When you were born, your soul knew the answer to this question. Living in the fog, you may no longer feel connected to your soul, and it may seem like you have forgotten what your message to the world is.

Now is your time to remember ...

# PART I
# SEE THE TRUTH
## Reconnect to age-old wisdom and build a solid new foundation of understanding

*"You never change things by fighting the existing reality. To change something, build a new model that makes the existing model obsolete."*

— Richard Buckminster Fuller

**Truth**

In this book, I share ideas, wisdom, messages and realities, and I call them "truth" in a definitive, direct way. I make no apology for doing so. I am writing and speaking as part of my own purpose for being in this world, offering what my soul resonates with as truth from a place beyond what my logical mind can explain to you. I share what has been passed on to me in life and what has been passed through to me in spirit.

I do not want you to buy into what I tell you. I do not want you to subscribe to my view of the world. I do not want you to believe that what I am sharing with you is true because I put a label on it called "truth" and therefore you should feel compelled to agree with it.

Instead, I want you to experience *your own truth* in life, to willingly undo your mind of what you currently accept to be true and real, just for a moment, and to allow yourself to see yourself, life and this world from a different angle. Then, from that moment of new perspective, I wish for you to make up your own mind afresh about what you see presented before you and notice what resonates with you at a deeper level far below your thinking mind.

## Tuning into Your Soul

In everyday life, heavy emphasis is typically placed upon the use of logic, fact and intellect. And without diminishing their critical place in our experience of life as tools for interpreting, understanding and decision making, there remains a massive gaping hole if that is the only way one perceives and navigates life. You are not just a physical body with a mind. You are a soul having a human being experience. Your soul uses the vehicle of your body, with your mind and feelings, as your navigational system on the journey.

Your body and mind are well versed in functioning with five powerful physical senses through which they receive this three-dimensional life experience. And yet, there is something called intuition, your soul sense, which is your sixth sense for recognizing valuable information and guidance to support your journey. Some people call it your inner knowing or inner voice. It comes from the soul aspect of who you are, beyond your mind and body. It is the part of you that is intricately connected to, indeed that which comes from and is one with, infinite universal wisdom and higher consciousness. That part of yourself has the ability to decipher truth in ways that your logical mind cannot explain or understand, and likely never will. Moreover, your logical mind will often do all it can to suppress or ignore that intuition, particularly so in cases when intuition does not align with the foggy paradigm your mind is so used to operating from. If your intuition grates up against the limiting beliefs, expectations, fear and societal conditioning that your mind accepts as real, then it is no wonder it gets ignored.

As you read the truths presented in this book, I encourage you to tune into your own intuition to *sense* for yourself the validity and benefit of the information. Pay attention to whether the truths *feel* true and real for you, and whether they *feel* applicable and beneficial in your own life.

## Never Hold Hard and Fast to Anything

*"A mind is like a parachute. It does not work if it is not open."* — Frank Zappa

Keeping an open mind is guaranteed to serve you well. The second you close your mind to other perspectives, you lock in your existing paradigm and freeze-frame the reality you are experiencing. Nothing new can enter your life experience that does not align with your paradigm. It simply cannot. You will not see it, you will not hear it, and you will not perceive it— because it does not align with your version of reality.

Have an open mind while reading this book. Be willing to see yourself and life from a new perspective. Have an open mind as you formulate a new foundation of truths that best serve you as you walk your path forward.

I encourage you to have an open mind to the extent that you remain completely unattached to these truths that you are about to read. Even if they lift you up and appear to be the best possible reality you could live from, please do not grip on to them like they are your new saving grace. Why?

Because it benefits you to never be wedded to any perspective so hard and fast that you limit yourself from considering and exploring even greater, deeper, wiser views and truths that may be presented to you on your journey forward in this world. Every moment of your life is an opening for new insight, but only if you allow it.

Consider the idea that you can have a new foundation of truths that serve you in this life as a powerful paradigm, and at the same time have a completely open mind that continuously welcomes further insight, different perspectives, evolving understanding and deepening wisdom through ongoing reflection and resonance.

Life is a constant process of learning, growing, letting go, exploring and elevating understanding, shifting realities each moment as you come to see yourself and life in new light. This happens constantly. Why? Because you are not a static being. You are a dynamic, evolving being by your inherent nature.

As the seasons of your mind evolve, so the seasons of your life change. Each time, your version of reality refreshes. Then the next scene in the movie of your life begins to play out. If you want to progress in your movie, and not keep replaying the same old scene, then you must continue to evolve in your paradigm; this is best achieved with an open mind.

## 166 Truths—A Solid Foundation for Thriving in the New World

Having established that your paradigm dictates your reality, to shift into the New World right now, shift your paradigm. That is—shift your perception. That perception is based on what you believe. Therefore, if founded upon limiting beliefs and illusions (untruths), you are stuck.

To enter into and thrive in the New World, connect back to age-old universal wisdom, to spiritual truths that will create a solid new foundation of understanding from which to live your life. These truths will dispel the fog, thus opening the most important door you will ever pass through ... the door into your new soul-aligned reality.

As you read the forthcoming one hundred and sixty six truths, I invite you to notice if your mind wants to control the reading experience by analyzing the information and lining it up for comparison against your present circumstances, your past experiences or your limiting beliefs. It does that in order to accept or reject everything it observes in accordance with its current limiting paradigm. This is habit. Your mind will process in the way it is used to processing. That is what it does, at least until you teach it a new way.

- To create room for a shift to take place within you, simply open your mind and heart as you read, and say to yourself, "What if this were true?" Be willing to take these truths and "try them on for size." Let yourself absorb and *feel* your way through the material.
- You may wish to write down any questions or concerns that arise from within you as you read, to empty your mind as things come up, with plans to revisit your notes

after reading the book. Writing in this way, as you read, will help free up space inside of you, mentally and emotionally, to focus all your energy instead on discovery and exploration.

- You may also wish to write down any new insights that these truths unlock, about yourself and your life. Notice what new possibilities and paths open up for you in relation to each area of your life as you review these truths.
- And, finally, whenever you notice any of the following terms, please know that they are all referring to one in the same—source, source energy, universal energy, the universe, divinity, highest consciousness, creator, God.

## Energy

### Truth #1—Everything Is Energy

Everything that exists in your experience of life is energy. The planet, every human, every animal, every plant, every physical object, every living and nonliving thing—at their core foundation, they all consist of energy matter. The way in which that energy behaves is what causes it to show up in different forms and densities.

Not only is all of creation a fabric of energy seen in various physical forms and densities, but creation also consists of unseen waves of energy. Your own consciousness is constantly creating and sending out energy waves, based upon your beliefs, thoughts and feelings. You cannot hold your beliefs, thoughts or feelings. You cannot see your beliefs, thoughts or feelings. And yet, their energy is real, and their creative power and influence is real.

The fabric of universal energy, underpinning all of creation, is nothing short of miraculous. It is intelligent, divine and self-organizing. It gives life and supports life. As source energy is miraculous, and you at all levels of your being are comprised of that same energy, you are also miraculous.

## Truth #2—Everything Is Energetically Connected

While all people and things have physical form independent of each other, completely separate as far as your eyes can see, because all of creation has the same underlying substance (energy), everything is, in fact, intricately connected.

No matter what physical reality shows you, I am intricately connected to you, and you to me, because we have taken form out of the same fabric of energy. We are just like drops of water taken from one large pool of water, each drop holding its own shape and form. Yet, all are intricately linked because of their shared origin, fundamentally identical in their core substance.

## Truth #3—Shifts in Energy in One Place Have Influential Ripple Effects

Due to all aspects of life sharing the same one energy source, manifest into different forms, that interconnectedness means that a change in energy in one place has a ripple effect, flowing outward to influence all energetically connected matter.

Having established that you are energy and that you are energetically connected to every other person and aspect of creation, and having acknowledged that all nonphysical aspects of life are also energy, including your beliefs, thoughts and feelings, this means everything emerging out of you impacts all of creation. Nothing is separate.

When you shift your energy in a new direction, for example changing your consciousness to a different way of believing, thinking and feeling, that new wave of energy creates a real ripple effect in the world around you, generating shifts in your experience of life as a result. In this way, you influence life from the inside out.

## Truth #4—You Have a Unique Energy Vibration

You have a personal energy vibration or energy signature. It is comprised of the energy of your soul, mind and body.

Your soul is operating at a high level of consciousness; it is not of this world as you know it. Your soul is intent on what it came here to learn and contribute in this lifetime. Your soul will never forget this and it holds its intent despite whatever is occurring in your life at the mind and body level. That soul clarity has an energy.

Your mind also contributes to your energy vibration, via what you believe and think.

You also have emotional responses that you experience, rising up and running through your body, in connection with your beliefs and thoughts.

All of this is happening all of the time, forming an energy vibration that goes out like waves, intersecting with and influencing the fabric of universal energy that you belong to.

## Truth #5—Your Energy Vibrates Positively or Negatively

Energy vibrates at different frequencies. Your nonphysical energy of beliefs, thoughts and feelings can be classified as positive or negative in vibration. Negative does not mean "wrong" or "bad"—notice that is just emotional labeling. We are not here to judge, just to speak about what is happening. In this context, positive means high vibration and negative means low vibration.

Positive vibration, at its highest point, is what we will describe as pure love. Negative vibration, at its lowest point, is what we will describe as inner pain. Your beliefs, thoughts and feelings all have positive or negative vibration, and they combine together to form your energy vibration at any given point in time.

## Truth #6—Your Energy Vibration Influences the Type of Actions You Take

Your beliefs, thoughts and feelings impact the decisions you make and the actions you take. Your actions contribute to life outcomes.

If you hold predominantly positive beliefs, thoughts and feelings, you make different choices and take different actions than what you would if you held predominantly negative beliefs, thoughts and feelings.

Not only do your beliefs, thoughts and feelings contribute to your energy vibration, which is constantly being sent out as waves, energetically influencing all of creation, but that "way of being" (beliefs, thoughts and feelings) directly influences your "way of doing" (your actions), thus tangibly generating results.

You are, in every way, an inside out creator.

## Truth #7—You Can Adjust Your Energy Vibration, Thus Adjusting the Core of Your Creative Power

The key is that you have the choice as to what type of energy you generate through your ability to consciously alter the components that make up your energy vibration.

You can change what you believe, think and feel. It might seem, on the surface, that you do not have control over what you believe, think or feel, but look more closely ...

As you are a conscious being with awareness, you have the capacity to observe your own beliefs, thoughts and feelings. When you are able to witness your own beliefs, thoughts and feelings as they play out, you are not lost in them and that awareness allows you to see that they do not define you. This gives you the power to change them.

When you exercise your power to change your beliefs, thoughts and feelings, you change your energy vibration.

## Truth #8—Resolving Your Negative Energy Will Cease an Exhausting Yo-yo Cycle

Imagine if you hold a set of negative beliefs about yourself, your life and the world. You view life through the filter of those beliefs. They are like a pair of tinted glasses you wear. You cannot see anything as it truly is; rather you see it in alignment with your beliefs. As you see life occurring day to day through these beliefs, you are unconsciously looking for evidence to support your beliefs or seeking to align with other people, things and situations that resonate with your view of the world. As you notice things happen in your life and you interpret them, it gives rise to thought patterns (all founded upon your beliefs). Your beliefs and thoughts then account for the vast majority of your arising feelings.

Most people have a mixture of positive beliefs and negative beliefs. Like a bell curve, there are outliers to the majority at either ends of the scale. Some have mainly negative beliefs and may also hold a few isolated positive beliefs, like a little ray of light shining through. Their overall internal experience of life feels negative as a result and they predominantly stay in negative vibration energetically speaking. Some people have mainly positive beliefs and few isolated negative beliefs. Their overall internal experience of life feels positive as a result, and they remain predominantly in positive vibration energetically speaking. The vast majority of people have an equal mix of negative and positive beliefs. The positive beliefs are enough to keep them in relative ease and flow in their lives, but the negative beliefs are the foundation of ups and downs along the way. In particular, these negative beliefs are triggered when life doesn't go smoothly, giving rise to a cycle of negative thinking and feeling. All of this causes a vicious yo-yo cycle in attitude and outcomes, and this puts a ceiling on the inner peace, freedom and success they experience.

One of the most important things that you can do in your lifetime is to recognize your limiting beliefs as the source of your own pain and to choose to resolve them. Resolution of limiting beliefs is what brings inner peace. Inner peace is healing for you. You are connected to all of creation and you are an inside out creator. Therefore, your inner peace creates outer peace. Outer peace is healing for all.

## Truth #9—Your Energy is Constantly Creating Your Life

You are always creating and influencing your life. You do this when you consciously use your energy vibration in a way that serves you. For example, when you have your heart set on a goal and you foster positive thoughts and plan the actions necessary to achieve it. Or, when you are faced with a difficult situation and you choose to proactively look for solutions and remind yourself of your ability to overcome adversity. But what you must understand is that you also create and influence your life through your energy vibration even when you are not consciously aware of it.

You cannot stop your energy from weaving its way in the world and doing its job of creating, influencing and attracting outcomes every moment of your life. It is an inherent part of being human. You cannot shut it off, because you cannot stop believing, thinking or feeling.

You don't need to think about how to breathe, it just happens. You don't need to think about your heart beating, it just does. You don't need to think about feeling, it just happens. You don't need to think about thinking for that matter, you just do! Likewise, you don't need to think about creating in order to create … you were built to create and so you do. You simply either do it consciously in a way that benefits you, or you do it accidentally and by default, and that may or may not benefit you.

You either choose to generate and hold a predominantly positive state of vibration that serves you or you will default into the vibration you get based upon unconscious reactions to whatever is happening in your life. When you default into unconscious reactions to life, your energy vibration may suddenly seem outside of your control, as it fluctuates in response to what is going on around you.

You also attract other energy (people, things, situations) that your personal energy resonates with and aligns to based upon common vibrational frequency. This is true both for high vibration or "positive" energy, as well as low vibration or "negative" energy. You do not do this by conscious choice. It is part of the natural flow of energy.

## Truth #10—Where Your Attention Goes is Where Your Energy Flows

Your conscious awareness directs your energy. You are aware, and you can focus that awareness on whatever you choose. As you choose what to focus on, turning your attention to it fully, you send waves of energy toward that focal point. Those waves of energy, whether they are of positive or negative vibrational frequency, are creative and influential.

Therefore, simply said, where your attention goes is where your energy flows, and because energy is always creating, it is in your best interest to be conscious about what you predominantly place your attention on. Consider, do you put your attention primarily on what you don't like about your life and what you don't want? Or, do you put your attention primarily on what you do like about your life and what you want to create?

Negative energy intensively focused in any area of your life can be incredibly destructive. Positive energy intensively focused in any area of your life is just as powerful, but in a transformational way. It is both the frequency of your energy, and the sustained focus of it, that fuels outcomes.

## Truth #11—You Have Unlimited Divine Energy

Your soul is not bound by the physical laws of the world you live in. You may be here in the body you are in, with the mind you perceive through, but as a soul having a human being experience, you always remain part of the divine highest consciousness of all creation to which you belong, which itself is infinite. Therefore, your energy right now, at the level of your soul, is also infinite.

You are encoded with and forever connected to timeless wisdom, unconditional love, unlimited creativity, endless passion, boundless inspiration and infinite intuition. Your soul provides all of this to you in your daily life, and that unlimited divine source will never run dry. There is only one thing that can block you from sensing and harnessing this— the fog.

## Truth #12—You Have Limited Human Energy

While you are a soul with infinite divine energy at your disposal, right now you are also human, and, as such, your mind and body are bound by the laws of the world you live in.

You have limited physical, mental and emotional human energy to draw upon and give into the world each day. You know this, because when you have depleted your reserves in any one day, or consistently over a period of time, you feel that depletion show up painfully as tension, stress, burnout, exhaustion, confusion and imbalance. You must ask yourself, then, "If I only have so much human energy to expend each day, what will I give it to?"

You can give it to your past or you can give it to your present. You can channel it into worry or you can channel it into action. You can focus it onto your problems or you can inject it into solutions and new paths. You can expend it on negative habits and conversations, or you can reserve it for empowering, uplifting rituals and engagement with others.

You must make conscious choices about what to give your precious energy to, and how, if you want to make the most of your life experience. If you do not make conscious choices, you may expend all of your physical, mental and emotional energy on things and people that are not meaningful to you, in ways that leave you feeling negative and which deplete you of your reserves.

Do not be fooled for one moment, though, that this limited amount of human energy you have available to expend each day is not enough. You have more than enough physical, mental and emotional energy to achieve what your soul came here to learn and contribute. Having limited human energy actually serves you extremely well, because it compels you to be acutely aware of what you are doing and why you are doing it, and to make specific choices. Not everything needs to be done. Not everyone needs you. You are called upon to discover what you really most need and want, and who or what really most needs and wants you, and to then give yourself wholeheartedly to that. The energy you have available is more than enough for your mission.

## Truth #13—You are Fully Responsible for Your Energy Expenditure

You are the only one responsible for how you expend your energy day to day. If you don't understand your energy and how to use it, and you are in a low vibration state, you might accidentally fire your energy off in all directions, causing chaos for yourself and others, without any idea that you're the cause. You have to learn how to manage and channel your energy with precision, in a way that serves not only you but also everyone around you.

It is a moment-by-moment choice. It is a conscious decision as to what you believe, what you think, how you feel, what you do, where you place your attention, and how you respond to what life presents to you each passing moment.

No matter what happens in life, no one else and nothing else is ever the cause of your response. In all situations, no matter what is occurring, you choose how you respond. What you give your energy to (with belief, thought and feeling, feeding into actions) and how you give it (positively or negatively, directing your awareness) are freewill choices, ones you must take full responsibility for. If you do not take responsibility for these aspects of your consciousness, then you have victimized yourself and denied your true creative power.

## Truth #14—You Control Your Own Energy, and That Is Always Enough

You do not control life. You do not control other people. Control over others is futile. It is an unevolved, Old World model of attempting to create inner peace, freedom and success for yourself by using external force. That force shows up in many guises, such as domination, manipulation, judgment, demands, agenda-driven tactics and power over others. It is low vibration energy. When you consistently deliver low vibration energy into the world, you sabotage your own potential. When you revert to control as a way to create your life outcomes, your energy and actions are a statement to the universe that says, "I do not believe in my own creative power. I do not have faith in my ability. I am left no choice but to try to control, because I do not understand how the universe really works."

While you do not control life or other people, you influence everything in the world with your consciousness and its inherent creative nature. What you focus your energy on and the way you focus it (positive or negatively) has ripple effects that influence other people, things, situations and your circumstances.

There is a big difference between this type of influence and control. Influence is a dance, between yourself and the world, where other people are equally participating. Control is a dictatorship, where you are lost in the illusion that the world revolves around you and that you are the only one with creative energy. You are not the only one.

Moreover, you do not *need* to control anyone or anything. There is only one thing you truly control, and it is more than enough. You were gifted the ability to control it when you were born into this world as the precious soul you are. That is your ability to control your own energy.

This ability to control your energy is always enough for you to live a life of inner peace, freedom and success. Anytime you feel that this is not enough, it is because you have fallen into believing your power rests outside of yourself, evidenced through power over others, rather than your power exists inside of you.

## Truth #15—Unexpressed Energy Becomes Destructive

As important as it is for you to understand that you have limited human energy to expend each day, it is equally critical for you to understand that the reason you have that energy in the first place is so that you can use it. Nothing exists in our world without purpose.

Given that you have precious physical, mental and emotional energy to use each day, if you do not use it, then it is pent up and has nowhere to go. Human energy seeks to move. Flow is its natural state. Energy exists in order to create, shift, generate, produce, light up and bring momentum. It seeks to fulfill its purpose.

When it cannot fulfill its purpose, that pent up energy disrupts your natural balance. Your natural balance is to expend energy, replenish, expend energy, replenish, expend energy, replenish—in a constant cycle. You nourish yourself with what your physical, mental and emotional self needs, and you do so in order to fuel your physical, mental and emotional exertion. If you are fuelling yourself, but not expending yourself, then you suffer imbalance.

The imbalance shows up in different ways. If you are not expending your physical energy, you may notice physical problems show up, or you may feel restless; this can impact your mental and emotional state. If you are not expending your mental energy (creativity, inspiration, ideas, intellect), then you may feel frustrated, bored or "stir crazy." If you are not expending your emotional energy (feelings and self-expression), then you may feel blocked or suffocated.

When experiencing pent-up energy and the resulting imbalance, if you don't understand the cause then you may engage in unhealthy behavior as outlets for your feelings, and it may seem like you are momentarily not in control of your own choices and actions—being destructive in your relationships, your finances, your work or your health. Or, when feeling imbalanced you may seek an outside-in external fix to make yourself feel better, rather than the required healthy expenditure of that energy from the inside out. Such outside-in fixes include stimulus such as food, alcohol, drugs, sex, shopping, television or other brain candy.

## Truth #16—Opportunities and Synchronicities Are the Natural Flow of Energy

When your soul is able to fully express through you, uninhibited by the fog, you are in your ultimate state of being. It is a natural flow, where your soul partners with your mind and body to bring your passion, inspiration and intuition to life in the physical world. This is how highest consciousness creates through you.

When this occurs you are in what might be called your slipstream. It is a state where your soul energy and your human energy are in sync with each other, and in sync with the universal energy to which you inherently belong.

In this state, your personal energy vibration is at its peak. You become automatically attuned to, and attract, energy of a similar high vibration. You create powerfully from this place, and you allow support from the fabric of universal energy into your awareness. This support manifests as opportunities, synchronicities and helpful coincidences, along with people and things coming into your path just when you need them, triggering new insights and propelling you forward.

To get into your slipstream and benefit from everything on offer, you must align to your soul. You do this by unblocking the channel through which your divine soul energy seeks to flow. That is, you must unblock yourself. Specifically, you must clear the fog of limiting beliefs, expectations, fear and societal conditioning, which acts like a dam.

## Truth #17—Every Interaction Is an Energy Exchange

Every moment in life you are interacting with the world around you—your environment, people and things. As you engage, you constantly participate in an energy exchange with these different aspects of life. Your energy intersects with their energy, and the quality and vibration of the exchange contributes to the quality and vibration of your outcomes and your life.

You interact with nature as you breathe air, drink water, absorb sunlight and walk upon the earth beneath your feet. You are given these gifts on a daily basis by nature to support your time here on the planet, and in that interaction you exchange your energy in return. What energy are you giving back? Gratitude or obliviousness? Support or resistance? Love, nurturing and protection, or disruption and destruction?

You are professionally involved in studying, working, volunteering, learning, contributing vocationally, doing business or whatever it is that you spend your time doing. As you do so, you constantly interact with individual people and/or with organizations. Organizations are simply groups of people formed together under brands and collective names. Others give you opportunities, education, space, time, knowledge, growth, payment, feedback and, in return, you offer your time, space, intellect, ideas, emotions, skills, talents, wisdom, love, passion and authenticity. Or, alternatively, there may be low vibration (negative) exchanges of energy taking place, such as apathy, frustration, manipulation or control.

You are personally in relationships with other people, connecting through family, friendship, companionship, partnership, marriage or other forms of romantic and/or physical engagement. You give of yourself and you receive from others. These energy exchanges can be of high or low vibration energy, and therefore mutually beneficial, or not.

You exchange your energy with every aspect of creation. The more you come to understand this, the more you will realize that you leave an imprint upon life every moment of every day, and the imprint you leave is contributing to your own life experience and the experience of every living and nonliving thing in existence.

### Truth #18—You Have the Capacity to Protect Yourself from Low Vibration Energy

You may notice that you feel quite emotionally affected around certain people's energy, without realizing what is actually happening to you. You may start feeling down when around people who are down, feeling negative when around negative people, or feeling sad for seemingly no reason. You may be confused about why you feel that way. It may be that you are picking up on energy and feelings that simply don't belong to you.

Similarly, it is also possible to enter a physical environment without people present and feel certain low vibration energy, because of what has taken place in that space previously. If low vibration (negative) energy has been there, and you are highly attuned to energy, which happens when you live consciously as a practice, you may sense it.

If you find yourself in the presence of something, someone or somewhere that has low vibration energy, and you do not want to be affected by it, your conscious awareness allows you to protect yourself. You can literally state to yourself, as a declaration, that the negative energy you sense does not belong to you and that you do not wish to carry it. You protect your own energy space this way.

Awareness is all it takes. In this highly interactive world with many different vibrations of energy surrounding you, you can be with low vibrations without being adversely affected by them.

## Truth #19—Everything Beyond Source Energy and Soul-level Is Impermanent

The source energy, which all of creation consists of, is the only infinite aspect of life.

Every physical aspect of creation is impermanent. Everything will come and go, will evolve and then devolve, will expand then contract. Every aspect of nature and every physical person, animal and thing is impermanent in your life. Either you will cease to exist in your human being experience, therefore they no longer exist in your experience, or, they will cease to exist period, and you will live without them in your experience of life.

This is the reality of your human being experience. It is natural to feel sad when facing this reality. Yet, from that sense of sadness, it is possible to also remember and resonate with the truth that all beings are far more than mere physical forms. When you know that you are a soul embodied in physical form having a life experience, then you know that you are infinite and that you transcend this body and this life. You also know that this is true not just for yourself, but also true for all other beings whom you love dearly in this life. You know therefore that you are never without souls you love, even if you cannot experience them on the physical level.

When you try to grip onto a form that by its inherent nature is impermanent, you know logically that pain will of course arise at some point when that something or someone no longer exists. You can enjoy and love wholeheartedly who you are with, what you have and what you experience in this life, without gripping onto it in the fear that you might one day lose it. Because, one day you will lose it. It is inevitable.

You may, without even consciously realizing it, live your life slightly on edge, on guard because of this fear. You might try to control your external life (people, things, situations)— holding on tightly in order to keep what you desire constant and close to you, for safety and for enjoyment. When you're happy you don't want anything to go "wrong"—for example your job or business, your relationships or your finances—so you unconsciously build little fortresses to protect yourself and to exert as much control as possible, with all good intent.

Whether you realize it or not, you already sense that all things outside of yourself are fleeting and impermanent. That is your soul sense. The more consciously detached you are, the more peaceful your experience of life will be. Do not, however, mistake detachment for lack of love, lack of joy, lack of care, lack of consciousness, lack of engagement, lack of passion, or lack of fully living your life. You can be completely loving and loved, deeply passionate, highly creative, incredibly influential, joyous, and totally detached at the same time.

Detachment simply means knowing that all you are experiencing and loving about your life does not belong to you. You do not own anyone or anything in the wider sense of this life experience. All that you are experiencing is a gift to you, a gift from creation. It may fade, shift in form, change in nature, disappear, die, or leave you before your mind wants it to, or you may do the same before your mind says you are ready to. But your soul will always be ready for whatever comes. Your mind and body are asked to detach and come into alignment with this soul knowingness. Then you can fully embrace life without needing to grip onto the illusion of permanency.

## Truth #20—Source Energy Nourishes You

The energy that lies at the source of all creation is not just a spark that brings each "thing" into existence in the first place, but it is the life force that also sustains each "thing."

Source energy is therefore the life force, or the lifeblood, of the universe. You are a part of that universe. Not only is this source of energy the substance from which you came forth and to which you infinitely belong (both as a soul and as a physical human being), but it is also what nourishes you and gives life to every aspect of you (your soul, your mind and your body).

Source energy gives life to all the aspects of nature that physically nourish your body—air, water, nutrients, sunlight, and shelter.

Source energy has the capacity to support the balancing of your mental and emotional state, if you are present and still. By stopping your frenetic activity, your frenetic thinking and your emotional rollercoaster, and starting to see the truth (not the illusions you are used to believing in), then you will witness the miracle of your being alive and the miracles that exist all around you. You acknowledge in those moments of stopping and stillness that the fog is an illusion, that your soul, mind and body have a special connection, and that divine highest consciousness is seeking to channel through your soul into this world for learning and contribution.

In that stillness, and from that perspective of truth, by placing your awareness on the more expansive nature of who you are (a soul first and foremost) and by acknowledging that source energy is the core of what nourishes you, the very power of your consciousness invites a rebalancing of yourself at every level, by declining illusion and accepting truth. The more you do this, the more balanced you become.

## Truth #21—Your Connection to Your Source Is Never Broken

You were born with your connection to source energy. This highest consciousness is where you come from and is what you are a part of. You are a reflection of it in every cell of your being. It is not separate from you. It is in you. It is you.

You do not need to try to create a connection or work anything out. You do not need to fix anything. Nothing is missing and nothing is broken. If you *feel* disconnected, it is simply because you are in the fog and so perhaps feeling somewhat distanced from your source because of that fog.

The experiences you've had over your lifetime are what slowly built up to create that feeling of disconnection—forming layer after layer of limiting beliefs, expectations, fear and societal conditioning—building, thickening and deepening the fog of your limiting paradigm and burying your true nature. The more you identify with the fog, the greater the distance you sense between yourself and your source. From there, it is challenging to really know and accept with your mind the divinity that you are.

When this sense of disconnection occurs, the feeling shows up as the uneasy void within. It feels like a gap inside, and your mind/body reaction is to go seeking something to fill that gap. As many people do not understand what that void-like feeling is actually telling them (a calling home to your source), they mistakenly look to the external world around them to make them feel better. Again, such outside-in fixes like food, alcohol, drugs, sex, shopping, entertainment and other momentary highs, create momentary relief by stimulating a positive emotional reaction within you that temporarily Band-Aids that void. However, these external fixes were never truly "needed" by the mind and body. Source nourishment, a connection to your soul, is always what is needed.

When you physically, mentally or emotionally take on too much of anything that you do not need, you create imbalance. This will eventually show up as negative side effects, which then have the potential to spiral out of control and create an even greater sense of void and feeling of disconnection from source. It is a vicious cycle, one that cannot be broken until there is an awakening to the fact that these behaviors, choices and external fixes stem from a void within, a void that does not need external fixes. Upon that realization, you can then start filling yourself with what you really need ... soul nourishment, by strengthening your conscious awareness of your soul and source, through stillness, presence, and acknowledgement and practical application of truth.

## Love

### Truth #22—Love Is Your Natural State

Love is understood by most people primarily as an emotion, which stirs in response to external experiences and interactions—for example, in relationships, or when perceiving beauty and nature.

However, ultimately, love is far more expansive and transcendent than just being an emotional response that you experience in reaction to certain external factors.

Love is an energy level, a frequency you operate from; love is a state of being. It is who you naturally are. The only thing that gets in the way of your natural state of love is the fog. Be clear about this—the fog of limiting beliefs, expectations, fear and societal conditioning is *not* who you are. You are love. You accumulated the fog, but below that fog you remain, always, as loving consciousness.

To return to loving consciousness, you simply focus on dispelling the fog; what is left whenever the foggy elements cease to impact weightily upon your mind, body and soul, is love.

You may already notice moments when you exist in that state of love, yet also notice that you spend time consumed by the fog. Love is not reliant upon the *absence* of limiting beliefs, expectations, fear and societal conditioning. Rather love is the acknowledgement of them, the detachment from them, and the transcendence beyond them. Love is witnessing them and choosing not to have them control your life.

As you evolve on your journey through life, becoming more conscious and clearing the fog as you do so, you naturally return to and hold your inherent state of love more frequently and for longer durations.

## Truth #23—Your Life Is a Journey into Love

The journey of life is not about having the full willingness to be love and the full strength to live out of love from day one, and to automatically stay that way uninterrupted for your entire lifetime without any hiccups.

Rather, the journey of life is to allow for your soul to evolve, and it does so through the vehicle of life experiences. Those experiences trigger a decision point for you; you have to choose willingly to exist and respond from the state of love or to react out of the fog, thus, they provide the opportunity for your progress *into* greater awareness depending on the choices you make.

It is through your life journey that you build the strength to be love no matter what you may face. You are learning the costs to you when you are not in the state of love. You are learning what you prefer. You are learning what works for you and what does not. You are coming to see the possibilities available to you in your life, inside and out, of choosing to return to the state of love. All life experiences, whether deemed by you to be positive or challenging on the surface, are beneficial assignments for this conscious practice of being love.

Your entire lifetime is a walk into love—into knowing that you are love at your core, and into knowing that love is who every other person is at his or her core also. The journey into love is to come to realize, recognize and honor your soul essence in this way, and to return to its state of love through conscious daily practice. Through this moment-by-moment practice, you further clear the fog, because limiting beliefs, expectations, fear and societal conditioning do not have the power to sustain themselves in moments when love becomes your predominant state of being. They need more of their own kind of energy (low vibration) to feed on. Such obstructions will not dissolve immediately, but with sustained exposure to love, they begin to lose their grip over you. Love is not toxic, and the fog needs toxicity in order to maintain its grip in your life.

## Truth #24—Love Is Remembrance of the Soul in You and the Soul in All Others

Love as a state of being, and as a way of living, acknowledges that you are a soul walking this earth, one that is divine and part of the miracle of life. Love as a state of being and way of living sees the soul in every living thing on this planet.

When you remember your soul, and when you simultaneously see and acknowledge another's soul, regardless of whatever fog is present, and no matter what pain plays out because of that fog, love triumphs. Love is the higher awareness you have. Love is the wisdom that helps you rise above it all. That loving wisdom says, "I see the fog that I have and how it triggers me. I see the fog that you are experiencing and how it is triggering you. I know the pain for both of us is because of the fog. I see my soul, and I see your soul. I know our true nature, our oneness and our shared humanity. And that is the truth that I choose to focus on right now. It is that truth that will underpin my choice in this moment, in how I speak to you and the actions that I take. I will not be defined by the fog."

In that choice, to notice both your loving awareness and your fog coexisting, and to choose to live from the state of love, you further dispel the fog.

## Truth #25—There Is No Lack of Love

It would be easy to fall under the impression that there is a lack of love in this world. You could assume that the negativity and problems you see present in our world are due to a lack of love. However, love is not lacking. Not at all.

Love is at the core of every person, no matter how sad, troubled, negative or destructive an individual may be, as a result of living within the fog.

Love is your natural state and it is the intent of your time here on earth. It is the intent for your own learning and evolution, and it is the intent for your contribution. As it is for you, so it is for every other person. Therefore, it is impossible for love to be lacking.

There is only ever a lack of *awareness* of that love, or a lack of *expression* of that love, due to an unwillingness to be it and share it, both of which arise because of one thing only—the fog.

## Truth #26—The State of Love Uplifts Your Actions

When you are living from your natural state of love in any given moment (pervading your beliefs, thoughts and feelings), that energy flows directly into your actions. Actions stemming from loving consciousness are powerful, energetically speaking. They are free of the encumbrances of low vibration limiting beliefs, expectations, fear and societal conditioning.

When you operate from the state of love, your actions are effectively your soul reaching straight through you to touch the world. In those moments you act as a clear channel— divinity playing in the physical world.

Words, tone, body language, actions, relationships, circumstances, outcomes, products, services, careers, businesses, finances, health ... anything that you create in external expression in this world from your natural state of love, becomes infused with love vibration, and is therefore magnetic and powerful in and of itself, in how it impacts upon everyone and everything in this world that it intersects.

Infuse all you do with love.

## Truth #27—Loving Consciousness Heals

Given that the fog is not your natural state of being, it creates imbalance and blocks your soul energy from freely flowing; that blockage impacts your physical, mental and emotional systems. You are a holistic being, and the burden of limiting beliefs, expectations, fear and societal conditioning is both real and considerable.

On the flip side, your natural state of love is incredibly healing—physically, mentally and emotionally. It is a state of equilibrium in which your mind and body balance, and thrive, and your soul is free to channel through you fully expressed. It is free-flowing energy. This is healing not only for you, as you are holding and living from that state, but for all those who you encounter, because of how they intersect and exchange with your unique energy.

As others pick up on your energy, they benefit from it because the natural state of love has the power to transmute pain. This doesn't occur consciously. It is not something you choose to make happen or something the other person has to want to receive. It is simply how energy moves between two people. Loving energy transmutes pain because it calms and creates space in another person for them to feel their own soul, to feel seen and heard by you given your level of conscious awareness. Loving energy is present, peaceful, anchored, unwavering and assured.

Those living from the state of love are what we might call "free souls"—living their days clear of the fog. They are magnetic, light and compelling to others. Their energy has an indescribable quality that draws people to them. The reason people long to be around free souls is because it reflects to them and therefore reminds them of what they deep down know is possible for themselves. Through their foggy paradigm they still intuitively sense possibility for themselves to return to loving consciousness as well, and when they see it embodied in another person and feel that unencumbered energy, their soul resonates with it and they want to be around it. Their own soul recognizes their natural state of love, as witnessed in another person. This is the miracle of energy weaving.

There is no state of being, therefore, that you can hold that is more healing for yourself and others than that of love. It is in this way that your full focus on yourself, on your evolution to no longer being controlled by your limiting beliefs, expectations, fear or societal conditioning, is a direct service to everyone you interact with. You don't need to heal others by healing them, you can heal others by healing yourself, and your energy drastically influences them.

## Truth #28—You Are Called upon Now to Embody Love

Each day you have the opportunity to return yourself to loving consciousness, even in small moments, and, as a result, raise the collective consciousness of humanity.

Yet, it is a daily challenge to practice love, especially when the world presents you with many opportunities to feel challenged and triggered, enticing you further and further into your fog. Your soul evolution, however, occurs through the moment-to-moment choices you make. There is always the chance to make a new choice, a different choice.

You may congratulate yourself for your loving consciousness around people you deeply care for, and therefore being a positive contribution in their lives. Without denying that value, you must understand it is easy to be this way around these people for whom you naturally feel human emotional reactions of love—perhaps your family, friends or a companion. You resonate with them. You can look beyond their blocks, their challenges and any unconscious actions they may take, and you can see their soul. It requires little effort from you to embody love in those relationships, when emotional love feelings are present.

But being love in this way is not all you are called to do in this lifetime. You are called upon to be love in relation to *every* person and in *every* situation, including the ones that challenge and trigger you the most. You are called upon to have loving consciousness in the face of people who you do not love emotionally.

Do not confuse this truth with a suggestion to love what people do, what they say, how they behave or how they treat you. For there will be people who offend you, grate upon you, hurt you and who are not loving in any respect toward you. And yet, while holding your boundaries, you are called to be love in the face of that experience anyway, to love them ... not for how they are being, not even for who they are in mind and body, but for the soul that they are.

We are all in this together, as souls here having a life experience. Any pain they inflict on you or others is simply a reflection of the pain inside them being projected outward for lack of any consciousness on their part. They may be so lost on their journey they are not even able to help themselves or see the truth the way you can. And in that situation, you are asked to embody love. Love does not tell them why they are wrong. Love does not tell them what or who they should be. Love does not judge them. Love does not pity them. Love does not feel superior to them. Being a state of love in relation to other people is simply to acknowledge their souls, be present, peaceful and nonreactive in the face of their pain, and to momentarily consider what it must be like to walk a life in their shoes with their suffering.

Love simply takes the expansive view, detaching from the mind-made fog that would drag you into their pain, and your own.

## Truth #29—You Are Infinitely Loved, Supported and Never Alone

Just as source energy gives life to all aspects of creation, such as nature, plants and animals, and loves and nurtures them with what they need, so it is for you. You are infinitely loved, not just for the timeless soul aspect of yourself but also for every moment that you walk this earth in this lifetime, with the trials and tribulations you face, in all your humanness.

This highest consciousness of source energy to which you belong guides and supports your journey at all times, from the moment of your birth to the moment your physical heart stops beating, and beyond. You are supported when you see the support show up in your physical life as people, situations and synchronicities that clearly love and leverage you. And you are also supported just as much when you are seemingly completely alone. Unseen helping hands stand behind you every moment of your life.

You could not separate yourself from your source if you tried. Your connection can never be broken. You are loved, supported and connected when you feel the connection, and you are equally as strongly loved, supported and connected when you do not feel any connection at all.

Even if you stand right now in the middle of a storm of challenges, with no one and nothing, you are never unloved, unsupported and alone. It is only when the mind takes control of your life, thus overpowering your soul, that you feel disconnected, and it is that disconnection that creates further turmoil in your experience. However, that process of feeling disconnected in itself serves an important purpose—it triggers your awakening and forces you into the wise questions that lead you to remembering the existence of something greater to which you belong, something beyond mind and body.

## Truth #30—You Already Completely Love Yourself

If you ever have moments when you do not love yourself, when you believe that it is not possible to truly love yourself, or that self-love has to be conditional, then know this ... you already do love yourself fully and unconditionally at soul-level. That aspect of yourself is expansive and one with the highest loving consciousness of your source. You, at the level of your mind, are blocked from living in this knowing and all-encompassing self-love and self-acceptance, because of the fog.

Your mind has gotten in the way of truth, and you have been lured into an illusion—that you must somehow be different or better in order to love yourself fully, that you cannot love yourself just as you are, that what you have done in the past and what you do next makes you more or less worthy of self-love. You judge yourself. You dislike parts of your physical, mental or emotional self. You see your situation, actions, your past and problems as definitive of who you are, rather than the fact that they are simply experiences and circumstances, not who you are.

You are not what you do. You are not where you live. You are not what you said or didn't say. You are far beyond any of that. With all your beauty, strength, light and wisdom, alongside all your challenges, quirks and darkness, you are a soul divinely orchestrated to be here in life, as a perfectly imperfect human being, as every human being is and will ever be. And, you are no less loveable because of it.

The only reason you fall into bouts where you lack self-love is because your connection to your soul, where full self-love already resides, feels broken or suppressed. The fog makes it so you no longer feel the existing love within yourself for yourself. But it is still there. The connection to self-love does not need to be created. You simply need to clear the fog and you will find your original truth and connectedness.

## Truth #31—Your Relationship with Yourself Is the Most Important Love to Nurture

If you want to honor your life, honor your divinity, and be of best service to yourself and everyone else you encounter, then you must realize that your number one relationship is with yourself. You need your own consciously delivered loving thoughts and feelings as a priority. These nourish you, lift you up, replenish you and anchor you in your daily life.

Whenever you give anything to other people, you give from within yourself. You cannot give them high vibration energy from within if it does not exist within. You cannot give them the fullness of your love for them if your inner space is void of love.

At any moment, you can consciously choose to give yourself support. You can practice self-love in how you speak to yourself, in how you treat yourself, in how you care for your physical, mental and emotional self, and in what you do. The more your behavior aligns with your already unconditional self-love at the soul-level, the more your mind will also come into alignment.

## Humanity

### Truth #32—There Is Enough for Everyone

There are enough resources on the planet for every person to be fed, watered and sheltered. It is because of human beings and the divisive decisions and systems we create that there is lack.

As humans we created the concepts of borders, countries, regulations, laws, classes, processes and systems. Some were created with good intent for order, security, safety and well-being, but others were not. Many are legacy systems that have stayed in place throughout the ages, morphing as we grew in intellect and technology over time, and as we individually and collectively grew in ego, greed, power and control.

The fog of many individuals was collectively combined to create governing systems, which, in many cases, do not serve the wider needs of humanity. Those needs, of course, are for every person on this planet to have his or her basic human requirements met physically and emotionally—to be fed, watered, clothed, sheltered, to be safe, to be seen and acknowledged for how precious they are. Indeed, to be cherished.

Many of the divisive systems we now have, which we may not necessarily even realize exist, were largely created from a paradigm of lack and self-protection, stemming from an illusion of separateness. These systems were not, and are not, always maintained or furthered with pure intent for the good of all.

The resulting divisions between people, families, communities and countries, and the apparent abundance in some spaces and the complete lack and desolation in other places, can easily lead you to believe that the world is not abundant.

This is not true. The planet we live on is abundant. It is each person's choice to view and use that abundance in ways that create apparent lack as a result. There is enough of everything for everyone's fundamental needs to be met.

Resist the urge to painfully dwell on the fact that this truth is not yet embraced by everyone on our planet. You are simply asked to live with awareness of the truth. You are asked to not fear lack. You are asked to not buy into mass messaging that seeks to condition you and perpetuate the illusion.

## Truth #33—Collaboration Is More Powerful than Competition

Due to the paradigm of scarcity that many people live from, importance has been given to competition in order to not only thrive, but simply to survive.

What could be quite healthy goal setting, achieving and financially thriving in the career and business arena in particular, has turned into a fear-based competition mind-set—characterized by "every man for himself" agendas, with a war-like approach to "take down" the competition, in order to get as big a slice of the pie as possible. This is a purely ego-driven need for more, with constant comparison to others combined with a deep fear of missing out and not having enough. This is when one's sense of self-worth is defined entirely by external success and amassing of resources.

If this is the reality you live within, then the mere thought of someone else getting what you want is a perceived threat, which is met with defense and, in many cases, the counterattack of full-blown competitive force delivered with low vibration energy infused into everything you do and create.

Competition as a pure fact of a situation (not a mind-set and attitude) is simply two or more people or groups competing for the same thing. That is in no way harmful or negative. We can absolutely all be in the world and create what we desire and some of us will be creating the same things and desiring the same things and selling the same things. We can compete in the same market and be collaborative in spirit. We can compete for the same jobs, awards, sporting outcomes or creative achievements, and be collaborative in spirit. But competition as a mind-set and attitude, where one is driven not just by the desire to succeed or win, but also by the desire to do so at the expense of another, is a problem.

Many people are living with the perception that they must fight for what they need, metaphorically and sometimes quite literally, and they are driven by the notion that if they have not attained something, then they have lost because someone else has clearly won and stolen their opportunity. There is no possible space for inner peace, freedom or genuine New World success when this mind-set exists en masse. When one person or group steps on another, literally or with their energy, there are no winners in the bigger picture.

Collaboration stems from loving consciousness and is a core fundamental of human life that allows *the whole* to thrive. When one helps another, both thrive. When one allows another to thrive, without making it mean something negative about themselves and their own situation, then both thrive. When one succeeds at something with a perspective of embracing all people they meet along the way, even embracing those people who are intent on the same outcome, then everyone involved has the energetic space to thrive. In this way, everything being done and created is infused with high vibration energy.

### Truth #34—You Uplift Humanity when You are Willing to Be of Service

When you are willing to be of service in this world, giving fully of yourself to each moment, in all that you do, you play your part in uplifting humanity.

Being of service to others in any small way, be it giving fully and positively of yourself in a conversation, in your personal relationships, in your paid work, in voluntary engagements, with complete strangers you pass momentarily, be it with a smile, a word, a gesture, an exchange of energy, a transaction of any nature—all of it energetically creates an uplifting ripple effect for humanity whether you realize it or not.

There is one thing that interrupts this—the misperception that you are here to get, not to give. That is part of the fog—an illusion that this world exists to serve your needs, rather than this world exists for you to serve the needs of yourself and others by giving fully of yourself in each moment, in all that you do.

The beauty is that when you are willing to be of service and you give fully of yourself, in return you will actually get what you need at the level of your soul, as a natural flowing consequence. Giving, however, comes at the forefront.

## Truth #35—How You Give Is More Important than What You Give

Being of service to humanity is not a quantity matter; it is a quality matter. It is not about what you give; it is entirely about *how* you give. The energy behind what you do matters most, in every respect.

Be it in your personal life or professional endeavors, give from love. Give with intent to learn as you go. Give to enjoy the feeling you get from giving. Give because you know that giving is one of the most fulfilling acts you can engage in. Give knowing it is part of your contribution, which is part of your soul journey. Give without concern for what, where, why, and without judgment about quantity, reach and recognition.

Be of service in whatever ways you feel inspired to, whenever opportunities arise, and know that every small moment of giving from positive energy makes a difference.

## Truth #36—Giving and Getting Is a Circular Flow of Energy

You are here to give and to receive in return, not to get and then to give as a result. This is not semantics.

Those who believe that the world owes them and that life is about getting more (of anything) and only then will they feel duly paid and able to spare excess (love, knowledge, insights, opportunities, time, money or resources) to give back into the world—these are the people who will never feel like they have enough. The energy of a getter is like a blocked river, where a dam interrupts the natural flow—the flow of energy and abundance. Those who solely seek to get for themselves may experience great abundance in some regards, and yet they will experience the energy blockage show up in other areas of their life. The universe flows uniquely for each of us, so that we may be triggered to see and learn these truths for ourselves in a way that will aid our own soul evolution.

Those who understand we are givers, who receive in return, are contributing and being of service in the little moments of their day. They are letting the energy of their being flow freely, letting it cascade outward to all those they encounter, giving willingly of what they have capacity to give and feel inspired to give, and because the floodgates are open for energy to flow, they put themselves right in the midst of the circular flow of the universe.

Interconnected to everything, you are either giving and receiving within the natural flow, or you are solely looking to get whatever you can and are blocked from the greater flow.

## Truth #37—Healing Yourself Comes before Healing Humanity

Healing is the resolution of anything that causes blockage, pain and suffering.

There is great need for healing across our world. Healing physically, healing mentally and healing emotionally. Healing divisions, rifts and relationships in the micro networks of each person's own experience of life, and at the macro level in terms of healing across communities and countries.

The foggy paradigm that individual people are living within is where the most extensive level of healing is needed in humanity—the healing of limiting beliefs, expectations, fear and the pain caused from buying into and desperately trying to live up to societal norms, which have no true meaning or value.

What many people don't understand is that healing at the individual level *will* heal humanity. Mass healing at the micro level will radically impact the macro level. After all, humanity is just a collection of individuals. Heal the parts, and you heal the whole.

If you want to make our world a better place, your reason might stem from one of two personal motivators. The first motivator is what we might call "a wounded need to fix." This means that from your own sense of incompleteness, pain, wounding, hurt, and your conscious (or unconscious) desire to be healed yourself, you feel driven to focus on healing the external world. You can see the pain others are suffering just as you are, and so you focus on supporting their healing without necessarily owning or supporting your own need for healing first, or simultaneously. When you do this, you are avoiding part of your soul path, which is to learn and evolve in yourself, as well as to contribute.

The "wounded need to fix," while driven from love and genuine desire to be of service to others, will never be enough to resolve any inner wounding you feel. We must all face our inner darkness in and of itself, so we can then better support anyone else we encounter in their own healing process if we choose to.

The second personal motivator is what we might call "a conscious mission to heal." This means to wholeheartedly own your inner healing process, to clear the fog as a priority, to bring conscious awareness day to day as you grow through the phases of your life, and to simultaneously, or later, share whatever you notice and learn in order to support others in their own healing journey. This path is about a commitment to heal yourself as much as you are committed to helping heal others. This is about having your energy equally focused within (where your center of creation and reality begins—

from the "inside out") rather than solely focusing your energy "out there" in the world.

# Soul

## Truth #38—You Are a Reflection of Divinity

There is no need to seek or try to connect to your source, divinity, highest consciousness, creator, spiritual home, God or the universe.

The human desire to go seeking in this way stems from the misperception that your source is not within you, that divinity is not who you are and therefore it resides somewhere outside of yourself. Due to that misperception, it is only natural to seek the divine externally.

In fact, everything listed above that you might go seeking actually refers to who you are, where you came from and what you will always belong to. The divine is everywhere, in everything, giving life force to every aspect of creation, including you. You are highest consciousness made manifest into human form. You are a living, walking, talking miracle that embodies source energy. The magnificence of God is in every cell of your being, and in every aspect of creation. You are the greatest achievement of source energy ... as we all are.

What you seek lies within you. It exists below the fog.

## Truth #39—Your Soul Is Not the "You" That You Know Yourself to Be

Your soul has no name. It has no gender. It has no ethnicity. It has no age. It has no personality. It has no body. It has no face. It is not the "you" that you know yourself to be right now. It is an essence within the oneness. It is an expression of divinity. Highest consciousness knows no bounds or identities like we know them in human experience.

Your mind may want to create an identity for your soul, to picture it with a face, to try to name it and define it. That is normal, because that is what your mind is used to doing—making sense of things.

It is not easy for your mind to accept the concept of your soul nature. It goes beyond logic. It is not something that has been scientifically proven. There is no way you can verify it. Your mind cannot process data in order to make sense of it. But your mind is not your only tool for navigating life.

Your soul nature can be sensed using your conscious awareness and your intuition, which go well beyond your logical mind.

## Truth #40—You Are Soul First, Body Second

Your body does not exist without your soul giving life to it. Your soul, however, exists infinitely, beyond your body, beyond this lifetime.

It is possible for you to experience the expansiveness of your soul and know from firsthand experience that you are more than your mind and your body. This can occur in certain states of heightened consciousness, such as meditation, dreaming and during extreme circumstances including near-death experiences, when your consciousness is able to perceive your mind, body and current life from an entirely different, elevated perspective, outside of your mind's perception.

No matter how fleeting those moments of sensing and perceiving from the expansiveness of your soul are, you realize that you are more than your mind and body. This consciousness, or soul essence, that you are able to perceive from momentarily, is actually who you really are at your core foundation.

However, it is easy to forget this. Living in a physical world, ruled by physical laws, the mind and body easily dominate the "mind, body, soul" equation. They are, of course, the most easily intellectually understood aspects of your being.

You do not need to have moments of expansive soul realization in meditation or other states of altered consciousness in order to know you are soul first and body second. You can simply remind yourself of it. Remember that the experiences you have as a physical, thinking human being are because the higher consciousness of your soul came into this life due to the world needing your contribution and your soul needing the world as a playground in order to learn and evolve. This exchange is the reason that you have a body and a mind. They make contribution and evolution possible.

Considering that your soul needs your body in order to experience this world, your physical body could be considered as a vehicle that carries you through life. Your soul needs your conscious participation in caring for that physical body with a great deal of love and respect.

## Truth #41—Due to Being More Soul than Body, You Must Nourish Yourself Accordingly

When lost in the illusion that you are primarily a body, you end up nourishing yourself according to that paradigm. For your well-being, therefore, you may focus primarily on your physical needs. That will serve you greatly, but not holistically. Your physical body will thrive, and yet the most nourished physical body can be wracked with inner pain and suffering at the level of soul, when the soul is ignored in the equation for well-being.

If your soul is ignored in a significant and longstanding way, the unease and stress it endures can take a toll on your mind and body, because no aspect of yourself can be viewed as independent of the other.

You are more soul than you are body, and you must nourish yourself accordingly. That means learning what your soul needs and giving that to it, just as you have learnt over your lifetime what your physical needs are and you attend to those. For example, when your body cries out in physical pain, you seek answers and treat it via whatever health solutions you most resonate with. When your soul cries out in pain or imbalance, which is simply the soul asking to clear the fog and to experience the evolution it came into life for, many people ignore it. The intuition shouting out, the unease niggling at you, the void-like feeling within, the emotional upsets triggered by situations, the suppressed passions due to limiting beliefs that skew your perspective of yourself and life, the expectations that weigh you down, the fear that keeps you stuck—your soul needs care, too, to heal and be set free, which is the process of learning and evolving. This is core to your reason for being here.

To nourish your soul, you must learn to tune into your intuition—notice how it speaks to you, then listen to it and follow it. You can allow for time in solitude and silence to hear what rises up within you. Be willing to look at what causes you the most pain and then ask questions about why that is and explore what might help you move forward.

Be willing to dedicate your time, energy and resources to your own soul healing throughout the phases of your life, and remember that this is how you truly create sustainable inner peace, freedom and success ... from inside out transformation.

## Truth #42—Spiritual Is Who You Are, Not Something You Choose or Become

Pain arises when you get lost in one of two perspectives about your spiritual nature. Firstly, you may latch onto the idea of being spiritual and label it as "a way of life," or grip onto an image of a spiritual person and then endeavor to live up to that image, with expectations of what you think a spiritual person should be doing, how they should be feeling and what they should look like. Overall, you will not experience sustainable inner peace while identifying with a stereotype, because you will forever feel like there is some way you need to be, something you need to do or somehow you should be feeling in order to be a spiritual person, other than who you are naturally. The fact is that spiritual is who you are, no matter what you say or do, because you are a soul (spirit).

Secondly, you may resist this truth of your inherent spiritual nature and attempt to disconnect as far away as possible in belief, thought, word and deed from your soul and source. You may claim yourself to be against or skeptical of spirituality. You may well have been driven in that direction due to societal conditioning, or, alternatively, you may have rejected the idea of your spiritual nature as a result of feeling disconnected while within a structured spiritual, faith-based or religious system. Sometimes, being within churches, mosques, temples and other houses of God can support one to feel deeply connected and loved. Just as often, those same places can lead to painful divisions among people, and lead to a sense of painful division within oneself. If you feel connected in such a place and feel moved to be there, answer that calling from within. Just know that you don't have to go into a structured spiritual, faith-based or religious system, nor live by set rules or required beliefs, in order to feel and nourish your inherent connection to divinity.

If you accept that you are spiritual by your inherent nature, then there is nothing you need to try to be or attempt to do to make yourself spiritual or to resist that spiritual nature. From acceptance and allowing yourself to just be, you will find great peace and freedom within yourself. If from that place of acceptance you then wish to actively foster a greater day-to-day *awareness* and celebration of your divine nature, to cultivate that inherent spiritual aspect of your life, you may enjoy rituals such as meditation, presence practice, prayer and gratitude.

### Truth #43—There Is a Design for Your Awakening

Why do we face so many challenges in life and have so many questions, and drift so far from our true nature at times? Why do we not retain the conscious awareness we hold at birth, of who we are and why we came into life, into adulthood?

Because you are here in life to evolve, and your evolution— an expansion of understanding—occurs through the process of awakening. It is a process, not a moment in time. And, there is a design to trigger that awakening.

The design is this ... whenever you feel disconnected, like something is missing, it is then that you are being called to awaken. Awaken to remember you have a soul, which has the intention to learn and contribute in life. You first *feel* a sense of disconnection from source like a void within, and then you experience the results of that disconnection in the world around you, as you perceive life from within the fog and seem to come up against blocks and challenges that cause you frustration, pain and results you do not like. When experiencing the results of seeming disconnection, you start to ask questions. You may pursue answers in order to move beyond what you are experiencing. When you begin looking in your day to day life for answers, you will eventually find. When you find, connecting to age-old wisdom, you come back to your inherent soul nature.

It is a cycle, beginning as a bright, clear soul energy when you first arrive, journeying forth, losing touch, rediscovering, and reconnecting—all the while learning as you go, and contributing from that increasing wisdom as you go, facing each newly arrived moment (challenges and opportunities) from your evolving perspective. This entire process of awakening aids your soul evolution with precision.

## Truth #44—Your Soul Can Have Numerous Lifetimes; You Have Much Wisdom Within You

Your soul may have lived numerous lifetimes. The number of lifetimes you have had is irrelevant. Who you were and what you did in those lifetimes is also not of primary interest. The point is this—your soul comes and goes from lifetimes for several reasons: to aid its own growth, to aid the growth of other souls, and to contribute to the collective.

Wisdom, gifts, preferences, experiences, challenges, pain, learning—they all carry an energetic imprint that your soul conveys from lifetime to lifetime. Each lifetime allows the opportunity for healing pains and blocks that have been encountered along the way, which in turn deepens the wisdom, and feeds into the contribution your soul can make.

Resist the urge to think about yourself in other lifetimes, because you will try to mentally perceive the "you" that you know now in name, personality and body, to be the person in those other lifetimes you imagine. That is not the case.

## Truth #45—You Have Soul Shadow and Soul Light

When you arrived in this world there were already two clear aspects to your soul energy: your soul light and your soul shadow.

Soul light consists of all the learning, insights, deep wisdom and gifts that carried with your soul from previous lifetimes, and everything you were imbued with in personality and traits to aid you on your journey in this life. Everything is energetically woven into your soul essence and is present in every aspect of your being. It is all available to you in this life, to support your learning and evolution, and to support your contribution to the world.

Soul shadow consists of all the unique lessons you are here to learn, including the energy of unresolved challenges your soul may have carried from previous lifetimes. It is also woven into your soul essence and is available to you in this life, for your healing of self, so that you can evolve. As you experience resolution and growth, you feed that wisdom into your contributions to others whom you encounter in this life.

One aspect of your journey is to find your soul shadow exposed through experiences and challenges triggering you, in order that you can see those blocks and wounds within, and have the opportunity and choice to heal them and grow as a result.

The other aspect of your journey is to shine your soul light, by tapping into, developing and fully expressing your passions, gifts, skills, talents and wisdom, so you can contribute.

Imagine these two aspects of your soul essence, shadow and light, like the two sides of a zipper. They are designed to come together, fitting seamlessly as one simultaneous healing/learning and contribution process. However, to pull these together you have to be willing to offer both sides of your soul attention—to consciously choose to see, understand and heal blocks and limitations you notice within yourself (for your learning), and willingly seek to express your gifts (for your contribution). Living divided where you focus only on one or the other, is a recipe for unease.

Your soul learning and soul contribution are a cycle, each one feeds the other. As your soul evolves through the life experiences you have, the wisdom you gain influences and informs how you are and what you do, thus guiding your contribution to the world.

As you contribute to others and the world around you, those interactions and ongoing exchanges of energy constantly enhance your personal learning and evolution at the same time.

The two aspects of your soul path here in life, learning and contribution, are inextricably linked together, feeding each other in a continuous circular motion.

## Truth #46—SOUL LEARNING: You Have Unique Soul Lessons to Learn in This Lifetime

Your soul has a unique set of lessons to learn, and evolutionary stages to go through, in this lifetime.

There is no getting around it, and there is no free pass. You either learn through being open and willing to evolve, seeing the challenges you face as ways to aid that evolution; or, you deny it, resist it, see challenges as curses and do your best to avoid anything in this life being about your own need for growth.

The former path is the one where inner peace and freedom are available to you. That path will support your success at all levels. The latter path, the one within the fog, limits you considerably and will not support any sustainable sense of inner peace or freedom.

## Truth #47—SOUL LEARNING: There Is Information Available to You about Your Unique Life Path and Soul Lessons

Your life is not something you have to navigate blindly. Wisdom about your life path is not hidden from you, but you may not know it exists, or you may not choose to seek it, to accept it or to indeed allow yourself permission to utilize that wisdom because of the fog you live within.

If you are trapped in the fog, then your intellectual mind reigns supreme, and may outright deny that your soul is real or that your soul intention can be found anywhere. Over your lifetime, your mind has likely been conditioned to believe only in what you can see, hear and touch through your physical senses and what can be analyzed and reduced to facts, statistics and evidence. This is all quite valid in many respects, but leaves no room for the magic and truth of your spiritual essence.

There is wisdom about your life path and soul lessons, available to you right now should you so choose to draw upon it. There are various access points, such as the science of numbers and their wisdom imbued within your name and date of birth, accessible through numerology, through to the position of the planets and stars at your time of birth, which reflect your soul intention as laid out in your astrological charts. You need only open your mind long enough to allow in new perspectives—to allow yourself a moment to consider the value and possible power of life path information.

Notice any hesitation, judgment or skepticism as they arise within you as resistance to any of these ancient sources of knowledge, and recognize that you have been conditioned to that disbelief through a society that beholds logic first, and dismisses all else. Notice when and where you see mass media portraying negative perspectives of spirituality or "spiritual people." Notice when and where you have been exposed to superficial and commercialized versions of such life path wisdom as numerology and astrology—stripped of their depth and chunked down into bite-size pieces of relatively unusable content to fit the masses for mainstream media consumption.

You may fear accessing wisdom regarding your life path if the source of that information lies outside the bounds of what you consider "normal." You may want above all else to feel "normal" yourself, to be seen as "normal" by others and to stay within the socially acceptable standards you were raised to believe in, rather than venturing out with an open mind to see what soul information might resonate with you. It is okay to feel fearful, and it is okay to feel skeptical. That doesn't stop you from keeping an open mind.

While it may not seem "normal" to give serious consideration to this type of life path wisdom that is accessible to you right now, let's be honest in recognizing that inner peace is also not the norm of the societally conditioned mind. Confusion, pain and suffering (either of infrequent mild bouts or persistent conditions) are the norm of the societally conditioned mind. Standing within your societal conditioning does not always serve you well.

Often the people outlying the norm are the ones experiencing the peace that eludes so many, because of their willingness to understand their soul essence and their soul journey, to access life path wisdom and bring greater depth of understanding to their life challenges and possibilities.

These types of life path wisdom, such as numerology and astrology, are part and parcel of how our universe functions. They were always intended to guide you in your physical human being experience, offering you a map to your own evolution and helping you make sense of the journey.

When seeking out such wisdom, you may wonder how to find someone you can trust to give you accurate information. Finding, vetting and then booking a session with a numerologist or astrologist, for example, can be a similar process to that of engaging any other service provider. You might research to identify experienced practitioners and review testimonials from people who have benefited from their service and wisdom, or you might choose a practitioner based on word-of-mouth referral.

Allow yourself the chance to simply review and consider your own life path wisdom. Trust in your own ability to make sense of it. Trust in your own judgment and ability to discern. Allow yourself to notice what resonates. Let yourself assess the information with both your intellect and intuition combined. You do not have to believe it, or disbelieve it. Simply notice what new insights about yourself fall into place. See what is triggered within you as areas for your development and learning. See what answers you find to your questions. See what intrigues you and aligns to your curiosities, preferences and passions.

Be willing to treat your life like a mystery and an adventure that you are exploring wholeheartedly.

## Truth #48—SOUL LEARNING: The Recurring Patterns in Your Life Can Point You to the Lessons You Are Here to Learn

Beyond the soul path information that you can access, your life experiences to date are often a trail of footprints to point you toward the lessons your soul is here to learn and evolve through.

When you look at your life to date you might identify recurring patterns of challenges, emotional blocks or fears. Major soul lessons have a tendency to play out over and over again as themes—in different forms, in different areas of your life, in different relationships and guises, until you pay attention and learn from them.

Seemingly negative themes in your life can help you evolve if you look objectively at what they might indicate about your own internal blocks, or your perspective of yourself, other people and life.

## Truth #49—SOUL CONTRIBUTION: Your Purpose in Life Is to Be the Full Expression of Who You Are

Aside from learning for your soul evolution, you are also here to contribute. Your major contribution in this life is through the major gift you were blessed with when you were born.

That gift is *being you*. No one else has that gift. Only you can be you. Gifts are for expressing. If *being you* is the gift, then *expressing* you is what you do with your gift. Expressing yourself fully, unapologetically, uninhibited and without limitation.

You are not here to judge yourself, judge your value, compare yourself to others, silence yourself, diminish yourself, hide yourself, downplay yourself, adapt yourself, suppress who you really are, do what you think you should do or meet the expectations of other people.

The world will never see another human being like you. Your uniqueness, in every respect, is your gift. Highest consciousness, your source, asks one thing of you ... to be the full expression of yourself so that you can leave your unique imprint on all those you encounter and upon the world.

Never underestimate the power of your energy and how it ripples outward to affect everything and everyone around you when you are being your full, authentic self.

If you do not open yourself to the magnificent truth of what you can offer this world by *being* who you are, expressing your passions, acting on your inspirations and honoring the intuition you feel nudging you inside, then you will come and go from this world, and your unique expression will be suppressed and lost forever.

There is no need to work out your unique expression. Just acknowledge that you *are* a unique expression, be willing to allow yourself to let that out into the world. That is your purpose. That is your contribution.

**Truth #50—SOUL CONTRIBUTION: You Were Born with Everything You Need to Achieve Your Purpose**

There is nothing you are missing. Before you were born, you were imbued with everything, and I mean *everything*, that you needed to fulfill your life purpose.

You came in with DNA that is unique to you. You came with soul wisdom, talents, a creative nature, a unique personality and traits infused into every cell of your physical being and every level of yourself energetically. You came with eyes that see the world in a way that only you will ever see it. And, you came with imperfections. And all of it, imperfections included, is divinely organized for you, to help your soul live in this world in your humanness, to make your unique contribution.

There is no need to frantically and fearfully try to become more, be more, do more or get more. You are whole and complete already, your beautiful imperfections included. As you move through the phases of your life energetically and physically, you grow into your gifts and talents. You grow into your insights and wisdom. You experience more of life and you start to come to know yourself in greater depth. Some wisdom, talents and passions that you have within you may become apparent early in life; others show themselves later in life. Some insights only become clear to you once you have certain life experiences that unlock such wisdom from within you. You must trust in the way your life naturally unfolds.

**Truth #51—SOUL CONTRIBUTION: To Honor Your Purpose, Act upon Your Soul Language of Passion, Inspiration and Intuition**

How your soul speaks to you and through you, so that you sense and align to your soul, is done in a way that your mind and body can understand—through the language of feeling. More specifically, through the feelings of passion, inspiration and intuition. Your soul is giving you these as signals to notice, follow and act upon to lead you into your most successful, fulfilled experience of life.

Passion is feeling. Inspiration is supported by powerful feeling. Intuition is feeling guidance. The language of your soul is all part of your unique expression, seeking to make its way into the world.

With conscious awareness you notice these specific feelings as soul messages, and you are able to process them with your logical mind and choose, with your freewill, to act upon them—to decide, to move, to do and to create out of the passion, out of the inspiration and out of the intuition.

It is your purpose to honor these aspects of yourself and give expression to them. Practically speaking, that means you pay attention to what you are passionate about, what inspirations come to you and what your intuitive sense is telling you. Then you bring these soul urges into reality through action. The more you pay attention and act, the better your energy is flowing freely from the inside out, the greater the space there is within for more to come in—more passion, more inspiration and more intuition. Your divine energy is unlimited.

The only thing that blocks it from flooding through you is your own lack of consciousness, and/or lack of willingness to act upon it. These ways that your soul communicates with you and through you are equally as valid as what your logical thinking mind offers you, and as real as anything you see and hear in your physical world.

## Truth #52—SOUL CONTRIBUTION: Your Soul Asks that Your Mind not Judge or Block Your Unique Expression

In relation to being your unique expression, including giving life to your unique passions, inspirations and intuition, you do not need to know exactly where this will lead you, or who might benefit from this, or how quantifiable that benefit might be for others and for yourself. Your mind wants to know, because your mind has an important job that it is used to doing—assessing, rationalizing, planning, plotting, strategizing and protecting.

Your soul asks that your mind not judge and block your unique expression. Nothing exists without purpose. Your soul language exists to be expressed.

When you honor your soul by being your full and unique expression, you directly support the natural unfolding of your life by allowing your soul to lead the way (getting out of your head and into your heart). This creates the conditions for inner peace, freedom and success from the inside out.

## Truth #53—SOUL CONTRIBUTION: Your Full Expression Has the Power to Unlock the Potential in Others

Simply by being your full expression, you will touch other people's lives in ways you might never fully understand.

This is because as one soul freely fulfills its purpose by letting its uniqueness shine out into the world others resonate with that freedom of spirit. They resonate with it because they are seeing their own potential being played out in another person. It energetically unlocks a remembrance (at a deep level below the mind) of their own soul and their own possibility.

On a more conscious level, it gives them the sense of hope and permission to do the same for themselves—to be fully expressed, to say no to their own limiting beliefs, expectations, fear and societal conditioning, and to instead say yes to their own passions, inspirations and intuition.

## Truth #54—You Are, and Always Have Been, Enough

You are enough. You always were enough. You were born enough. Neither limiting beliefs nor arising thoughts and feelings you have because of the fog you were conditioned to live within will ever diminish the fact that you are enough.

You were not put on this planet as an incomplete person to make your contribution. Your imperfections do not make you incomplete in any way; they are part of your completeness.

Everything about you is miraculously designed to aid your learning and your contribution.

Others, from within their own fog, do not get to say that you are not enough. There is nothing that has happened in your life circumstantially that can change how whole, complete and enough you are.

There is nothing that you need to be, do or have in order to be considered valuable, worthy, whole or complete. Your value is inherent.

If this is not your sense of yourself, and you feel incomplete and lacking, then as you strive to create external success in the world you are always doing so, even unconsciously, out of a need to complete yourself, validate yourself and prove yourself to yourself and/or to others. That energy is low vibration and is not reflective of who you truly are, and as such the process of creating your success will be a rollercoaster of highs and lows based on whether the external world (people, things and situations whose energy is outside of your control) is giving you the validation you seek.

To experience truly fulfilling outward success in the material world, you must first come to sense your own completeness within yourself—to know that who you are, just as you are, is enough. From that secure and grounded sense of self, you can go about creating whatever you wish in your external life experience, and infusing all of your endeavors and creations with high vibration energy.

That sense of completeness goes where you go and supports your inner peace. It remains whether the sea of your life is easy sailing or stormy. While external people, things and situations will come and go, and be positive or negative because that is the nature of life, your chosen inner landscape is something no one and nothing can dictate or take away from you. It is yours and yours alone to rule. When this inner landscape is a healthy reflection of truth, success outwardly will flourish, because even during trials and tribulations you will have the presence and sense of self to know that nothing diminishes who you are.

## Truth #55—You Are Not Creating Your Life Alone, You are Co-Creating It

The you that you know yourself to be in name, personality, mind and body is clearly "of this world" and in this world creating—building relationships, building products, services and offers in career and businesses, developing health, well-being and balance, and building financial resources, experiences and outcomes. There is an endless list of what you create day to day, month to month and year to year. You apply your physical, mental and emotional energy to these creative endeavors, and you get certain results. From your human perspective, you may assume that you are the only force at play in the creative process.

However, you also know that energetically you are connected to the totality of the universe, to everything tangible and intangible stemming from the source of highest consciousness. You know you are a soul, as well as a mind and body. You know that your soul has intention for being here—for learning and for contribution—from a much bigger perspective than just what your mind wants to do. Highest consciousness, to which you belong, supports you being here and supports the unfolding of your soul's journey.

Please notice that, due to this integrated structure of life, you are never creating alone. You are never the only point of energy that is working in your favor. You could only create alone if you were separate and independent. You are not.

Highest consciousness co-creates with you by giving you what your soul most needs. This does not always align with what your mind wants. At times the co-creation process means you will be given assignments in life to lovingly challenge you into your own much needed growth, which will in turn aid your intended contribution to the world through increased wisdom and greater proficiency in your inner and outer strengths and talents. Other times the co-creation process means you will be given divine signals to guide you forward in the best direction to achieve your goals, beyond what your mind may come up with on its own—this happens most frequently, fluidly and seemingly miraculously when your mind-made goals and freewill are stemming directly from you being the full authentic expression of who you really are. From that space, you may notice that what you need shows up when you need it—practical support, leverage, opportunity and openings, synchronicity and coincidence, people and things turning up in your path at the ideal moment—all helping you to fulfill your goals in alignment with your soul-led passions, inspirations and intuition. This is co-creation.

## Truth #56—Divine Signals Help You to Navigate Your Path in Life

Highest consciousness provides, through energy flow, constant guidance for "the whole" to thrive, seeking to support every aspect of creation. This energy has what we might call an ongoing feedback loop, information dissemination or messaging system, so that all components of the whole can thrive. You are part of the whole, as is everyone. Highest consciousness is guiding you.

Like a brain sends signals to the cells of the body, like a speaker sends out messages to an audience, like an animal uses agreed signals to alert the rest of its tribe, highest consciousness supports all souls on their journey with ongoing feedback by way of the natural flow of energy. Energy guides you if you pay attention, informing you as you move through life, by way of reactions and responses, messages and signals.

You do not need to believe in anything in particular in order for divine signals to exist for you. They exist irrespective of your beliefs. You do not need to believe in energy, or in the one core source of all energy, highest consciousness, divinity, creator, God or the universe —all of which are simply descriptions of the higher intelligence from which all life stems. The signals will be there to guide you whether your mind believes in them or not. Why? Because belief or no belief, you are part of a collective, and you cannot disconnect yourself from your originating source even if you tried. You are highest consciousness manifest in human life, and highest consciousness communicates with its collective.

While your beliefs don't impact the signals, your beliefs can get in the way of you recognizing and harnessing those divine signals, as the fog clouds your view. If your conditioned paradigm is that you have no soul, that you are neither divine nor guided and that life has no deeper meaning, then you will naturally perceive life through that fog, and you will find evidence to support your perspective. If you don't believe that you are guided with signals, you will miss the signals completely, either because they will never show up on your radar or you will dismiss them as meaningless if they do.

If, however, you do believe in divine signals, your mind will attune to them and recognize them, because you always perceive reality (and indeed create reality) in alignment with your beliefs.

It is not that your beliefs make the signals appear or disappear. They are always there. It is just your perception that changes everything.

## Truth #57—You Are Taking Two Journeys Simultaneously, Internally and Externally

In a society dominated by the tangible and outward experience of life, many people first awakening to this co-creative process of divine support and signals become primarily interested in what highest consciousness, or the universe, can *give* them in terms of their ability to create their life in the physical, material sense—wanting more success, more money, more material possessions, more holidays, more experiences and so on. They work hard to get in alignment with the universe so they can get what they want when they want it.

Indeed, the co-creative process with divine support and signals can guide you on that external journey to create the reality that you desire in the physical environment in relation to the goals, dreams and success you envision for your life (when it is founded upon you being the full authentic expression of who you really are).

However, all of this external success is secondary to the primary journey you are here to take as a soul. External success is meaningless and hollow if you do not have inner peace and genuine happiness within.

The co-creative process with the universe will always, without fail, occur to guide you on an internal journey within yourself, to develop and grow as a person by clearing the fog. You will be lovingly triggered to see your fog, which could be interpreted as life beating up on you or things not going the way you want. What is really happening is that co-creation as a process is helping you to see and to shed everything that doesn't serve you, guiding you back within yourself to know who you truly are.

Why? Because you cannot create genuine and sustainable success in the New World, indeed you cannot create magnificence "out there" in the world to enjoy, if you are not discovering and nurturing magnificence within yourself. Of course this directly speaks to your nature as an "inside out" creator—both the fact that your beliefs, thoughts, feelings and actions (all stemming from your internal landscape) create life outcomes (external), and the fact that your soul intent to be here for learning (internal) is what draws to you some of the challenges you face (external) in order to trigger and aid that evolution.

When you focus on your internal journey just as passionately as you do on your external journey by looking honestly at yourself and dispelling your fog so you can be a clear channel for your soul to express through you into the world, then you reveal the person you were born to be, and the external journey to create the life you desire then becomes a *natural flowing consequence*.

## Truth #58—The Universe Will Always Give You What You Need to Grow

Everything in your life triggers your learning or your contribution. Your specific experiences are uniquely designed for you.

It is simple to identify how positive experiences and opportunities are a gift for your evolution. These are easy to embrace. You are likely to express gratitude to the universe for delivering these experiences to you.

However, it is also possible to see seemingly negative experiences in the same way. If you live from the paradigm that your soul is here to evolve, challenges take on new meaning. Breakdowns become clear conduits for breakthroughs. Every time you are triggered, you realize that you are being given an assignment for seeing yourself, others and life in a new way. You accept that you are being given an opportunity to see, and to shed whatever no longer serves you so that you can be a clearer channel for your soul to express out into the world. You notice that the challenge presents a platform for practicing a new way of being. Each experience can trigger new learning, generate new questions, new insights or new choices, and thus carry you in new directions.

Strangely enough, challenges may also be your opportunity to contribute. What looks like a storm in your life may well be someone else's storm, and your role is to learn from it and to shine the light of your consciousness—perceiving and behaving from the state of love—in order to support them.

Until you come to realize this particular truth, you will witness challenges in a one-dimensional way, through the narrow standpoint of your mind alone, one that says life "shouldn't" be doing this to you. This thinking is guaranteed to cause you pain.

## Truth #59—Both Your Soul Intention and Your Human Freewill are Occurring in Unison

Freewill is the reason that your life has the power to go any infinite number of ways. Your life is not written in stone. And yet, your life is also not solely determined by your mind.

Your soul's intention for being here and your freewill occur in unison. A fine dance goes on between the two. No one and nothing can force you in mind/body to play your part in this dance. If you do not dance, you may not learn, or, rather, you may learn the hard way. If you do not dance, you may not fully contribute. This means you may not align fully in mind and body to your soul intention. If, however, you do dance (being led by your soul—your passions, inspirations and intuition), you can rest assured that you will derive maximum benefit from the co-creation process with highest consciousness, and that you will journey into the greatest possibilities available for your soul in this life.

## Truth #60—What Your Soul Needs and What Your Mind/Body Want May Differ

Your mind and body wants are of this physical world. You may direct these with your freewill. Your soul needs come from a higher perspective. When your soul wants one thing and your mind wants another, pain arises. This happens in two ways.

What your soul needs shows up, and yet your mind may resist and reject these challenges, experiences, openings for change and opportunities presented to you.

Or, what your mind wants may not show up. Your mind may hold onto a desire to have something—a possession, an experience, a situation, or a particular goal or end outcome. Your soul, from a bigger picture and infinitely wiser perspective, may need something quite different. Therefore, anytime you do not get what you want, never feel that you are forsaken and that what you desire is not available to you. The showing up of unexpected challenges, experiences, openings for change or unrelated opportunities are simply part of your unfolding in that moment, an unfolding that must take place to prepare you in learning and contribution to experience your fullest possibilities.

What your mind perceives as delays is never evidence that you cannot have what you desire. Delays are divine in order and timing, to help you evolve *into* what you desire.

## Truth #61 - Divine Order and Divine Timing Exist

There is magic in the way life unfolds. When you least expect it, and sometimes seemingly without any effort on your part, there can be opportunities, good fortune, progress and helpful chance encounters. Life, at times, seems to conspire in your favor. And, yet, at other times, you do your best and work hard to create something, and nothing seems to happen the way you want it to when you want it to.

But know this—you will always receive what your soul needs when you need it, not a moment too soon and not a moment too late.

In divine organization, as highest consciousness weaves all of creation, there is an exacting nature to what you receive, which you cannot possibly wrap your logical mind around. What is necessary to leverage you to the next stage of your life journey will arrive right on time as part of the co-creative process. You are called upon to have faith and trust in the complex tapestry and how energy guides you and every other person on the planet.

Divine order and divine timing, as inherent functions of highest consciousness, are always working in your favor.

Without understanding divine order and timing, it is easy to assume that any delay in creating what you want in your life is somehow evidence that you cannot create it. However, delays are a part of your soul's growth. Something special happens in the gap between deciding what you want to create in your life and the point of actually achieving that goal—after setting a clear vision based on your passion, inspiration and intuition, and after taking every action you could take, if there is a delay in achieving your goal, there comes a moment when you are forced to do one last thing ... to trust. You are forced to trust deeply in yourself, in your own capability and in your own knowing of what is possible, and to have deep faith in the co-creation process with the universe, remembering that you are not forging this path all on your own, remembering you are not the only creative force at play.

Delays ask you to clear your mind of the fog. They are another mechanism to trigger your unfolding into your true nature by ditching whatever doesn't serve you. They force you into either giving up or fully aligning to your inner knowing about what is possible for you.

The delay between consciously creating and then experiencing and/or receiving is where your growth and learning occur.

## Truth #62—Dead Ends Are Never Truly Dead Ends

From your mind's perspective of how life works, you see yourself on a linear path from the moment of birth to the moment of death, from point A to point B. You have a picture of how your life should look, and you spend your time and energy striving to create that vision.

From this linear perspective, it's easy to fall into the belief that you are only moving forward if you are experiencing tangible evidence of your progress in the sense of creating the external life experience, goals and outcomes you want.

You have an idea in your mind, which is mind created (not soul created), of the most expedient path to your desired outcome. This will typically always be a straight line from your current position to that desired outcome. Based on that perspective, anything that sidetracks you from your goal appears as an obstacle to your mind's carefully crafted plan. As a result, whatever tangent you end up on feels like wasted time, wasted effort, an annoyance, a mistake or a dead end.

Whenever it feels like you have woven a path away from your desired destination, consider that your perspective could actually be warped. It's possible that your apparent tangent is actually part of the most direct path you could take, from your soul's perspective. For example, there may be learning available to you during your tangent, or at your seeming dead end, which is essential for your evolution in order for you to move forward into your original goal better equipped, as a wiser, clearer and stronger person.

There are no dead ends in your life. There are only temporary stops for learning and contribution, along your winding path.

## Truth #63—You Are Here to Intuitively Resonate with Higher Wisdom, Not Just Intellectually Understand Facts

As you walk your life path, you have experiences. You seek to make sense of those experiences so that you can better understand yourself, life and the world around you. You are conditioned to do this primarily through intellectual understanding. Society worships intellectual understanding.

You look for facts. You process "data" that you perceive through your physical senses, and you accept or reject what you see, hear and experience based on your intellect and how it considers, compares, contrasts, measures, rationalizes and analyzes. This is all valid and valuable as an approach. It can, however, at times be a forced process of reasoning to make life fit in a box that you can make sense of and, worse yet, to discount the aspects of life that just don't seem to fit in that box.

Aside from the power of your intellectual capacity, you have an equally powerful way of navigating, through your soul resonance. There are times in life when you come to sense something, feel something and know something. Or, you are nudged by an inner knowing to move in certain directions, which goes beyond any intellectual understanding and may defy logic. It may not make any sense to your mind, but, to your soul, everything is perfectly in order.

Soul resonance is beyond thought and words. It is when you can feel and experience something as true, without any intellectual way to explain why or how you know that truth. It is your intuitive, sixth sense. It is an automatic resonance that rises from within you, without a mind-based process initiating it. This is soul speaking through you. This compass of spiritual understanding is a gift every human possesses, the value of which has been largely overlooked and dismissed.

Due to the way society has conditioned you, and the fact that you see most other people around you as operating from intellect alone, it can feel challenging to give yourself permission to make soul-based decisions in your life. It can also be difficult to explain and be understood by others. Coming to accept your own soul resonance (intuition) is critical; being understood by others is not.

A moment of soul resonance will put you in a position where either your intellectual understanding is validated and now supported more deeply at the spiritual level, meaning your mind and soul are in unison of understanding, or, alternatively, where your intellectual understanding is set aside as not feeling right. Perhaps you may suddenly see aspects of your own foggy paradigm limiting you, which opens the door to new insights, new possibilities and new pathways forward.

## Truth #64—You Must Be Present to Receive Guidance

When you place your conscious awareness fully in the present moment, paying attention to how you are being, to what you are doing, to what you are sensing and feeling, and to what is going on all around you, then you are far more receptive to your guidance—both your soul speaking through you, and the divine signals showing up in your life.

Most people do not live anchored in the present moment. Instead of having your awareness here and now, you send your awareness off into past or future moments. When this occurs, you are not living in your life; you are living in your mind. You become busy revisiting, replaying, worrying about or being upset over something that has happened previously, be it five minutes ago or five years ago. Alternatively, you are busy rehearsing something that is going to happen, worrying about, preparing for and strategizing over coming moments. In this way, the present moment becomes a means to an end for you to project yourself into a mind-created experience of life. All the while the only real access point to your life, this moment, continues to pass you by unrecognized.

The present is the only place you can access your guidance. Your soul is not seeking to live in the past, and it is not seeking to live in the future. It seeks to express through you right now. It needs your attention and speaks to you through the language of feelings. You will only notice it if you are also here, with your conscious awareness in the present moment. The same goes for the divine signals being given to you. These can pass you by completely unnoticed if you are lost in your mind.

## Truth #65—It Is Never Selfish to Follow Your Intuition and Do What Is Heart-led

Whenever you authentically act in alignment with your intuition, carrying yourself with compassion and integrity, doing what is loving and heart-led for yourself, it is never a disservice to anyone else.

The notion that you doing what is best for your mind, body and soul is somehow selfish or in any way the wrong thing for someone else, is an illusion that you have been conditioned to believe in, which focuses on narrow circumstances without any consideration for the bigger picture of soul journeys and the interconnectedness of all souls energetically weaving together for mutual learning and contribution.

Even when following your intuition means having to put your needs before the needs of others, or when following your intuition means someone else does not like what you decide to shift into or away from, you must understand that it is of highest service to the world when you bring your full unique expression to every moment of your life. This is your purpose.

Other people may not like it, particularly if it disrupts a former falsified sort of equilibrium that was based upon you living as a suppressed version of yourself from within the fog. They will naturally experience an adjustment of some type in response to the real version of you that listens to your soul language. How people respond to that is not something you can or need to control. This doesn't mean not caring about how those people respond and feel. You can follow your intuition, and stay in the state of love, all while being aware of the ripple effect on others and how they choose to respond.

## Truth #66—Your Life Is a Process of Undoing and Removing Layers, Not Adding Them

The journey of growth—spiritually, mentally and emotionally—is one where you remove layers that have blocked your soul from expressing itself fully out into the world, and living its intention for learning and contribution. The journey of growth is not about adding layers.

In a world that promotes having more, being more and doing more, it is easy to become lost in thinking that your personal growth is a process of adding something to yourself in order to become more, become better or to complete yourself, like something is missing.

You are already enough. You are only here to grow into the fullness of who you already are. To expose that true you and to evolve yourself into knowing that person and living as that person, the process of personal growth is actually about removing what you no longer need, ceasing what no longer serves you and letting go of what blocks you. You are clearing away unnecessary layers, like peeling back an onion, which has sour outer layers, to get to the core, where the sweet center exists, so that any action you take is authentic and soul-led.

## Truth #67—As Long as You Are Breathing, Your Work Here Is Not Done

When your soul is ready to leave, it will. As long as your heart is beating and you draw breath in this world, your soul is here for a reason and your work is not done. There is learning to be had. There is passion, inspiration and intuition to act upon. There is your unique expression to be given into this world wholeheartedly.

This is your work. This is your calling. This is your purpose.

## Conscious Creating

## Truth #68 - Consciousness is Your Greatest Tool

Consciousness is a gift and a tool. To benefit from it, you have to choose to accept it and use it. If you do not, you will default into unconsciousness, which is to live in autopilot mode where your mind takes over and runs you.

It is with your consciousness that you influence your life outcomes. You consciously choose to adjust your unique energy vibration by molding your beliefs, thoughts, feelings and actions in ways that serve you, to create the inner and outer experience of life you prefer.

Your consciousness defines you as something other than an object, a robot or a puppet, and as something more than a passive recipient of gifts, a victim of challenges or a mouse on a wheel.

The most liberating benefit of your consciousness is how it allows you to observe your own mind as it runs its automatic thought processes, and how it allows you to witness your own feelings as they arise. Consciousness allows for the separate identification of these parts of yourself as just that ... parts of yourself, but not who you are in sum total. The fact that you can witness your own thoughts and feelings, and make choices about them, means that those things are not entirely who you are, and therefore they do not have to define and control you.

You have the choice to live from conscious awareness, instead of from identification with your automatic thinking and feeling.

This is how your conscious awareness is your greatest tool for creating inner peace, freedom and success. You are able to use it to create a paradigm you prefer, to align to your soul language and to live your highest possibilities.

### Truth #69—Conscious Living is a Choice and a Moment-by-Moment Practice

You can be physically awake and medically considered conscious, but from an energetic and spiritual perspective you can be sound asleep at the same time, if you identify primarily with your mind, stay stuck in the fog and do not apply awareness to your life.

Your consciousness makes you both an observer of yourself and life, and it makes you a creator of yourself and life. It gives you choices.

Living from your conscious awareness is a choice, not something that just magically happens to you. Many times you might have accidentally lapsed into unconscious living, spending a lot of time lost in your mind and probably noticing that it didn't benefit you.

Therefore, you must choose consciousness in order to benefit from it.

Choosing to live a conscious life does not mean that you choose once to be a consciously aware person, and forever after that moment you are living in awareness.

Your life is a constant moment–by-moment practice in awareness. The more you practice, the more familiar conscious awareness becomes. The more familiar it is, the more natural it feels and the more you notice how liberating it is to observe yourself and life in this way.

The more you select and embrace conscious living consistently, the more sharply you will notice the contrasting feelings of contraction, restriction, confusion and numbness that occur if you accidentally fall into unawareness, and, thus, the quicker you will return to awareness.

You do not need to plot, plan or strategize about how to live your entire life journey as a consciously aware person, nor how to make all the changes you want for yourself happen right now. You do not need to fight old habits, limitations or obstacles that seem impenetrable and pervasive as if life is an arduous long-running battle. Why? Because your life is simply a moment-by-moment experience, and change comes about through a moment-by-moment strategy. The present moment is the only point from which you bring about the change you desire. Being consciously aware in this moment is your primary access to all you desire.

Right now, you can be aware and make a choice that serves you and, in the next moment, you can repeat this. If you are accidentally unaware and make a choice that doesn't serve you, in the next moment you are presented with a brand new opportunity to be consciously aware again and make a different choice, one that serves you.

## Truth #70—Enlightenment Is an Ongoing Process, Not a Status to Achieve

Through the practice of conscious living, you learn to let go of mind-identification, feeling-identification and body-identification. As you do so, you become more enlightened about who you really are, who others really are, why you are here and how best to navigate your life. You become more empowered by your spiritual nature.

One moment of consciousness does not equate to enlightenment. Many moments of consciousness also do not equate to a status (label) or ongoing state of enlightenment, one based on prior moments. Not even the most holy of holy can declare themselves to forever be in a state of enlightenment with regards to the future. The reason is because the next moment has not happened yet, and it is in the face of that coming moment, in the face of new experiences, challenges and triggers that every human being is asked to make choices. Those choices are what create, expand and hold enlightenment, or not.

Each choice you make through your human perspective either further opens you up to be a clear channel for your soul to express from its expansive and loving awareness, or it closes you down and blocks that flow.

Each moment you choose conscious awareness, you enlighten yourself further. Your personal process of enlightenment in this lifetime never stops, until the day your heart stops beating.

## Truth #71—Your Beliefs, Thoughts, Feeling and Actions Are a Creation Equation

The process of how you experience and create life runs in a constant cycle, as an equation. This happens whether you are consciously aware of it, or not.

It starts with your beliefs, positive beliefs and/or limiting beliefs, as a key part of your paradigm. They are the way you uniquely perceive, filter and then interpret the world—you will experience the world in direct alignment with your beliefs.

As you notice life and process what you notice both consciously and subconsciously through what you believe to be true and real, this produces a response at the level of thought and feeling as a result, both of which will obediently align to your beliefs.

You then take action based entirely on what you believe, and on the resulting thoughts and arising feelings. This cycle goes on continuously for as long as you are alive.

It is a process that requires no conscious awareness to occur. It will happen in healthy and positive ways, or destructive and negative ways, based entirely upon the nature of your beliefs.

## Truth #72—Your Beliefs Are an Internal Code That Run You

Your beliefs are an internal code that run you and thus run your life experience. They do so in two primary ways.

Firstly, your beliefs dictate the way you experience whatever is happening in your life. They define how you perceive yourself, other people and every aspect of your day-to-day life. You filter and interpret everything through these beliefs. They define what your circumstances mean, what story you tell yourself; this all forms the foundation of either all your pain and suffering, or all your peace and happiness.

Secondly, your beliefs underpin all your thoughts and feelings, with the exception of soul-prompted feelings of passion, inspiration and intuition, and those thoughts and feelings are (a) part of your energetic vibration that is constantly influencing your life by intersecting with the fabric of universal energy you belong to, and (b) those thoughts and feelings influence your actions, which directly produce tangible results in your life.

This belief code runs you much like the operating program that runs a computer. Just like computer code is written and drives the whole functionality of the system, your belief code does the same.

Every person has different beliefs, and every person has a different experience of life. Even two individuals encountering the same people, things, situations, circumstances, challenges and triumphs experience them uniquely because their belief code filters what is occurring.

Limiting beliefs are a major fog component; they will cloud you, suffocate you and completely warp your experience of yourself, others and life. If you change your external life experience—moving, changing jobs or switching relationships for example, but you continue to experience all of that newness from the same old beliefs, then life will continue to occur to you in much the same way because your beliefs remain unchanged. Despite some improvement and relief due to external circumstances being more palatable or different, you simply carry your inner limiting belief code with you into your new external experience.

A healthy new positive belief code will literally transform your life. You could live exactly the same life situation, with the same physical day-to-day life experiences, and yet life will occur to you in an entirely new way because of your new belief code.

The sooner you understand what your own belief code is and realize that you have the capacity to change it, the sooner you will take control of your experience of life (how life occurs to you) and be in a position to create and hold a state of inner peace and inner freedom no matter what life throws at you.

### Truth #73—Limiting Beliefs Are the Core Foundation of the Fog

You know the four key components of the fog are limiting beliefs, expectations, fear and societal conditioning. And now is the time for me to share with you the stark truth of what this really means ...

Limiting beliefs are limiting beliefs.

Most fear arises from limiting beliefs, and fear has the power to generate more limiting beliefs.

Expectations arise out of limiting beliefs and have the power to create more limiting beliefs.

Societal conditioning creates limiting beliefs.

Limiting beliefs are the foundation of the fog.

*Limiting beliefs are the only thing you need to focus on in terms of clearing the fog.*

### Truth #74—You Hold Both Conscious Beliefs and Subconscious Beliefs

There are beliefs you have that you are already aware of, both positive and negative (limiting). You say them quite freely and easily. You can voice what you believe about yourself, what you believe about people in general, what you believe about your life and what you believe about the world.

You also have beliefs that run much deeper and are not part of your conscious awareness. They are like an undercurrent below the surface of a river; they direct the flow and are a powerful force, but they are not visible on the surface. These are your subconscious beliefs.

## Truth #75—Your Beliefs Were Created and Cemented Due to Frequency and/or Intensity

Consistent, repetitive thought and feeling processes are part of what creates your underlying belief systems. Experienced often enough, a thought and feeling combination can become so familiar that it becomes your habitual way of experiencing the world, formulating as belief code due to frequency and repetition.

Intensity of thought and feeling processes are another part of what can create beliefs. Something that occurs one-off but is traumatic in a passing moment, processed in thought and feeling, can be influential and effective in creating a deeply held belief about who you are, who others are and what the world is about.

## Truth #76—Your Limiting Beliefs Can Be Identified in Three Powerful Ways

While the majority of your beliefs are attributable to experiences you have had in this lifetime, there is an undeniable energy that is based upon your soul history—your soul light and soul shadow.

It doesn't matter where the belief stems from, this lifetime or soul energy you brought with you, the way to find the limiting belief is the same.

If beliefs + thoughts + feelings + actions = the majority of what generates your life experience and outcomes, then you can work backwards from the results you create, to the actions you took, to the thoughts and feelings you had, to the beliefs upon which it all rests and was driven by.

The first method to help you identify your limiting beliefs is through reviewing your life to date for patterns or themes. Limiting beliefs will often play out over and over again in different areas of your life, until resolved. You can consider your actual experiences, outcomes and life path to date retrospectively in order to see what repeating negative patterns there might be, and to consider what beliefs those patterns may point to.

The second method to help you identify your limiting beliefs is to look at the middle of your equation for creation, not at the actions or outcomes that have occurred, but at the thoughts and feelings you have right now, irrespective of how they influence your actions. Your thoughts and feelings, whether you consider them positive or negative, always arise as messengers. If you pay close attention, they will point you back to the originating beliefs from where they stem.

The third method to help you identify your limiting beliefs is through targeted conversation for the purpose of discovering those beliefs. Two-way conversation is a remarkable tool for accessing deep beliefs, if the right questions are asked and the conversation is within a trusted and loving environment where you feel free and supported to be honest with yourself. Such conversation, informally with a loved one or formally in coaching or therapy, acts as a trigger, and beliefs will come up from within you that you didn't consciously realize were there.

## Truth #77—Your Limiting Beliefs Do Not Belong to You

If who you are is a soul manifest in human form, a spark of divinity, a reflection of highest consciousness—then there is no way that any low vibration limiting beliefs truly belong to you. They are mind-created misinterpretations that led you away from your true nature and shrouded you. Accumulated from one time or another, from one place or another, from one person or another, from one source or another.

As limiting beliefs are not in any way reflective of your true nature, you cannot hold on to them. They simply do not belong to you. There is no room in your true nature for them. They are weighty baggage, excess, burdens that sadden, restrict and make you feel uneasy for a reason—they simply don't gel with who you are. You don't want them, and you don't need them. That is enough impetus for change.

## Truth #78—Your Limiting Beliefs Are Not a Roadblock to Your Success, They Are the Signposts to Your Success

As you learn about your limiting beliefs, it would be easy to suggest that they are your enemy, a roadblock to all you desire. This, in fairness, is somewhat accurate. However, there is one absolutely critical realization about your limiting beliefs that will transform your understanding of life.

Your limiting beliefs provide signposts to your success. When triggered, they provide you with exacting guidance as to what internally is holding you back from your success so that you have the power to proactively transform your paradigm. They show you the way to move forward by showing you what is in your way. Whatever stands in your way is the place to move into, to face, to shine the light of your conscious awareness on, to give your attention to, for the pure purpose of transforming that block. In this way, your limiting beliefs flaring up and getting your attention is actually of benefit, because they show you what to resolve in order to create greater inner peace, freedom and success from the inside out.

## Truth #79—Your Limiting Beliefs Can Be Changed

Just as they were formed in the first place, your beliefs can be unformed, or, more accurately stated, they can be transformed.

It is the replacement of one energy with another energy that brings about transformation. It is the substitution of one perspective for another perspective that brings about inner peace and freedom.

Once you have identified the limiting beliefs that were keeping you stuck in the fog, your empowerment lies within your ability to choose, from your conscious awareness, a replacement set of new uplifting beliefs, which resonate deeply with you, inspiring you and evoking a sense of positive emotion.

There are three factors that loosen the grip of old limiting beliefs and support the embedding of replacement positive beliefs.

Firstly, awareness. Understanding what those limiting beliefs are (literally naming them specifically) and understanding how they have been negatively impacting you and your life, allows you to see the ludicrous nature of those limiting beliefs as a complete contradiction to who you really are in light of all the truths you now know. That in itself is enough to release their full power over you. Awareness of truth is the starting point for your unleashing.

Secondly, the high vibration associated with consciously chosen positive beliefs is part of what overwrites the low vibration, unconscious way of perceiving the world that has previously been your experience. This high vibration is a counterbalance. And, it simply feels good. Once you know it exists, you cannot help but move toward it.

Thirdly, as consistent and repetitive negative thought and feeling processes are a part of what created your limiting beliefs in the first place, then the same process of consistent, repetitive, consciously chosen positive thoughts and feelings in alignment with your new beliefs supports the embedding of those beliefs. You can create daily rituals and practical tools to support this consistent and frequent repetition, such as verbal, audio or written reinforcement of your new beliefs.

These three factors support the formation of your new paradigm, aligned to truth, making your old paradigm obsolete.

## Truth #80—You Must Act from New Empowering Beliefs for Them to Come to Life in Your External Reality

While you control what is within you, and you have the power to form this new paradigm, you are still living within a world that is filled with triggers that may previously have hit the nerve of your old, limiting beliefs.

As you go out into the world as it is and always has been, with newly chosen beliefs, and you notice your old paradigm flare up in reaction to people, things and situations, your conscious awareness (your greatest tool) is required in order to bring your new beliefs to life. In that moment of feeling triggered, noticing the residue of your old beliefs lingering, you have a conscious choice to make in that moment—give airtime to that old paradigm, or reinforce your new paradigm by responding out of the lens of your new beliefs. Your real-time practice of your new beliefs, putting them into action in the heat of the moment, is what helps to consolidate your new paradigm, and bring it to life in your external reality.

It is easy enough to proactively think and feel in alignment with your new beliefs when in moments of isolation, peace and quiet, when life is going smoothly, but the way you deeply ingrain those beliefs is through the moment-by-moment practice in your busy and noisy daily life.

The more you practice responding to life from the position of your new beliefs, the more your old, limiting beliefs continue to fade away. The more you see your new beliefs in action, because you consciously directed your mind to perceive from that new perspective, the more your thoughts and feelings naturally lift to and cycle within higher vibration. The more empowered you feel, the more your ongoing actions naturally come into alignment. The positive flow-on effects in your life (from your energy vibration) then act like a positive feedback loop, reinforcing the value of your new paradigm.

## Truth #81—Your Mind and Feeling System are Navigational Tools

You are not your thoughts or your feelings. Your mind and feeling system are tools to help you navigate life and create life. They are designed for your use. The aspect of "you" that is using these tools is your soul through conscious awareness, which exists beyond your mind and body.

You may find it challenging to believe that you are not the thoughts in your head or the feelings in your body, especially if you have spent your entire life to date identifying with them.

There are many parts of yourself that help you navigate through life, but they are not entirely who you are either. For example, you have a liver, but you are not your liver. You have a set of lungs, but you are not your lungs. You have feet, but you are not your feet. You have a brain but you are not your brain. These aspects of who you are—your mind, your thoughts, your body, your feelings—they are all a vehicle through which your soul experiences life, and they are tools to help you function as a human being. They provide you with a sensory experience of life.

Focusing now primarily on your mind and feeling system, but also applicable for certain aspects of your physical body as well, these tools can take instruction from you on what you want them to do for you. But, they can also, without being invited to, provide you with important messages to help you learn, expand, contribute and navigate this complex world as a human being.

For example, regarding your mind, you can consciously focus your awareness on something in particular, which redirects all your attention to that focal point. You train your thoughts onto whatever it is you wish to experience, proactively helping to form a paradigm that works for you. You create your life in this way. And, you can also take feedback information from your mind as it throws up unwanted automatic thoughts. Their unwanted nature, in low vibration, helps you understand that you have limiting beliefs. Your thoughts are clearly signposting the way for you to find those limiting beliefs within yourself.

Regarding your feeling system, you can consciously uplift your emotional state based on what you choose to focus your awareness on. As you shift your attention, it shifts your thoughts, and that impacts your arising feelings. You can create certain emotions within yourself by utilizing your consciousness in this way. Your feelings in turn are also providing feedback to you in a loop to help you navigate. You have the feelings of passion, inspiration and intuition, which are your soul speaking to you, in a way that your mind can understand. You also have low vibration feelings, which are incredibly powerful messages that help you to understand that you have limiting beliefs or which help you to discover what and who in life you do not naturally gel with, what you do not like and do not want. That clarity helps you to hone in on what you do prefer.

Growing up, the majority of people are not taught that their thoughts and feelings are navigational tools. As such, they become immediately and completely identified with their automatic thoughts and feelings, as if these are who they are. Instead of owning and using their tools, they are owned and used by them. Conscious awareness is all that is required to break out of this cycle.

## Truth #82—Your Mind Is Not Bad, It Is Simply Misused

When discovering more about the relationship between your true holistic nature and the role of your mind in creating your experience of life, it is glaringly obvious to see the role of the mind in pain and suffering.

This does not make the mind bad. This makes the mind a misused tool.

Your mind needs you, the conscious awareness you are, to provide it with leadership to guide it into optimal performance. If you practice presence in the moments of your daily life then you will start to disidentify from your mind, coming into your conscious awareness such that you can observe your minds automatic thought processes. This then gives you the capacity to start to change those processes, training your mind by consciously shifting your attention, and thus using your mind to your advantage.

## Truth #83—The Majority of Your Emotional Pain Stems From Your Perspective

There are many triggers in life, which may appear to cause you to react negatively. Something happens, someone says something, or something doesn't go the way you expected, and that triggers a reaction within you. Often times, you might consider the external person, situation or thing to be the cause of your negative reaction and therefore responsible for your pain.

You must realize this—in the majority of cases the external person, situation or thing is not the cause of your pain. It is only the trigger.

What is it triggering? You. More specifically, it is triggering some part of you that is unable to be with the world as it is, that is unable to accept what it does not like or approve of. The cause is often within you.

The root cause is typically what you believe about what is occurring. Because you have the power to shift your beliefs, you have the ability to transmute the cause of your pain. Shift your paradigm, unleash your life.

You have been conditioned to believe that life occurs outside of you, and you react to that with your internal thoughts and feelings, and if those thoughts and feelings are unpleasant then you might extrapolate that to mean that the external experience is at fault, and that life is happening to you. While there may be extreme circumstances where external events or people literally inflict physical pain or emotional abuse upon you, in the majority of situations day to day the inner pain is generated primarily from your perspective (how you perceive and interpret life), which leaves you powerless and victimized to the external world.

It is an empowering realization to discover that the cause of most of your emotional pain is within you. Even if your interpretation of a situation appears to you to be understandable, rational, realistic and valid, you are encouraged to remember that in most situations no person or thing can *make* you feel anything. No person or thing can *make* you think anything. Your thoughts and feelings are your sacred territory. They are the one space in your life that you can hold for yourself irrespective of what goes on around you. Do not give your power away by saying that someone or something else dictates what you think and how you feel.

That said, it is not realistic to anticipate that you will *never* be triggered into a painful reaction. Life is challenging at times, certain things happen that are outside of your control. You are human and you are not meant to be perfect. Rather, you are on a journey to practice your awareness, to practice choosing perspectives that support you.

This does not mean that you need to continue to be in the presence of the person, situation or thing that triggers your reaction. By all means, if possible, move away from the trigger, but simply understand that the root cause may be within you, and so while you can shift away, if you carry the cause within you, there will be new triggers waiting for you wherever you go.

## Truth #84—Life Is Not a Race

Whenever you discover something new about yourself, and about life, it is all too common to think that the time before your discovery was wasted, or that mistakes could have been avoided by knowing these things earlier. There is also a sense of wanting to live the optimal life as soon as possible, both in terms of having inner peace and happiness and regarding external success and achievements.

Anytime you wish you knew something earlier, realize that you would not be where you are now if you had. You might think that would be a good thing if you don't like where you are right now, but that is viewing the present from the limited perspective of your human mind. You were born to grow into your realizations, not to come fully equipped with them from day one. It is part of the design for awakening. There is nothing wrong with you for acquiring wisdom and knowledge later than your mind deems ideal. Where you are right now is going to lead you to your next realization, your next insight, your evolving wisdom, your learning and your ongoing contribution. Where you are right now is part of the journey and it is key to the unfolding of your life.

Life is not a race. There is no need to sprint. Learning, growing into and living from truth is a lifetime's work. That is, you have been gifted an entire lifetime, however long that is for you, in order to practice this. The entire journey of life is a practice. An exercise in conscious awareness. A practice of your natural state of love. A practice of learning, growing and contributing.

## Truth #85—You Are Living in Natural Cycles of Expansion and Contraction

A life is made up of seasons. You move from season to season, like nature does. Just as the seasons change from summer's creative flourishing to winter's restorative hibernation, as the tides of the ocean ebb and flow, as the sun rises and sets, you also go through your own natural cycles.

Your life from birth to death is one cycle of your soul—birth brings you into creation, death returns you home on the soul journey, with lessons learnt and a contribution made along the way. Your soul may go through many of these cycles, having multiple lifetimes.

Within this lifetime you are having mini cycles of expansion and contraction. These mini cycles are ones of outward creation and inward reflection, of action and stillness, of motion and rest, of waking and sleeping, of new discovery and assimilation.

At certain times of your life, you will be contributing more than learning. At other times, you will be learning more than contributing. You will have periods of time where you are predominantly externally focused, doing, and periods of time where you are predominantly internally focused and going within yourself for reflecting, recharging and simply being.

Expanding and contracting, expanding and contracting, expanding and contracting—this is the natural flow. Life cannot be continued expansion. That is exhausting and would be imbalanced. Everything has an opposite, a counter balance. This is the way all of nature is designed; it is a fundamental to life in our universe, and you are not exempt from this.

For balance and well-being physically, mentally, emotionally and spiritually, you must understand that your life has these energy cycles and that you are being called upon to flow with them, rather than to resist them. In our modern busy world, which is focused primarily on the creation of more and better, and material standards of success, most people are trying hard to stay within a constant expansion phase, and little to no value is placed on the concept of a contraction phase. What this mode of operation fails to account for is that the power and momentum of a creative expansion phase is fuelled by the recharging and insights that come out of a contraction phase.

Bringing presence to your life, a greater level of conscious awareness, will help you tune into your cycles. If what your soul needs is restoration, reflection, going within and a focus on your being, then you must listen to your inner voice. Your intuition will guide you. If what your soul needs is to express, to do, to contribute, to create, to move, to speak and to evolve outwardly in the world through external action, then you must listen to that passion, and those inspirations and urges that come to you.

The ancient science of numerology also clearly outlines for you a nine-year cycle that continues over and over during your lifetime. Each year in the cycle carries a specific type of energy that you are living within and influenced by. This information can help you to tune into your flow.

## Truth #86—The Life You Desire Is Possible, but First You Must Be Willing to Let Go of the Life You Have

The access point to all that you desire is your willingness to let go of what no longer serves you; this includes your limiting ways of being (beliefs, thoughts and feelings) and your limiting ways of doing (actions). It may also include letting go of external circumstances, arrangements, people and things that you no longer wish to have in your life.

If you desire a different type of life experience, that means you don't desire the totality of the life experience you are having right now; therefore, there is no point in clinging onto it.

You cannot walk into the new aspects of life that you know are possible while dragging behind you the old aspects of life you no longer want or need. You will not have space within your life or yourself physically, mentally or emotionally to do so. You will not have time, energy or attention free to give to what you desire if you are fully immersed in a mind-set, or engaged with actions, situations, people or things that are not reflective of the possibilities you want to create.

You simply can't live two different life experiences at once. You either have your present experience, or you create a new one. The act of willingly releasing your inner attachment to what you no longer want and need is energetically what shifts you forward. Willingness, though, is not an action; it is an attitude. Willingness is an inner release. It does not necessarily mean that you must literally let go of anything. Rather, it is allowing your life to flow and unfold naturally without you holding it back, funneling and restricting it. Willingness allows energy to move as energy wishes to move, like a river that wishes to follow its curves and gravity, to move as nature intended. So, too, your life can flow and unfold as your soul intends, working in unison with your conscious desire and freewill to create. But you have to get out of your own way. Your grip on what is familiar and what you have, even if it is not what you want, is what stops the flow. Any desire to create a vision, met with your unwillingness to actually allow that vision to become a reality, means you enter a stalemate. You want it, but deny it the chance to come into existence.

The life you desire can be both a perspective of life and an actual physical external experience of life. Often the life people desire, which is not their current experience of life, is both a desire for inner peace, sense of freedom and happiness, as well as some type of change in their external circumstances. The new inner perspective of life is available to you right now, if you willingly let go of your old paradigm, actively and consciously choosing to clear the fog. Your reality literally transforms from the inside out, in the sense that while your physical, external life experience may remain exactly the same (the same environment, same people, same circumstances, same day-to-day routine and the same resources), your paradigm has changed so you interpret everything with new eyes. Remarkably, the "sameness" can start occurring to you in a completely different light.

New external circumstances, be it where you are, what you do, who you are with or what you have, only become available to you when you are willing to exchange your energy out there in the world in new ways. To be in a new location, you must be willing to leave your current location. To have a new job you must be willing to leave your current job. To have a new intimate relationship you must be willing to either leave your current relationship or leave your situation of being single. To have new health and well-being, you must be willing to say goodbye to the unhealthy habits you have. To experience greater financial freedom you must be willing to function in ways (inwardly and outwardly) that generate greater flow of income, and/or less expenses. There is always an energy exchange going on, which carries you forward, and that exchange requires your willingness in order for it to take place.

# Reality

## Truth #87—Your Entire Reality Is Unique

The planet is. Life is. Things are. People are. Situations are. Fact.

And, reality is none of these things. Reality is how you personally and uniquely perceive your world through the filter of beliefs, which were conditioned by experiences.

It is your unique paradigm that filters "what is" (fact) and makes meaning of it (interpretation), creating reality for yourself.

No one experiences the same reality as you. In this way, what you think "reality" is, is completely unique to you.

## Truth #88—There Are Countless Versions of Reality Occurring at One Time

Your version of reality shifts over time, based on your evolving belief system, which is changing in response to your experiences. The more experiences you have, the more your beliefs further embed or change. Therefore, over this lifetime, you will experience many versions of reality, because the shifting lens of your beliefs colors how you perceive others, life and the world.

As it is for you, so it is for other people. There are over seven billion people on the planet. That means over seven billion versions of reality are going on at one time, due to over seven billion unique belief systems shaped by each individual's own personal path of experiences. As each person evolves over time, having more experiences, belief systems shift too, creating different versions of reality along the way.

## Truth #89—While Every Person Is in a Different Reality, There Is Common Ground for Love and Understanding

With every person experiencing a different version of reality, it could seem on the surface that this would create a sense of separation, isolation and conflict among all people.

All conflict does arise because of different realities, based on different belief systems. But it is not the difference in belief systems alone that creates the conflict. It is the unconsciousness of the people involved that leads two vastly different belief systems to clash. The clash occurs because people are unable to see their common ground, often because they do not seek it in the first place. They have no higher awareness of their energetic connectedness and shared source, and thus no awareness of their commonality as souls or as human beings.

Instead, they are lost in their own distinct fogs; they grip onto their belief systems from the perspective that their lives depend on them. That is, their entire version of reality is based on what they believe, and anything that opposes that view is a threat to life as they have come to know it. If someone or something suggests their version of reality is not real, it threatens to cut off any sense they have of who they are. Some people will die to protect their sense of who they are, even if that sense is warped.

Two different belief systems meeting in a state of unconsciousness—be it two individuals, two groups, two businesses, two families, two communities, two religion or faith bases, or two countries—are live wires ready for escalation to spark from initial misunderstanding, disagreement and arguments, to hate, bigotry, violence and war.

However, whenever consciously aware people come together, living from their natural state of love, they can have different beliefs, experience their own unique versions of reality and still be at peace with each other. This is because consciousness and love allow for the full sight and sense of the commonality in all people—they see the energetic connectedness, the oneness in all things, the shared source from which we all spring. Consciousness and love see this because they seek to see it.

When you are conscious to your own true nature, and why you are here, and why all souls are here, then you look for resonance in the world around you. You become more allowing of all people to be their own unique expression, rather than the unconscious default position you fall into in the fog, which is to desire and potentially force others to express themselves in alignment with your reality, to mirror what you believe.

Loving consciousness does not ask this of others. Love asks others to be their unique expression, so that they may make their contribution to this world and learn their lessons along the way. Love understands that this is why we are here.

## Truth #90—You Will Always Find Evidence to Support Your Perspective of Reality

You can find evidence to support whatever perspective you take in life. Just notice whether your perspective creates a limiting life for you or a limitless life, whether it creates inner peace for you or pain for you.

If you believe the world is unfair and you are not supported, you will easily find evidence to support that perspective. If you believe the world is full of miracles and endless possibilities, you will easily find evidence to support that perspective. If it is true that you find evidence to support your perspective, then it goes without saying that you would do well to choose a positive perspective.

You could debate that particular truths in this book are not certain and cannot be labeled truth. You could say that they are not fact and there is no evidence in your life to date that supports these statements. You could choose to say there is no guarantee that these age-old truths will provide you with the type of life experience you desire. And, yet, you could also look at each opportunity for growth with problem eyes or solution eyes, with a glass half empty or a glass half full mentality, and the quality of your life experience will undoubtedly be a reflection of the perspective you choose.

If how you currently perceive yourself and life does not work for you, and a new perspective allows you greater peace and flow, regardless of whether you can qualify or quantify it, it seems insane to choose a proven limiting perspective over an unproven limitless perspective.

## Truth #91—Miracles Are Everywhere, Every Day

Miracles surround you. Nature is a miracle in every respect. You are a miracle. The ability to shift your paradigm is a miracle. The ability to create out of your imagination by consciously directing your energy is a miracle. The fact that you were born is a miracle. Your body with its incredibly complex, finely tuned system for living, breathing, nourishing, thinking, feeling, alerting you, supporting you—it is all a miracle. Your soul is a miracle.

When you stop trying to force life to look a certain way, based on what society tells you life "should" look like (part of your conditioning that led you into the fog), and instead you tune into your one true guiding compass—your soul—you will start to notice miracles everywhere.

It is not that miracles appear from thin air, it is that you perceive reality in a way that suddenly allows them to be seen. The beauty of this is that you can shift your perspective in an instant, with little effort and immediate impact, and thus life can appear to you in a whole new way. It is like you took off a blindfold.

## Truth #92—Time Is Not Real, Now Is What Matters

Time is an illusion. You are conditioned to think of your life in a linear fashion, like a timeline. You might imagine a long line and a point called the present that you stand on right now. The past stretches behind you and the future lies ahead.

This way of perceiving time is a man-made construct. Human beings created the calendar and clock timekeeping systems to reflect the movements of the sun, moon, other planets and stars, to account for and track day and night and seasonal changes. This is immensely helpful in terms of functioning as a society. Our systems of time allow us to interact and communicate in an orderly way. We can name the present moment, along with past and future moments, in an internationally agreed upon way for the purpose of collective understanding and communicating in day-to-day life.

Here are the facts. The planet is. People are. You are. Days turn into night. Nights turn into day. The sun and moon shift. Seasons change. That all occurs. That does not make time real.

While time as a construct has helped society function, it has also completely constricted people in the way they perceive themselves, because people experience their life in relation to time. When you experience life in relation to an illusion, you become stuck in a trap.

The idea that time is real gives rise to notions such as the "right time," the "wrong time," "not enough time," "time is running out" or "I've got plenty more time." These notions have the potential to lead you into treating the past and future like living, breathing entities, which then control you. These notions also have the potential to lead you into wasting the present moment in thinking and feeling states that don't serve you, such as resistance, fear, anxiety, panic, worry, lack of confidence and concern, or apathy, carelessness, laziness and dismissiveness. This all diminishes the value of the present moment, treating it like a portal to go off in your mind into past and future, or using it merely as a means to an end, to get somewhere else in your life.

There is only this moment. You can't physically go back into the past, and you can't physically go into the future. You will never exist in this lifetime anywhere apart from right now. Your only experience of your soul is right now. Your passion can only ever be brought into reality now. Your inspiration will only ever be noticed in the now. Your intuition can only be felt now.

As this moment passes, a new moment arrives. You will also experience that moment as now. The previous moment literally ceases to exist. The only place moments other than "now" can exist is within your mind as a perception.

## Truth #93—The Past Is a Memory and the Future Is a Mental Projection

You cannot show me the past or the future—you can only perceive it as an idea through your mind. The past is a memory. The future is a mental projection. Both are mind creations.

You can choose to dwell back in the past for learning and joyous reflection. You can choose to dwell in the future for visualization and practical planning. However, whenever your awareness floats away to the past or future frequently for low vibration thinking (giving rise to low vibration emotional reactions), you are suffocating your ability to thrive in the only moment you ever have ... the now.

Many people do not live their life in the now; they live their life inside their mind where they replay the past over and over again—what someone said, what someone did, what you said, what you did, what you didn't do, what you didn't create or achieve, what it felt like, what you regret, what you resent, what you wish you could do over, who you miss, all while wishing you could go back, wishing life was how it used to be, or living in fear that the present will be more of the pain of the past and longing to be freed from the past. As you do this, you send all of your precious energy hurtling out of the present and into a bottomless hole—the illusion of the past as experienced solely in your mind. You miss the now, and you miss the opportunity to use your energy for the fulfillment of all the possibilities the now offers.

People rehearse the future over and over again—what might happen, what you might do, what you might fail to create or achieve, what it might feel like, what you worry could happen, all the scenarios that could play out, preparing for the coming moment, planning all the things that need to be done in the future and hoping your future will be different to how your life is now.

Unless you are consciously using a memory of the past or a projection of the future for the purpose of feeling good or for conscious creation (reflecting on the past with gratitude and for learning, or visualizing your success), then you are trapped.

Past and future do not exist—this truth frees you. When you learn that the past and the future are simply constructs designed to help you make sense of your life experience, then you can use those memories and mental projections to your maximum benefit instead of to your total detriment.

## Truth #94—Time Cannot Run Out

Because time is not real, it cannot run out. Even when you die, time does not run out. Your soul simply continues in oneness with highest consciousness and exists beyond the physical experience you have right now.

A sense of scarcity, lack, comparison and fear, all underpinned by limiting beliefs and lack of awareness of your true nature, give rise to strong negative emotions and a sense that time is running out ... to find love, to have children, to achieve your goals, to live the dream, to accumulate "enough," to find meaning in life, to understand life, to become more and to do more.

There is never anything missing with where you are right now—not circumstantially, not physically, not mentally and not emotionally ... where you are is serving a purpose for your learning in this moment, so that your next moment can give rise to new insight and new contribution to yourself and to others. All of this aids your evolution.

There is nowhere to get to. There is nowhere to run. There is no ladder to climb. There is no way you need to make yourself be other than who you naturally are. There are no more things that you need to accumulate. You are not being left behind by anyone or anything. You are not "not where you are 'supposed' to be."

When you desire something other than what you currently have, it is not time running out that you need to focus on. It is your energy. From a soul perspective, everything you need arises when you need it. Beyond need, in terms of what you want, you are being asked to shift your paradigm, which shifts your reality, so that what you want has the chance to actually show up on your radar. You are being asked to live consciously, to be present to the now moment, to pay full attention to and act upon your soul language (passion, inspiration and intuition), to make choices that serve you moment by moment, and to trust in the natural unfolding of your life.

## Truth #95—There Is No Right Time

If time isn't real, then there can be no "right time."

There can be moments in your life that intuitively feel more conducive or less conducive to certain goals and dreams. There can be times that feel more instinctively like an opening for change. There can be times when inspiration rises most strongly and times when your energy has to focus primarily on inner learning rather than on outer creating, or vice versa. But none of these are the right time or the wrong time, as far as unleashing your life. The time to be in inner peace is always now. The time to experience freedom from the inside out, is now. The time to be successful as a human being, according to the New World model of success, is now. The time to clear the fog is now.

If you are waiting for the right time to have inner peace, freedom and success, this means you must feel like the present moment is not the time for these experiences, or for the conscious awareness and love that give rise to them. This must mean that you are busy being in pain instead of peace, shackled instead of free, and struggling instead of successful. You may feel forced to experience more of this difficult energy until "the time is right" for change. If that is the case, please let me know when you are done with the pain, shackles and struggle. Let me know when you feel the time is right. Your soul knows that time is not real and that the now moment is the one and only time to shift your paradigm. Your soul is patiently waiting for your mind to come to the same conclusion.

## Challenges

### Truth #96—Challenges Are a Natural Part of Your Life Experience

Life is not always easy. Stop resisting this, and you will discover inner peace. No person on the planet will tell you honestly that life is easy. It is a complex adventure. Challenges are a normal part of that adventure; they are a natural part of life, gateways to new insights and gifts for growth. There is nothing wrong with having challenges.

If you expect that your life should have no challenges, you will be in pain. You will resist any challenges that do arise, and you will make it mean something negative, such as there is something wrong with you, with what you are doing or with your life. This will lead you to beat up on yourself or to feel wronged. You will say it should be some other way than how it is, resisting the facts of the present moment. All of this is a waste of your precious energy.

Relax. There is nothing wrong with you. The process of learning and contributing is vibrant, satisfying and sometimes challenging.

While you needn't embrace and rejoice any challenge you face—you can still be at peace and cease from exacerbating the issue for yourself through a paradigm that makes you suffer. This allows you to reallocate that energy to identifying what learning might be available to you in that challenge and to focus on solutions for moving yourself forward through it.

## Truth #97—Drama and Chaos Are Not Real

Drama and chaos are not things that happen to you. You create them, but not at all in the way you might suspect.

Adversity, challenges, loss and problems—those all happen, but they are not drama, and they are not chaos. They are just situations.

Something happens, fact. You interpret it, and, because of your interpretation, you either witness the situation peacefully or you react to it; your perspective can make it dramatic and/or chaotic.

It is entirely your interpretation of, and reaction to, circumstances and events that creates the emotional cycle. The truth is that drama and chaos don't exist without you. They don't exist as independent entities. You cannot show me drama or chaos as objects. They exist in only one place— within yourself, as a result of how you interpret, and then respond, or react, to life circumstances based on your perspective. This is empowering, because you can shift your perspective, and thus eradicate the notion of drama and chaos from your life.

Of course, certain circumstances and events such as violence, tragedy, grief, loss and critical illness are deeply challenging and provoke strong, visceral emotion within us, which is natural. In such situations it can easily feel like drama and chaos are happening to you, especially when the events are outside of your control. The power you have in those extreme situations exists within your ability to respond to life with grace—allowing the fullness of your emotions to arise and flow, while also choosing a perspective that helps you come to terms with what life has presented, and thus allows you to consciously manage the intensity and direction of your emotional cycle. It is possible, with practice, to do this without generating an interpretation of drama and chaos layered on top of what are already challenging emotions.

Below all challenging emotions, inner peace exists. That inner peace is your natural state of love. It is always there and available. Your perspective can take you closer to it or further away from it.

## Truth #98—You Are Never Given More than You Can Cope With

Precious diamonds are forged under great pressure. Immense challenges are sometimes required to bring out the depth of your potential, your character, your strength and your greatness.

No matter what you face in life, you have the capacity to face it and to move through it. You were not born incomplete or lacking anything. You were not brought forth into creation missing the skills to live your life. You were gifted everything you need.

When in your own deepest of despairs, while experiencing the most emotionally distressing times, if it seems like nothing is working in your favor, know that many of the greatest contributions in history arose because of how the human spirit was forged through darkness, rising into light. That same spirit is within you. Your chosen perspective in the face of any challenge is what allows your spirit to shine.

## Truth #99—Loss Leads to Learning and Creates a Clearing

Loss can lead to deep pain—be it loss of resources, loss of possessions, loss of status, loss of position, loss of relationships, loss of purpose or loss of life. Through all painful experiences, you are called to develop new strength within yourself.

The pain causes you to question loss, to try to make sense of it. You are developed in your ability to adapt and to adjust, to learn how to stand in your life without whatever person, thing, situation or sense of self you have lost. Most importantly, you are silently drawn to consider your own identity in relation to what you have lost.

Loss is one of the deepest experiences human beings have. It aids your soul evolution because loss leads to learning. Loss is also one of the most powerful ways you develop your compassion and desire to contribute to others—wanting to share the learning you have experienced with others in a similar position. Loss in this sense serves an important purpose in your experience of life.

Loss also creates a clearing. Whenever something leaves your life physically, mentally, emotionally or energetically—at any level—it leaves a space of some type. No matter how tragic and painful that loss may be, and your grief for that loss entirely warranted, and the grieving process essential to help you adjust and work your way through learning to live without whomever or whatever is no longer in your life, the fact remains that in the clearing on the other side of that loss, new things can arise in your life—new people, new experiences, new situations, new sense of purpose, new insights and new contributions.

## Truth #100—The More Challenges You Face, the More You Have Within You to Contribute to Others

One of the greatest gifts challenges offer us is how we learn from them and use that learning to support others who are facing the same type of adversity. People all over the planet are experiencing their own versions of challenge—in health, fitness, well-being, career, finances, achieving goals, or perhaps in relationships, education, sense of purpose, self-belief, self-love—in everything you could possibly imagine. For those caught in a challenge, there is no greater light in their darkness than hearing from someone else who has gone through something similar and come out the other side. This reminds them of their own inherent capacity to do the same.

Your own learning from challenges becomes a gift you contribute to others. It may be your children you help; it may be your friend you support with your wisdom, or it may be a family member or colleague who witnesses you walk on with your head held high and your light within shining brighter.

Maybe you help strangers you encounter. Perhaps you give through a compassionate hug or smile, with no words at all, to express your understanding of the path you share. Or, maybe you encourage someone to remember who they really are and what they are truly capable of, so they do not feel defined by their circumstances. It may be more in-depth, complex wisdom shared in myriad ways, shapes and forms.

### Truth #101—Your Capacity to Cope with Challenges at Any Given Time May Vary Depending on What Else You are Facing

If most areas of your life are flowing well, and you experience one challenge, you may respond quite peacefully and effectively to it. If, at some other point in time, you face the same challenge but you are simultaneously faced with many other challenges, you may not feel as equipped to deal with it. It is not that you have any less ability to cope (which is inherent); it is that you have less capacity to cope (which is situational).

You only have a certain amount of physical, mental and emotional energy to give into the world every day, and the more spread out it is, despite your ability to practice presence and inner peace, you might feel less in control and capable. You may beat up on yourself for not being able to cope with small things that ordinarily wouldn't faze you.

Always remember that your ability to cope can be relative to what else you are facing at that time. It doesn't mean you are not capable, strong or wise, nor does it mean you are regressing. It also doesn't mean you have a free pass to not practice conscious awareness. It simply means you are human and you have a lot in that moment to process and make sense of. Be kind to yourself, and keep a bigger picture and compassionate perspective of yourself and your life situation. Remember that your growth and enlightenment is an ongoing process and each moment offers you the chance to make a new choice to aid that process. Doing so when you are facing many challenges is not always easy, but it is available to you and it is possible.

## Truth #102—Being at Peace and Being Successful Doesn't Mean Challenges Disappear

You can be at peace and have challenges. You can be successful and have challenges. Any peaceful, successful person will tell you that challenges do not disappear because of your inner peace and outer success.

If you become lost in the notion that you must get to some point in the future where you are "successful" (having everything you need and want) and without challenges, then you will never feel at peace. This is because even when you attain all you desire inside and outside of yourself, and yet you still face challenges as a natural part of your life experience, you will feel that you have somehow failed or you will think you still have further to go or somewhere to get to. That quite simply isn't true.

Holding a state of inner peace and operating from the New World model of success is not about being without challenges. It is about remaining conscious in the face of challenges, learning from them and being empowered to move through them.

## Truth #103—Challenges Do Not Limit Your Possibilities

Whatever challenges you face right now do not dictate or forecast what is possible in the coming moments of your life. Every possibility you can conceive of, with your imagination, can be created.

Not only is this truth despite your challenges right now, but quite possibly *because of* your challenges right now. Challenges have a strange way of proving to be major pivot points in life, which have the power to propel you into new understanding and new directions, unlocking something within you that helps you to achieve your aspirations.

All possibilities remain possible, always. That is why they are called possibilities! Every coming moment is a conduit for all those possibilities to be realized. They are creative potential, energy waiting to be made manifest into your reality. Their potential to come into your reality is found in your paradigm. This has nothing to do with your circumstances. You can be in the direst of circumstances, and hold beliefs, thoughts and feelings that positively contradict those challenging circumstances in every way, and that is how and why your circumstances will not obstruct your path forward.

In relation to realizing these possibilities, remember two things. Firstly, your soul will speak through you with the language of feeling (passion, inspiration and intuition) to help you navigate into the fullness of your potential in this life. Therefore, in the midst of circumstances you do not like, pay attention to your passion, pay closer attention to your inspirations and pay even more attention to your intuition. All are messengers to guide you out of circumstances you don't like and into the creation of possibilities you desire.

Secondly, because you are co-creating your life with highest consciousness, your job is not to logically work out *how* to have the possibility you desire from the position of your current circumstances and challenges. Your job is to act upon your passions, to give life to your inspirations, to follow your intuition, to actively open yourself to your learning along the way and to contribute to this world as the unique expression you are. This is the energy vibration that brings new possibilities to reality. This is your natural state of love at play. This transcends circumstances. You will be guided. You will notice divine support and signals. Your circumstances can shift more radically than you can possibly imagine. The universe takes no effort to support a precious and beautiful flower to expand and express itself through dirt. It also takes no effort to support a precious and beautiful person like you through the most challenging or seemingly limiting of circumstances.

You do not need to see how it can be possible for it to be possible. You need only bring your paradigm into alignment with the reality you want to experience—that is, you must believe. From your belief all else stems.

## Truth #104—Comparing Your Worst Day with Someone Else's Best Day Will Never Bring You Peace

It's easy to get caught up in thinking that you are the only one facing a momentary challenge or long running adversity, the only one with unanswered questions, or the only one who hasn't figured out how to create the balance, health, relationships, finances or career success you want. That is not the case. Others are also evolving in their own unique way, at their own pace.

One way you are conditioned into this sense of isolation, as if you are the only one facing challenges, is that you are led to believe everyone else has it together. Most people only show the sanitized and happy aspects of their life to the world—on social media, in social situations and in conversation. Many people keep the dark moments to themselves or share only with those closest to them. That is natural and of course in many cases quite appropriate. But it leads you into a false perspective of your own situation in relation to others. You can easily get lost in comparison and end up feeling alone and isolated in your challenges.

No one else on this planet is going to unfold in the same way as you. No one. No one else is uniquely like you. What you most need to understand when you go into comparison mode in your mind is that you channel all of your precious energy away from what you actually want. Instead of consciously focusing your thoughts, feelings and actions on creating positive outcomes for yourself, you focus all of your attention on others and what they are creating for themselves.

That said, while unhealthy comparison limits you, this doesn't mean you can't observe and admire the success of another person. This actually lifts your vibration through your love for others, through your joy for all they are being and creating; you may well feel inspired into the ongoing possibilities for yourself by witnessing them flourishing. You may see opportunities to learn from what they are doing. You may be able to apply that learning to your own path, in your own unique way, aligned to your passions, inspirations and intuition, to aid your success.

You will always know the difference between this form of positive observation and learning, versus pure painful comparison. The former leaves you feeling uplifted and the latter leaves you feeling deflated. Listen to the messages your feelings are giving you.

### Truth #105—Challenges Often Unlock the Deeper Meaning and True Value of Your Life

Challenges often prove to be triggers that guide you toward what is most meaningful and valuable in your life. Health issues may lead you to see the precious nature of life itself and the importance of your well-being, and may forge you closer to those you love. Career adversity might force you out of jobs or companies that were not in your best interest and push you to reevaluate what you are truly most passionate about and what to do with your time and skills. Relationship breakdowns may support you to see what you really value the most in other people and bring greater conscious awareness to what you want and need from the relationships in your life.

From confusion comes clarity. From clarity comes a renewed sense of purpose and direction. Challenges have the power to show us what and who is most meaningful to us.

### Truth #106—Solution Identification and Learning Are the Only Reasons to Dive into or Dwell in Your Challenges

Diving into and dwelling in your challenges has the potential to drag your thoughts and feelings into negativity, lowering your energy vibration and stealing away your focus from possibilities and paths forward. However, there are two valid reasons to dive into and dwell in your current or past challenges. Firstly, to fully understand the challenge and your options, so that you can devise appropriate solutions to move yourself forward, and secondly to discover what there is to learn from the situation.

For these two purposes, it is incredibly important that you do not cover up, run from, hide from, avoid, ignore or suppress the challenges in your life. It is by bringing challenges under the microscope, and shining the full light of your conscious awareness on them, that you then have the power to resolve them, go beyond them and expand yourself through the learning on offer to you.

## Truth #107—Your Challenges Will Be the Making of You

Challenges are like a helpful acid that eats away the unnecessary protective exterior that you have been wearing as armor since an early age. Challenges ask you to let your walls down and not be wedded to opinions and beliefs that limit you. Challenges ask you to be wide open to life, to be vulnerable.

In that vulnerability you can have a relationship with yourself in an honest, authentic way. Behind the labels, behind the roles you play out in the external world, behind the mask you might wear to protect yourself and appease others—you can look at yourself deeply in a way you don't ordinarily give yourself permission to do. Challenges often force this to occur, because they put you under pressure physically, mentally or emotionally; they weaken your ability to hold any façade together.

As you face challenges, you may pity yourself, and others may mistakenly have pity for you. Higher consciousness does not pity. Your soul knows no pity. There is unlimited support and love for you, and there will be universal celebration as you walk through challenges, because they are your pivot points, leveraging you forward to unleash your life as your soul intends, for you to become the fullness of who you were born to be.

You can resist and detest those challenges; they will still occur. You can be at peace with them, and at least ride more easily with the waves, rather than against them. For you to give your fullness during your lifetime, there must be mechanisms in place that allow you to breakdown any illusions and falsehoods that hide that fullness, forcing you to ask new questions, bringing you closer to truth. All of this allows you to breakthrough. If not for this process, the world would miss out on you. You would come and go, and your fullness would be lost forever. For this reason, all of creation celebrates those challenges, for they are the making of you.

## Inner Peace

### Truth #108—It Is Not Possible to Be Happy All the Time, but It Is Entirely Possible to Be at Peace

Happiness is typically an experience prompted by external events and circumstances. You react with happiness as things occur to you and for you, or you actively look for things in your external life to be grateful for, and you create happiness through that attitude and practice.

Inner peace is an experience prompted by internal perspective. You can hold a peaceful state irrespective of the circumstances.

It is not possible or realistic to anticipate that every moment of your life you will be happy. You will not be happy if someone you love dies. You will not be happy if you stumble multiple times on your way to creating the success you desire. You will not be happy if you have an accident and physically hurt yourself. You will not be happy if stuck in a traffic jam that causes you to be late for an appointment. You will not be happy if faced with any number of natural and frequent challenges that life presents.

However, it is possible and realistic to anticipate that every moment of your life can be peaceful. You can be peaceful when someone you love dies, while also grieving. You can be peaceful when you stumble multiple times in regards to anything that is important to you, because you know mistakes are part of the process. You can be peaceful when you hurt yourself, because you know that you will heal and move on.

## Truth #109—Being at Peace Comes with Practice

There is nothing wrong with you if inner peace is not a state you experience often. Inner peace is something you cultivate and practice.

It is a perspective that initially stems from having a healthy, truthful paradigm as you begin to clear the fog and remain clear of it. Secondly, it is a way of being that you nurture by practicing peaceful response in your daily life, in the face of whatever you encounter.

Whenever life triggers you to feel something other than inner peace, that is your opportunity to practice. You bring conscious awareness to the situation, to understand what is triggering you and why, and you then make a choice about whether to respond peacefully or to react painfully. The more you practice a peaceful response, the more familiar it becomes, and the more natural it feels.

## Truth #110—Peace as a Practice Returns You to Your Natural State of Love

Love is who you are. Love is your inherent nature. It is the fog of your mind that clouds you and carries you into other states of being.

To be peaceful in the face of a difficulty is to rise above your circumstance and see the bigger picture and the journey of your soul. This practice of being at peace is the process that helps you return to your natural state of love.

To be peaceful in the face of someone lost in his or her own pain and projecting it on you, is to see the soul in that person and to recognize your own self reflected, to know your interconnectedness. This takes you directly back to your natural state of love.

To be peaceful when you are not experiencing the version of reality you want, and to realize that challenges are vehicles for your growth, and that your reality is based upon your paradigm, is to see everything from your true nature. This places you in your natural state of love.

### Truth #111—No One Else is Ever Responsible for Your Inner Peace

Even though people, things and situations can stimulate pain or peace, happiness or sadness within you, your thoughts and feelings are yours and yours alone.

You were gifted consciousness and freewill when you were born. These gifts were given to you for one reason—so you could utilize them. Inner peace comes about through conscious living and the use of your freewill to choose your responses to life and therefore choose to create an inner space that allows for peace. No one else is ever responsible for your inner peace. This is an empowering truth.

When you know this as truth, and you practice the cultivation of consistent inner peace, you will realize that you can take that inner peace with you wherever you go. When you choose inner peace consistently, it becomes easier and easier to access it when you are presented with triggers.

### Truth #112—If You Cannot Accept the Present as It Is, You Will Not Be at Peace

If you can accept how things are in any given moment, allowing the present to be just as it is even when you don't like it, then you will be able to experience a degree of inner peace.

If you cannot accept the facts of a situation, and you think resistance will somehow change the present moment, then you will automatically experience inner pain of some nature—be it frustration, tension, anxiety, anger, hurt, upset, fear or any other form of pain and suffering.

The present moment is. That is all there is to it. Resisting it is futile. You don't have to like it, but you must allow it before you have any inner power to create change. Non-allowing and non-acceptance force you into a corner where you cannot escape, where your mind keeps you in turmoil.

## Truth #113—Accepting the Present, Is Not about Embracing the Present

Being at peace with the present requires you to accept the right-now-ness of it. It requires you to allow it to be, knowing full well that any resistance to it will lead you nowhere. But peace in the face of the present moment does not mean you have to embrace it.

Peaceful non-resistance is not endorsement, enjoyment, enthusiasm or endurance of something or someone you do not wish to have in your life. You might be having difficulties in a relationship, or problems at work, or health challenges or issues with your finances. No one is asking you to love these challenges and to remain within them. This is not about bearing a burden and trying to find an upbeat perspective that will somehow allow you to perceive these unsavory experiences as positive things. You are not asked to accept difficulties as part of your life going forward. Not at all. You are simply asked to accept that the experience is in your present moment right now.

## Truth #114—Giving Over Is Essential for Both Inner Peace and Effective Change

You cannot effectively create change in your situation going forward if you are not able to accept where you currently stand. Two detrimental things happen when you fight against the facts of the present moment: You have no inner peace because you are full of resistance and low vibration thoughts and feelings; and, you have significantly reduced ability to create positive change, as you are giving all your energy to resisting what you don't like about the present, instead of directing your precious energy into the change you want to create.

When you peacefully accept your present circumstances, you can turn your full focus to the creation of what you desire. You do this by aligning your beliefs, thoughts, feelings and actions (your creation equation) to that desired change, which generate outcomes in your life and at the same time influence the fabric of universal energy that you belong to, making you a magnetic point of attraction for all like-minded people and like-vibrational situations and experiences.

As you go about creating change in this way, from a position of acceptance and inner peace, understand that there is a definite difference between passionately channeling your energy to that which you want to create, versus pushing, forcing and demanding that new creation arise in your life to meet your expectations. Remember—you are co-creating, so you are working in unison with the universe to weave energy as you move through the days of your life. There is a divine timing and order that helps your life to unfold. No amount of pushing, forcing or demanding will change that—in fact it will delay it, because you are not a vibrational match with what you want to experience if you are stuck in a negative way of being and doing. This way takes you out of peace and back into pain. This yo-yo cycle from pain into peace and peace back into pain is common and is one of the most important things you can become aware of, and empowered to mitigate in terms of harnessing your nature as a true creator.

Without realizing it, you can end up flip flopping—making peace with the present circumstances (accepting and allowing), then turning your attention to the creation of what you desire (passionately focusing your energy on change), but you have an exacting idea of how you want your change to happen, what you want your outcomes to look like, and when you expect it should happen, so much so that you are unwilling to waver on that concrete vision should the universe show you other more magical, expedient and possibly quite unexpected ways and paths to get what you want. Of course, due to those expectations you have, when your desired change doesn't happen in those ways or in those timeframes, you become frustrated and disillusioned. What are you frustrated and disillusioned with? Your present moment. So you become stuck again, back in resistance of your life as it is right now.

Your access to sustainable inner peace is to both make peace with the present, and, regarding the creation of your desires going forward, to turn over the "how and when" to the co-creative partnership you have with the universe. This is known as surrender or letting go, and it is a vital part of the creation process.

Surrender, or letting go, is not about giving up. Far from it. Giving over is not about apathy, caring less, desiring any less, or doing any less. It is not closing yourself off from what you want. It is not about leaving your life to fate. It is not about making your life the universe's responsibility.

Giving over is about realizing you are not the only creative force at play in your life. It is about ceasing your obsessive attachment to how things must go, how things must look and when it must happen. Giving over is allowing life to be just as it is right now, while also passionately holding a vision of potentiality and freely letting that potentiality come into reality with passionate action, open-mindedness and natural unfolding. Giving over means not forcing, controlling or dictating the means and timing of such unfolding. Giving over means showing up every day in your life with the intention to be your best self, and to do the best you know how, without expecting life to go a certain way. Have goals, have dreams, aspire and take purposeful action, but detach from what life must look like along the way.

Whereas giving up would be saying, "I am done. I want no more of this. I do not care. I do not believe. I give up on myself. I give up on life," giving over says, "I want what I want with all my heart. I care deeply. I believe in myself and in my life path.

I act upon all my passions and inspirations. I step forward into all opportunities. I follow my intuition. And, I know that I am a co-creative being in soul, mind and body. I am guided, and I know that I need to get out of my own way (out of my head and into my allowing heart) and let the greater force of the universe do its part in helping my desires come to fruition."

## Truth #115—There Is No Destination, Only a Journey

When you believe there is a destination that you are supposed to reach, you will constantly feel uneasy with the present, like it is somehow not the fullness of your life. This uneasiness contradicts inner peace.

There is not meant to be one fixed destination point where you are all-knowing and all-perfect and have achieved everything. What would you do if you were at such a point? You would be done with life. You would have done everything, you would know everything and you would have given everything. Your learning would be complete and your contribution would be made. When those things occur, you would be ready to leave this life.

Reaching a destination is not the point of your life. The journey is the point. Journeys unfold, and they always unfold synchronistically, in divine order and timing.

## Truth #116—Practicing Peace in the Present Helps to Reduce Fear Response

If you lived your present moment for exactly what it is, you would not experience the majority of your fears. Most fear enters the present moment because your mind drifts into memories of the past, giving rise to fear in the now over whether the past will repeat, and because your mind drifts into a mental projection of the future, which gives rise to fear in the now over what might potentially happen.

What did not go well before does not dictate what will happen now. What you have experienced before does not have to repeat. Now is a fresh moment full of possibilities. It is your mind that brings the past and future to life and allows them to color the present moment with fear.

The more you remain in conscious awareness, and practicing peaceful acceptance and allowing of the present, the less fear response you will feel.

## Truth #117—Your Physical, Mental and Emotional Well-being Supports Inner Peace

Your physical, mental and emotional well-being is not separate from your experience of inner peace. In balance, they are designed to support your inner peace. You need to first understand the dynamics of all these aspects of yourself and appreciate how they link together holistically, and then make the choice to honor that link in the way you choose to live. If you do not nurture your physical, mental and emotional well-being into balance, then those aspects of you cannot effectively do their job to support your inner peace.

When they are out of balance, it shows up as feeling exhausted, drained and overwhelmed. From that state you suffer further negative consequences in the form of inner turmoil or pain, instead of inner peace. Why? Because you are less able to be present and thus peaceful in the face of challenges when you are exhausted, drained and overwhelmed. You are also more likely to fall into unconscious ways of being and behavior. You have less energy physically, mentally and emotionally to make healthy, conscious choices. Quite simply, your reserves are depleted. You are not fully fuelled to be at your best. You are not as equipped to help yourself. If you want to have inner peace, you need to commit to taking care of your physical, mental and emotional well-being, so that you can hold your presence and be fully empowered in your peaceful response to life.

There are rituals that can support every individual's holistic well-being, in a way that uniquely attends to one's particular physical, mental and emotional needs. Rituals are simply any experiences designed to aid your physical, mental and emotional balance that you consciously choose to create for yourself and execute on a consistent daily or weekly basis. They are not a "sometimes practice" for when you feel out of balance. They are an "always practice" to keep you in balance, so you never have to dig yourself out of imbalance in the first place.

Rituals do not rely on anyone else agreeing to participate with you. They are ways in which you can manage your own energy no matter what is going on around you, giving you the power to care for your own holistic well-being, irrespective of circumstances.

Rituals are a recharge and refuel, which allow you to be on top of your game. They are soothing and calming. They care for your physical body. They quiet and focus the mind. They bring your conscious awareness fully into the present moment. They support positive messages, drawing your attention to your soul, and drawing attention to your blessings and, thus, to gratitude. Rituals uplift your emotional state. They help you tune into what is most important to you, eliminating the noise of life around you.

Your rituals will be specific to you. Follow your intuition and allow yourself to explore and play with experiences to see what feels right. It may be forms of exercise or sport that allow for physical exertion and fitness. It may be certain healing, healthy and nurturing foods and drinks that you consume. It may be holistic mind, body and soul practices, such as yoga or Tai Chi. It may be expressive outlets such as writing, art, music or dance. It may be nature-based activities, such as walking, hiking or swimming, where you can be with the uninterrupted energy and beauty of the planet. It may be silence, solitude or stillness-based practices, such as meditation. It may be gratitude practices that tune you back into the bigger picture and the deeper meaning of your life, such as journaling or prayer. It may be emotionally calming, relaxing or uplifting practices, such as affirmations, visualizations, or pampering yourself with aromatherapy, baths or massage.

Your rituals are for your well-being. They are personal care and love for you, expressed practically.

Just as this holistic well-being supports a sense of inner peace, your resulting inner peace in turn directly creates positive effects back on your physical, mental and emotional state. It is a soul-nourishing cycle.

## Truth #118—Consistent and Sustainable Inner Peace Is Available when Your Actions Align to Your Values

You can perceive from a healthy paradigm, but if you do not follow through and act in alignment with that perception, then you will always feel disloyal to yourself, and that will continuously cause you unrest.

You cannot be at ease and have consistent inner peace when the way in which you execute your day-to-day life is in direct conflict with what is meaningful and true to you. Unleashing your life is about marrying a paradigm shift (seeing the truth) with an action plan that flows from that paradigm, and thus experiencing true inner peace, freedom and success at all levels.

If you behave in ways that go against your values, if you treat people in ways that grate against the love you know you are, if you are in a job that you know goes against what you believe in, value, are passionate about and inspired to do, if you treat yourself in a way that you know diminishes your true nature, if you stay in relationships that your heart has moved on from, if you give time, energy and light to things that you ethically and morally don't agree with, then you will always feel like something is missing.

What is missing is alignment of your mind and body to your soul. You are living your life as someone who you are not. You are masquerading. Sustainable inner peace does not arise during this masquerade.

A level of consistent and sustainable inner peace is possible when your actions align to your values, and you feel synchronized with the deepest part of yourself, and thus with the source from which you came forth and to which you eternally belong.

## Freedom

### Truth #119—The Most Important Freedom Is the Freedom to Live Outside the Fog

The greatest shackle you face in this life is the fog. There are three main scenarios of how your life will play out in relation to this shackle and your freedom.

You can be held prisoner by your own mind and never awaken to it, and live in pain as a result. You can awaken to the mind-made prison you are in and not consciously choose to take a journey to free yourself, and live in pain as a result. Or, when recognizing the fog, you can actively go about setting yourself free.

Ultimate freedom is a state you create inside yourself due to alignment with your true nature, without which you will forever feel trapped no matter how many external variables you try to change in your life. You can be free in your circumstances, and yet completely imprisoned within yourself. You can also be literally restricted in your life circumstances, and yet totally free inside yourself.

No one can stop you from experiencing inner freedom, and no one can take inner freedom from you. This truth is empowering, because it means you alone hold the key to the freedom you most need.

### Truth #120—Your True "Home" Is a State of Being, Not a Place

Despite how much your mind wants to cling to the fact that your home is a building with four walls and roof, a location where you go about the activities of your life in this physical world, or the location where your family and friends are—your home is not any of these things alone.

Your true home, as aligned to your soul, is not the place you sleep, it is not the place you work and it is not where your family and friends are. Where you physically live of course provides a sense of familiar comfort, belonging and security. However, your universal home as a soul is wherever, whenever and however you experience inner freedom. Freedom from pain, freedom from suffering, freedom from limiting beliefs, freedom from mind-made obstacles, freedom from what you perceive that traps you. Your soul knows that home is this inner position of freedom—where you can express your uniqueness without inhibition, where your passions and inspirations can shine out without suppression, and where you march to the beat of your own intuitive drum. This is home, because this is your true nature. This is you as a clear channel. This is your mind and body aligned to your soul essence. This is you directly tapped into highest consciousness without any restriction on that energy flow. It is you in physical life remembering your nonphysical heritage.

A person could have everything stripped from them, have no home base, stand in the face of great adversity, with nothing and no one, and still genuinely feel a sense of home within them.

While certain places and people may feel like home to you, it is typically because they are conducive to you finding your way to this true sense of home within yourself, as a soul.

## Truth #121—Your Value and Place in This World Are Not Defined by What You Do

Believing that your value and place in society are defined by what you do and how much you do, completely contradicts the truth that your value is inherent in your existence.

You are valid, valuable and valued based entirely on who you are, irrespective of what you do. That doesn't in any way diminish the magnificent value of whatever you do, nor does it mean that you will do nothing. However, it is important to discern if you want to be doing in this world for the joy of it, instead of doing in this world out of desperate need to feel validated and important.

Babies don't "do" anything. They just exist. In all their beauty, you know they are worthy and completely valid for the simple fact that they exist, not at all for what they do. This is something you will no doubt agree with.

Yet, as you personally grew up from that beautiful, worthy baby, you became conditioned to believe that your inherent value somehow disappeared. Your paradigm shifted, and you started to believe that your value had to be created, that your value and worthiness had to be proven and that your place in this world had to be earned. It became not at all about the value existing inherently in who you are; instead, it became all about the value in what you do.

If you believe that society will only value and respect you based on what you do, what you produce and what you achieve, then the inevitable conclusion is that without your actions and outcomes, you are not valid and worthy. In order to avoid that possible unworthiness, you enter a never-ending cycle of doing and achieving, and overdoing and overachieving, in the hopes of proving your value and feeling your worthiness, of having society reflect that back to you through recognition and reward.

When you try hard to create your position in this world, you deny that you already had a position in the first place. When you feel not enough just by being who you are, then you will do more in order to feel more, and you will try more in order to be more, and on and on it goes. Each action and achievement might give you a sense of progress, but ultimately it never completely fills that void within (which stems from a warped perspective), and you remain in the vicious cycle.

Consider this—if you attach your value and place in this world to what you do, then what happens when you stop doing what you do? What happens when circumstances change? What happens when what you do is no longer working well for you or when you simply cannot do what you have done before? For example, what if your job disappears, your company is in a downturn, you are not well enough to work, you are unclear on your professional direction, you retire, or you are nearing the literal end of your life? You will feel like you have no place, and you will feel like you are not of value; you will have nothing to "do" to generate your feeling of worthiness.

The problem lies in seeking to feel complete as a person within yourself because of something you do outside of yourself or seeking to fill an internal void with an external fix. Internal voids can only be filled with internal truths. You were never incomplete, unvalued or unworthy in the first place; there was never any gap to fill and therefore no need for validation. Nothing you do will ever be enough to meet an illusionary internal need. Unless you know this for yourself as true, the external cycle for validation will continue, and all too often it leads to stress, imbalance, burn out and soul deprivation.

## Truth #122—Freedom Is Expressing You for the Joy of It, Not for Validation

Whenever you are stuck in the validation cycle, without realizing it, you are always seeking to get something back from the world to make you feel good. You may smile at someone and want to see a smile back, but if no smile is returned, then there is no good feeling. You may tell someone, "I love you" in order to hear, "I love you" back; but if this response is not returned, then there is no good feeling. You work hard and want recognition for your efforts, but if there is no recognition, then there is no good feeling. This is crippling. You are expressing yourself for validation, making yourself completely reliant upon the world around you to help you feel good.

Your life is not happening from the outside in. It is happening from the inside out. Everything starts within, everything stems from you and your energy, and your entire experience of life relies upon your beliefs, thoughts and feelings aligned to your inherent value, worth and completeness.

When you cultivate the truth inside of yourself, knowing your value, worth and completeness, then from that feeling of completeness you will act in the world through pure passion, inspiration and intuition alone. You will smile because you feel like it, not to see a response back. You will tell someone, "I love you," because you feel compelled to express yourself, not because you need to hear it returned to you. You will work hard for the joy of what you give, not for what you expect to receive. This doesn't diminish the value of what you do receive back from the world around you as you interact with it; it is simply to say you cannot be reliant upon it.

## Truth #123—Perfection Is an Illusion

Society constantly creates and promotes images of perfection in marketing and advertising, and throughout the media. The illusion of perfection makes you feel like nothing you are or do is quite enough or quite right. This may leave you constantly trying to be more, do more and achieve more, to make things better and better, until one day you will be able to breathe easy knowing that you are perfect, that everything you have done is perfect and that everything around you is perfect. The quest for perfection either stops you from finishing anything because you are constantly trying to perfect whatever you are working on, or it stops you from celebrating what you do finish as you are too busy looking at what you wish you had done better. This torments you, it suppresses your natural creativity (why risk when you might fail?), it limits your progress and it slows the pace at which you produce anything (personally or as productivity in the workplace). It affects the outcomes you generate and drastically impacts the enjoyment you derive from whatever you are doing. It will cause you to focus on things that don't matter, at the expense of things that do matter. It will lead you to see faults, where right next to those faults complete beauty and miracles exist. It will even lead you to think that you are someone role modeling excellence, when, in fact, you are role modeling paralyzing overanalysis and complete imbalance in priorities. Perfection affects your home life and your career. It affects your self-esteem and your relationships, and it gives rise to unnecessary tension and stress.

If you believe perfection is attainable, you will seek and never find it; you will strive and never achieve it, or you will think you've got it, then something will happen and you'll realize you never had it to start with. The notion of perfection sucks the joy from life.

Striving for perfection is a hollow goal that can never be achieved, because perfection does not exist. You are a beautifully imperfect being, operating in an imperfect world; that is the way it is meant to be. Why? Because your entire life from birth to death is a process of expansion. Perfection goes directly against this process. If you were perfect, and your life were perfect, then you would be done! You would not need to be here. You could not fulfill the progression inherent to your human nature; what would be the point of your life?

The idea of perfection denies the value and uniqueness of all your imperfection—of your quirks and development areas, of your beautiful self that you know well and your loved ones adore. Perfection would make you vanilla. You were born much more flavorsome and colorful than that. Your job here in life is to give full expression to every ounce of who you were born as, not to try to fit yourself to a societally created, unattainable, plastic model of perfection.

By all means, strive for excellence. Face every moment of every day with the intention of being your best self. That will lead you into success. But don't confuse high standards with crippling perfectionism. They are completely different perspectives, and give rise to opposing life experiences.

## Truth #124—Your Circumstances Are not Who You Are

Who you are remains timeless—a whole, complete, worthy, loved and supported soul. However, people often extrapolate via a tenuous thread of logic that challenging life circumstances define them in a different light.

Interpretations such as "my life is a mess" easily morph into "I'm a mess," or "my life shouldn't be this way" morphs into "I shouldn't be this way," or "my business/relationship failed" becomes "I failed."

Your circumstances, no matter how they come about, are never who you are. They are experiences you are having. They are not your identity. They do not define you. They are outcomes, and that is all.

## Success

### Truth #125—There Is One Core Motivator Behind All Desire for Success

If you are not clear on *why* you truly want what you want, then you are not operating from your authentic core, with clarity, in order to create success. Instead, you are being run by your foggy paradigm, and, from that superficial level, you will find it difficult to navigate the path to the success you want to create.

Behind every desire you have for any type of external success lays one core motivator. No matter what endeavor you engage in, what your definition of external success is, what the result actually is, what you intend to do with that success for yourself or for other people—all human beings seek to create an internal feeling from an external endeavor.

The three most common feelings that people desire to experience, as their core motivator for almost everything they will ever do, are happiness, inner peace and love. Any other desired feelings, and any other motivators, sit on top of these fundamental, underlying, or "end state" feelings.

Even if you are driven by a desire for status, recognition, image, reward, money or material possessions, these are still not your core motivators. It all comes back to these external points of gratification being a path you use to create a feeling, or feelings, within yourself—of happiness, inner peace and/or love.

It is instinctive that you seek out ways to create and hold these feelings within yourself. Part of the mechanics of our universe, and part of your inherent nature as a creator, is that you will come to generate and learn more about these feelings through what you do, as this process helps to drive your overall soul intent for learning and contribution.

Most people are not aware of their core motivator, and they think they are striving for success for some other reason, focusing on surface level motivators. This leaves them blind to what is really going on inside. Once you understand why you do what you do in terms of seeking success in this world, then you are anchored in truth and you are in a far more powerful position to do what you do in a conscious, sustainable, highly effective and positively energized way.

The truth is that you can experience the happiness, inner peace and love you seek in any number of ways, not just via the particular activities you engage in or the path you currently walk in your life. Not only this, but you can create the happiness, inner peace and love you seek without *doing* anything at all in this world because happiness can be experienced out of a chosen perspective based on your paradigm (for example, a gratitude attitude), inner peace is possible in the face of anything through presence practice, and love is who you are.

Once you realize this, seeing that you don't need any of the external successes in order to give you those feelings you so naturally desire, then there is no longer an incessant need to try hard to get success in order to generate those feelings from external sources, thus you are suddenly free to create success just for the joy of it—reveling in the journey (not just working toward a destination), making more heart-led choices about what you do in each moment, as directly aligned to your passion, inspirations and intuition.

It is through seeing this truth that you realize that being your unique expression, and contributing, as your soul intended, is your primary driver, and external success is not necessarily a goal in and of itself, but rather a natural flowing consequence.

## Truth #126—The New World Model of Success Has Nothing to Do with Your External Life

The Old World model of success was based on the size of your house, car or bank account, the breadth and depth of your education and career, the extent of your awards, achievements and honors, your image, status and amount of recognition, combined with how hard you were willing to strive, compete and win at whatever you were doing.

While these were all typical marks of success by definition in the Old World paradigm, most people already know that model is outdated, in that you can strive for and attain all those indicators of Old World success and while you *might* have happiness and inner peace as a result, this model does not by any stretch of the imagination guarantee it. Nor does any of it make you a better person, a more worthy person, a more valued person, or a more complete, loved or supported person.

The possessions and experiences are not meaningless. They are not empty in and of themselves. But they are empty in the sense that they are not the core foundation of your life, despite what you may believe if you currently live your life from an "outside in" model of reality, where what you do, experience and own is what creates your feelings.

The New World model of what success as a human being looks like is actually what was intended for you, and for all of us, all along. The New World model goes well above and beyond anything that the Old World model could provide for you, because the New World model is based entirely upon what you really need and want at the depths of who you are— feelings of happiness, inner peace and love. It's an accurate model for who you are as a conscious creator, generating and interpreting your life experience through your unique paradigm—as an "inside out" model of reality.

Those external marks of success that have previously been viewed as important will still be present for you and add much value, enjoyment and inner fulfillment, but alone they are not a complete picture if you wish to experience *sustainable* inner peace and happiness in your life. Indeed, radically, these external marks of success need not even be present for a New World conscious person to be successful in the true sense of the word.

A successful human being in the awakened New World is:

- consciously living (with awareness and presence)
- owning their inherent completeness, with a secure sense of self
- committed to balanced, holistic well-being
- alive with a sense of personal purpose
- giving life to passions
- acting upon inspirations
- operating from intuition
- open-minded
- compassionate in perspective
- collaborative in nature
- connected and loving in relationships
- practicing peaceful response

Individuals who stand in this world adorned with all the shiny baubles they have accumulated in life but with none of the above, are not experiencing New World success. They are experiencing moments of fleeting and externally prompted happiness, interrupted by the turmoil of an unfulfilled inner landscape that is controlled by their foggy paradigm.

## Truth #127—Success Is First a Way of Being

As the way you create and interpret your life is always from the inside out via your paradigm, then any success you generate is entirely an inside out process as well.

It begins with your way of being (beliefs, thoughts and feelings), which directly flows into your way of doing (behavior and actions); these create your outcomes. The outcomes give you your desired sense of success, whatever success personally means to you.

The number one factor to consider when you wish to create external success in your life is your inner landscape. It will make or break your external outcomes, and it will dictate your way of interacting with, appreciating and sustaining those outcomes.

## Truth #128—Success Requires a Balanced Commitment to Both Your Way of Being and Your Way of Doing

If you focus entirely on your way of being, without considering your way of doing (actions), you will experience inner shifts, but, without action in this physical, tangible world, you will not create what you desire. You are a soul, but you are experiencing life as a human being in mind and body. You must work holistically as one unit to achieve what you want. Nothing can take the place of empowered action. There is no going around it. You have to get up and get out there into life and do what needs to be done.

If you focus entirely on your way of doing, without any consideration for your way of being, you will bring the same old limiting paradigm and negative energy to whatever existing or new actions you take, and as a result you will limit the possible outcomes.

For powerful shifts on your journey in this life, indeed to unleash your life, you team together an empowered new way of being that is grounded in truth (a paradigm shift), with new ways of doing directly aligned to your desired outcomes (a practical action plan).

## Truth #129—There Are Many Paths to Any Desired Result

A hangover from the Old World model of success is that there is only one true path of success for you, one destined career for you, one way in which you have to be successful and/or you must know exactly how to get from where you are now to where you want to go, and you must stick solely to that path without any deviation. This is not true.

There is a notion we are societally conditioned to believe in, which suggests that changing paths/direction is less than desirable, with a sense that it requires a step back or a step sideways. This notion is based on rigid linear thinking, which links to time, an illusion.

It is common in the Old World model to feel like a failure if you get far down a particular path only to realize it is not serving you. You may even be inclined to ignore that realization, to run from your intuition and stick to your current path just to satisfy the Old World model of success. In truth, all you need to do is clear the fog, enter the New World model of success and realize that switching paths in that situation *is* in fact the action that creates your success.

No path travelled is ever a waste. Ever. Every moment of your journey you learn something, you have new insights and you evolve. When it looks like you have made a mistake, going down one path only to realize it is not a path you want to continue down, consider that, in fact, you are exactly where you are meant to be, having the exact realization that your present moment calls for. Consider that everything is in divine order and timing, and your path is unfolding in the best way; the change in direction you are about to make is the next step in that natural unfolding. Consider that the seemingly mistaken path was actually critical for you to walk down in order to learn something, to unlock new insights and greater clarity within you and to prepare you for the next phase.

There are many paths to whatever you desire to experience in this life. There are many paths to your happiness, inner peace and love. There are many paths to the abundance you wish to create. There are many paths to the specific career or business success you want to experience. There are many paths to the relationships you want to form. There are many paths to the health and well-being outcomes you want to have. If you release preconceived notions of what your life should look like at any given point in time, and how the journey should go, all of which are based on expectations, then from where you currently stand you will suddenly have a more expansive view of your situation from which to see new paths forward.

## Truth #130—Mistakes and Stumbles Are Not Regression, They Are Part of the Journey

Society has strayed from understanding the value of mistakes, frequently placing mistakes on display with the labels, "Shame. Failure. Embarrassment."

While you may want to avoid mistakes, they are actually to be cherished as one of the ways you achieve your soul intent. They are vehicles for you to become wiser and stronger. They not only force your learning and inner growth but that growth will flow into your actions and may be evidenced in what you later create in terms of your external success.

The only way to not make mistakes is to stop living, to sit still and silent forever, and refuse to participate in life. Therefore, you are going to make mistakes and you will be whole, complete and wonderful in your imperfection as you do so.

In the moments when you are unable to consistently put all of your accumulated wisdom into practice, thus causing you to stumble, please remember this means you are human. It does not signify regression.

Many people become worried when they stumble that it means they have taken a step backwards, a sense of being further away from the success they wish to create in their external life experience. That is again based on linear thinking, which is based on the illusion of time.

When you stumble, you fall forward, closer to your goals and dreams, because within the stumble resides an opportunity for expansion. You experience learning and with new insight you pick yourself up, dust yourself off and flourish a little further in that moment of breakthrough.

It is, in fact, impossible for you to regress. Your inherent nature as a human being is progressive. What does that mean?

Every moment you face is unique, offering you something new, even if that moment feels and looks like many moments that have gone before. Every day you wake up as a fuller version of yourself because the day before you have experienced something more and/or new—of thoughts, feelings, situations, people, challenges and triumphs.

The key to stumbles benefitting you is the awareness you bring to why you stumbled, so you can embrace the learning held within as you step forward. Even if you cannot access the learning in that moment, the stumble adds weight and depth to whatever the forming lesson is that you are learning, which will become apparent to you in due course.

There may a period in your life where it seems like you stumble many times in close succession, over and over again. The accumulation of those challenges, which often feels like a storm of things going "wrong," and the associated inner pain building up to an immense peak, has the power to culminate in what is called a Pain Pivot Point.

A Pain Pivot Point is when there is such momentum and intensity to inner pain that it becomes intolerable and radically shocks you into greater awareness, causing a crack in the illusion of your fog, which provides you the most transformational opportunity to pivot your life in a new direction because of that awakening. The more stumbles, the greater momentum behind you to propel you forward into new insight, pivoting either your inner perspective and/or your literal outer life direction, which is a clearing for greater levels of success inside and out.

## Truth #131—Asking for Help Denotes Wisdom and Strength

Wisdom is understanding and living in alignment with the truth of your inherent connectedness, knowing that you are not a solo being operating in this life, set apart from everyone and everything else. From this knowing arises the logical insight that all beings energetically influence each other and would do well to work together in collaboration; the thriving of one supports the thriving of all.

No man or woman is an island. You do not operate independent of anything. You are not a fortress who requires nothing and no one to thrive. You were born into the collective of humanity. It is the collective that will challenge you. It is the collective that will inspire you. It is the collective that will trigger you to see life in new ways and reach out a hand when you fall down. But, you must also be willing to ask for that help, and you must be willing to grab the hands on offer.

You have been conditioned by society to believe that it is unacceptable to show your vulnerability. You think that you should have all the answers yourself, and that experiencing difficulty and personal limitations somehow contradicts the idea of being successful and is a weakness to be hidden. This keeps you stuck in a cycle of pretending to be fine while suffering on the inside.

Every person of great strength and success has courageously reached out to ask for help. Let us not pretend that great endeavors in life are possible by behaving like we are invincible and disconnected individuals.

The strong are not those who do not need help. They are the ones that have the wisdom to know when to ask for help and to willingly accept it, knowing that doing so does not make them any less capable or successful, nor any less of a human being.

## Truth #132—You Can Never Truly Fail

Failure is a word and a mind-set, nothing more. It holds strong connotations, because society has conditioned you to believe that certain circumstances make *you* a failure and that this somehow diminishes who you are and your value, wisdom, worth and position in the world.

If something you do does not work out how you planned, you can state that the plan failed or the situation failed. Instead, you might say you failed. Be aware of how you make a situation become who you are. Choose to label the experience a failure if you absolutely must, but never confuse that with meaning there is anything about you that is a failure.

Moreover, your soul-led goals cannot fail if you never stop believing, acting and living like they are possibilities. To continuously step out into life with the willingness to truly live can never be labeled failure. Ever.

## Truth #133—You Are Either Rehearsing for Success or Rehearsing for Disaster

The creative power of your imagination is immense. You are capable of generating incredibly vivid scenarios within your mind, with imagery, sometimes with sound, often with conversations happening and movement, and all of these visualizations give rise to certain emotional reactions in your body.

You can use your imagination to rehearse for success, in the same way actors rehearse scenes of a play before giving a live performance or athletes visualize the execution of their performance as a way to mentally and emotionally prepare for their sport or event. While living in the present moment is a critical and prominent feature of conscious living, targeted use of future visualization for short periods is a highly effective ritual to support success.

Not only does the purposeful and repetitive use of your imagination in this way let you see the possibilities for yourself in success, as you picture what you could achieve and what it would feel like, but you literally start to wire your mind to that possibility as being more of a reality than just a concept. In this way you are training your entire being to resonate with and accept that reality before it even shows up in your physical circumstances.

This visualization and resonance process starts to positively shift your emotional state, which begins to influence the actions you take.

On the flip side, your imagination can be used for just as much destruction as it can for positive creation. Left unchecked, your mind can rehearse for disaster. Most people who are not living consciously are accidentally rehearsing disaster most of the time, including in relation to their most cherished goals and dreams. Rehearsing for disaster happens in exactly the same way as rehearsing for success. Your mind has the power to conjure up possible negative scenarios, bringing them to life with images, sounds, dialogue and motion, which gives rise to emotional reactions within you.

Rehearsing for disaster entirely stems from a foggy paradigm, where your imagination works in alignment with your limiting beliefs, fed by fear. In the same way positive visualization can unleash your potential and help you bring to life your greatest desires, negative visualization can completely limit your potential and suffocate whatever you most want to create.

The answer is not to focus on how to stop you from rehearsing for disaster. That is just a symptom. The answer is to clear the fog that causes it in the first place.

### Truth #134—To Feel Fulfilled in Your Success, that Success Must Align to Your Values

Just as your actions must align to your values if you wish to have consistent and sustainable inner peace, so your success in terms of what you create and the way in which you create it must also align to your values, if you want to feel truly fulfilled in that success.

New World success comes from living your values, standing in this world as the authentic you. Anytime you cut your conscience as a means to an end, there will always be a niggling sense of emptiness inside. That niggling is because your soul and your mind/body are out of alignment. It means you just expended all of your energy striving to create external results in a way that was never going to be able to satisfy the one underlying motivator all people truly have behind desire for success—to experience happiness, inner peace and/or love.

If a path opens up before you as a way to achieve external success, and that path doesn't align to your values, your intuition will tell you—that path simply isn't for you. In the face of that path you then have a choice to make—to ignore your intuition and forgo your values, or to live in the New World model of success.

It is not idealistic to anticipate you could successfully and abundantly create what you desire in this world in an authentic way that is loyal to your values and loyal to your inner knowing. It is what your soul intended in every way.

## Truth #135—There Are No Sacrifices for Success, Only Choices

Every decision you make is a choice, made consciously with freewill, or by default—that is, at some points in life, if you don't actively and consciously choose, then your non-choice means life will push you into the alternative by default.

Some choices you make may involve you choosing one thing over another. Some choices may involve you putting the needs of yourself before the needs of others. Some choices may involve you putting the needs of others before yourself. Some choices may involve both opportunity and cost.

It is easy to fall into believing that with some choices, you are making a sacrifice. Sacrifice by definition means to lose or give something up for the sake of something better. You may believe you are sacrificing one thing for another, one person for another, yourself for something or someone. The truth is that sacrifice is a perspective, and an interpretation, of your choices. It is not fact. If you make a choice and you perceive it as a sacrifice, at the time of the choice or retrospectively, that is your belief system playing out.

Your mind-set about what decisions you've made and continue to make, and the outcomes you experience as a result, will either generate empowerment or regret and resentment. If you interpret a choice as sacrifice, it may lead you to have one of two experiences that eventually become like an identity for your ego or a burden you must bear. These experiences lower your energy vibration, and limit you.

If you believe you have sacrificed something (for example, yourself, your time, your resources or your opportunities) in order to give to something or someone, that label you give yourself as "someone who has sacrificed" has the potential to become payback to your ego, to martyr yourself, to walk in life as someone who laid down something of value as a sacrifice. If that perspective unleashes you, wonderful. However, if that at all causes you to get caught up in a story or negative emotion, then it is a limitation. That label you give yourself might also turn into resentment and/or regret—a feeling of loss and a sense of diminishing yourself, causing you to look backwards at the expense of the only moment available—the now.

### Truth #136—Your Dominant State Is What Matters Most

As perfection is an illusion, it is not possible for you to believe, think, feel and act in a perfect way all of the time. Your human nature is imperfect by design, as your imperfections are part of the method by which you evolve and grow. Therefore, you do not need to be concerned about holding yourself to an ideal state in every moment of every day.

What you do need to focus on is what your dominant state of being is and what your dominant way of doing is. You can identify your dominant state by simply reflecting on what your strongest beliefs are, what your frequent thought patterns are, what your most common feelings are and then what your habitual actions are. Listen to your intuitive knowing about whether the sum total of all of these is negatively slanted or positively slanted. That will tell you what your dominant overall energy vibration is.

Whatever is dominant will override whatever is not. Whatever is dominant tips the balance on the rest of your perspective and efforts.

Ebbs and flows in your energy vibration are natural in your day-to-day life. However, it is the swinging drastically up and down in your energy vibration, like a yo-yo, that causes exhaustion and confusion—you confuse yourself, but you also confuse the fabric of universal energy to which you belong, which is constantly listening and responding to your energy, seeking to understand clearly from you what you most need and want based on whatever your dominant way of being and way of doing are.

If you have no dominant state, because you are up one moment and down the next, or you are continuously down and have a negative dominant state, then your experience of life and your results will mirror this.

Give yourself permission to be human, and to forgive yourself for moments when you are unconscious and stuck in a negative cycle. What matters is your ability to bring yourself out of it. The moment you become aware again, you can make conscious choices to shift your way of being and way of doing into positivity. The more you practice that, the more natural it becomes, the more consistent it will be and positivity will start to dominate. This conscious practice helps you balance out any drastic yo-yo cycle of your energy vibration into a more natural ebb and flow.

## Truth #137—You Need Very Little in Order to Thrive

As a human being, you actually need very little in order to thrive. You are conditioned to believe that you need far more, particularly externally, than you truly do. That misperception leads you to attach to people, things and situations that your mind considers fundamentally necessary, when, in fact, you could quite easily survive, and even thrive, without them. You could release your grip on them in order to create space in your life to receive new creations, new people, new things, new situations and new possibilities more aligned to your true nature and to your soul-led passions, inspirations and intuition.

Many people are completely attached to what they *think* they need, rather than what they truly need. They are not willing to let go of anything as an energy exchange in order to usher in the life they really want. Consider the possibility that you could have what you most *want* in your life right now, if you were willing to loosen your grip on what you think you *need*. Consider, further, that what you think you need is actually a want, and what you think you want is actually a need. What does this mean?

The status, the recognition, the titles, the awards, the comfort and perceived certainty, the material possessions, and the demanded level of financial security beyond your actual requirements—these are not needs. They are wants. There is absolutely nothing wrong in any way with these natural, motivating and inspiring wants. By all means embrace them fully, but they are not to be confused with your core human needs.

Shelter, clothing, food and water are needs, not wants. Feeling loved, connected and supported in life is a need, not a want. Living in alignment with your soul is a need, not a want. Inner peace, a sense of personal freedom, and success as defined by the New World model—these are needs, not wants.

It can be frustrating and emotionally distressing when this equation is accidentally back to front, and you think your wants are needs, and your needs are wants. You have to start to reverse your want/need and need/want perception, and bring true perspective to your circumstances. Once you get clear on attending to your true needs first, you have much more empowered capacity to direct your resources to achieving what you want. Once you get clear that what you thought were necessities are really not, you will see that you can much more creatively weave your path, weave your resources and weave your decisions in a way that gives you more freedom and opportunity to achieve your goals and dreams and experience the fulfillment of both your needs and wants at the very same time.

If you are not willing to energetically let go of your grip on your wants, in order to attend to your true needs and create from the inside out the fulfillment of both holistically, then you will remain stuck.

## Truth #138—Things, Including Money, Are Simply Energy

You are not defined by the things you own, the clothes you wear, the house you live in or the car you drive. You may agree with this statement theoretically.

However, you may also experience a sense of uncomfortable personal diminishment and perceived lowering of your status, value and worth at the thought of not having those things. Your attachment to the things in your life is so subtle that you don't realize how attached you are until those things are damaged, taken from you, your access to them is limited or someone interferes with them, which fires up a painful reaction within you that reveals your true attachment.

You need to lift yourself above your current understanding of things, both material possessions and the paper and coins that are money, to consider for a moment a new perspective— a truthful one. When you do this, you will no longer feel owned by your things and instead you can own and enjoy them for what they really are.

Things are neither bad nor good. They just are. They do not make you more of a person or less of a person. They are nothingness. They are source energy vibrating at a certain frequency, which gives them their density and form, so they exist as physical objects and you can use them. In your use of them, they support certain external experiences and prompt certain internal feelings.

Having things or not having things is not the point. It's what you perceive the having or not having to mean about who you are and your life. Consider the truth that you could be completely thing-less, standing in the middle of nowhere, with nothing, and you would be just as whole and complete, worthy and valued, safe, supported and needed, with just as much possibility before you in every sense, just because of who you are, not because of what you have. That is the point.

Your attachment to things is because you believe they show the world who you are and, thus, you link them to yourself and your worth. This is false. Nothing, literally "no thing," defines your worth. When you realize things are not linked to your worth, they are just gifts to enjoy, you will cease to suffer the intensity of emotions associated with trying to accumulate them, grip on to them, maintain them, beautify them and control them like your existence depends on them.

When this truth resonates with you, not just intellectually, but emotionally at a deeper level, then the having of all your things is for pure joy without attachment, and things could come and go from your life and you will not be thrown around emotionally like a yo-yo as a result.

Further, when you realize that material possessions and money are simply energy, and energy by its inherent nature seeks to flow, coming into and out of form, you will realize that the coming and going of possessions and money in an ongoing circular flow in your life is quite natural. It is not something to fear or resist. It does not mean loss. It means incoming and outgoing, it means gain and expenditure, it means using and discarding, it means birth and death, it means shelf life and disposal—it means a constant flow and exchange of energy.

Remember that energy is literally the entire fabric of creation, it is ad infinitum, and completely abundant in every sense of the word; as material possessions and money are simply energy, there is no limit to what you can create, experience and enjoy. There is no place you can be in your life, literally and metaphorically, where material possessions and money are not available to you, and there is no limitation in terms of having to compete against anything or anyone else for them.

## Truth #139—You Came with Nothing and You Will Leave with Nothing—Release Your Grip

You were born as a baby without one single thing. Just you. Just your soul, mind and body. You were taken care of. You were given what you needed; even if in dire circumstances, you are here now because of how you were provided for up until this point.

When you die, you will leave empty-handed. Just you. Just your soul continuing on as part of highest consciousness, your mind and body ceasing to function. Your soul will be taken care of, as it always is, when you return home to your source.

Any things you have and experience as external to you in this life are gifts to enjoy, to marvel at, to play with, to experience, and to exchange one aspect of energy/possession/money for another. The less you grip on to any of it, the freer your hands are to be open to receive more, allowing you to relax, enjoy and flow.

## Truth #140—There Is Nothing but Uncertainty; Understanding this Liberates You

To give life to your soul language of passion, inspiration and intuition means taking action. At times, it requires action that carries you beyond your current experience of life— sometimes requiring changes to your circumstances. It is common to feel resistant to that idea of change, because you are so familiar with your current circumstances; that familiarity gives you a sense of comfort, and a perceived level of certainty.

Human beings are addicted to certainty. You are addicted to wanting to know what is going to happen to you and for you. As a result, you prefer to dwell within what feels most familiar and controllable. As preferable to the unknown, you may even be willing to dwell in complete discomfort if it is familiar to you and seems controllable. This is because it's a formula that you understand and feel safe with.

In instances, you may be unwilling to give up that perceived certainty for anything or anyone, not even for your passions, your inspirations or your intuition.

The absurdity is this—the certainty you choose over and above what is meaningful and soul-led for you, doesn't even exist, despite what you perceive. Your life can change in an instant. Not one thing is certain. Not your actual physical life, not your loved ones and relationships, not your environment, not your possessions, not your career, none of it. There is no certainty beyond this moment, despite your anticipation that the next moment is going to be much the same as the current moment. What you perceive to be certain is no more certain than complete uncertainty.

At first this truth can feel very unsettling. It rocks the foundation of how you have previously defined yourself, as far being safe and in control. However, once you come to terms with it, you begin to see that if everything is truly uncertain and there is nothing to grip onto or control, then, in fact, you are not at all risking certainty for uncertainty by stepping up to act upon your passions, inspirations and intuition.

The truth that there is nothing but uncertainty gives rise to all possibility and creates an immense sense of freedom.

## Truth #141—Uncertainty Is the Breeding Ground for All Great Possibilities

While you adore certainty, you also crave new possibilities. The curiosity, creativity and adventurer that lies within you knows there is limited room for any spontaneous and miraculous unfolding when you live your life within carefully constructed parameters of perceived certainty.

If are not willing to give up the "certainty" in your life, you make it difficult for anything new to arise. The contradiction that many people play out is they expend a great deal of effort wanting new possibility and trying to give rise to new creation in their lives, not understanding why nothing changes, but, on the flip side, they want everything to be familiar, comfortable and safe, and do little to create space in their life for newness to enter.

The confronting truth that most people don't want to acknowledge, is that if you want certainty, but you also want to give life to your soul language and achieve the goals and dreams that call to you, then from within the fog that clouds you, you will choose certainty every time. Your limiting beliefs will choose certainty. The expectations of others and your own expectations will sway you into choosing certainty. Your fear will choose certainty. Your conditioned mind will choose certainty. You will choose it to your detriment, and you will forgo the life you intuitively know is possible.

Instead, if you understand the truth that certainty is an illusion, you are left with nothing but a clear path forward to act in alignment with your soul as it speaks to you. And, as you stand in acknowledgement of all uncertainty, you will start to realize that within that uncertainty exists every great possibility. When nothing is locked in and locked down, then everything is free, open and available to you. Everything you could ever imagine is right there on the landscape before you, for your selection.

### Truth #142—Creating your Goals and Dreams Is Not Meant to be Easy, But it is Exciting

If making your contribution through being your unique expression, giving life to your soul language and achieving your goals and dreams were easy, then you would not learn along the way. It is the learning from challenges that allows you to evolve, becoming wiser, feeding further into your contribution to others and this world. This cycle is part of your experience of New World success.

Give away the notion that the ride to create success should be smooth. It is easy to buy into that illusion when you absorb messages in society that depict living your goals and dreams as a fast and easy process, selling you systems, techniques, methods, products and services that promise to take all the hard work out of your journey so that, in the instant gratification society that has conditioned you, you can have what you want when you want it, and with limited effort.

What your soul needs is not always what your mind and body want. And if you removed all the effort, there would be no evolution.

Just because life isn't always easy, doesn't mean it isn't joyful, exciting, creative, expressive, adventurous, incredibly meaningful and fulfilling. With all that, it takes effort. It takes willpower, strength, courage and the willingness to put yourself out there in life, metaphorically and in some cases quite literally. It takes going out on a limb to create what you want and to be open to receive what you desire. You can't play the game of life if you are not willing to suit up and get on the playing field to fully participate.

## Truth #143—No One Is Coming to Save You—You Are Totally Supported to Save Yourself

Your goals and dreams are not going to happen to you. You are going to happen to them. You are going to happen to life. You are going to bring your desires into existence through your creative power. There is nothing to wait for. It is you who must act.

You were not sent into this world as incapable of creating, or as missing anything you need to walk your path. You do not need someone else to ride in and save the day. Someone else making your life happen for you would completely steal from you the opportunity to face your own challenges, thus robbing you of the opportunity to learn from them and evolve through them as part of your soul intent. Someone else giving your goals and dreams to you on a platter by taking over your contribution for you, leaving you to reap the benefits at the other end, would steal from you the opportunity to directly give your own special gifts into the world. You would come and go from the world, taking your unique expression with you. You would not, therefore, fulfill part of your soul intent.

You were put here on this planet to learn and contribute; you do this by standing up in your life, fully showing up with every part of yourself, committed to forging your own path. It means the energy you bring to your life is one of personal empowerment, personal possibility and capability and utter dedication to owning your life in every way, shape and form.

This does not mean you are not wrapped in support every step of the way. Rest assured that you will be given divine guidance, love and support in divine order and timing, in the way your soul needs. Nothing will ever change that. But it is you who must act, and not when you get the guidance first, but now. Guidance will come when you move into alignment with your passions, inspirations and intuition. Your soul-led forward momentum calls in the guidance and allows the unfolding of your path. If you remain static, without taking action, without learning and without contributing, you block the unfolding.

Being responsible for making your own life happen doesn't mean that you can't depend on, lean on and leverage other people. Having people you know you can rely on when you need them is a fundamental part of being in relationship and connection on your journey. You are, however, asked to have an acute awareness of where you are participating in balanced and healthy interdependence, versus where you are in an unhealthy dependence on others, not living your own life. When you become so dependent upon something or someone that you stop exercising your freewill and avoid making choices, you have gone beyond the normal parameters of a healthy relationship or circumstance. This then becomes a block to creating the life you came here to live.

## Truth #144—Fear Is an Invitation to Shift

Fear shows up in different guises—such as worry, doubt, anxiety or panic. It can come as low-level unease or full-blown overwhelm. Fear is something you experience at multiple levels all at once—physically, mentally and emotionally. This can be a scary thing if you do not understand what is happening and why. The more you come to understand your fear response, the less of a grip it will have on you.

Fear can be triggered by external experiences or entirely internally generated by your own thought processes. It is always experienced to help you survive and/or to help you thrive, and it generally comes in response to three particular scenarios.

Firstly, if you are literally in harm's way and your physical life is threatened then your natural built-in human instinct will take over. That instinct is fear viscerally at every level within you, preparing your mind and body for fight, flight or freeze for your own well-being. Fear helps you physically save yourself. This is healthy, instinctive fear.

Secondly, either something non-life threatening externally occurs in your life and prompts fearful thoughts within you or you have self-generated automatic fearful thoughts arise— both in alignment with your limiting beliefs—and the fearful thoughts give rise to fearful feelings. The fearful thoughts and feelings then cycle and feed on each other. This is not fear in response to real threat. This is fear in response to *perceived* threat, based upon your paradigm. This is fog fear.

Thirdly, you face some type of uncertainty, even in relation to positive experiences like the creation of your goals and dreams, and because uncertainty goes against your deep desire for familiarity and comfort, it prompts fearful thoughts and feelings. This is also not fear in response to real threat. This is also fear in response to perceived threat. More fog fear.

When you notice fog-based fearful thoughts and feelings, the key is to remember that like all thoughts and feelings, particularly those you might deem to be negative, they are simply messengers. Fear helps you understand something important about yourself or your life, to aid you in expanding and thriving. It is as powerfully transformative as it is crippling, because it directly illuminates the fact that your perception is limiting you, thus giving you the empowered opportunity to shift that perception.

In all its forms, fear is an invitation to shift. With instinctive fear, it is an invitation to literally shift your body by taking action that will save yourself from real danger. With fog fear, it is an invitation for an inner shift in your paradigm and possibly also a literal shift externally by taking action on whatever you know you need to do. Fog-based fear always precedes expansion internally and externally. In this way, fear is something to celebrate, because it means you are facing a doorway into breakthrough.

When you witness other people creating change, bringing life to their passions and inspirations, and following their intuition, it is not necessarily that they are doing it without any fear. Those people simply make a different choice about what they do with their fear. They understand the message it is giving them. They use it to their advantage. It becomes a fuel for their growth. Instead of it stopping you, where you feel you must fight it, shy away from it or think there is something wrong with you or your path, you can partner with your fear to drive you forward.

The more you accept fear's invitation to shift, inwardly and outwardly, the more your courage grows as a result of acting despite the fear. The more you experience expansion and results in your life because of those shifts, the more confident you become. In every shift you further ingrain a foundation of truths as your preferred paradigm and become a clearer channel for your soul to express through you into this world.

## Truth #145—You Do Not Have to Literally Leap in Order to Make Leaps

If you want to bring about big change, it is easy to get lost in thinking that the only way to achieve that change is through taking one giant leap. That is one way of looking at it.

Yet, equally, every journey is made up of many small steps. You can make transformational leaps in your life without ever having to literally leap. This approach requires you to make small shifts in your paradigm and small shifts in your actions, consistently and with dedication. This has a cumulative effect, and eventually you will notice that you've made a significant leap forward in your life, not from throwing yourself head first into one big leap, but from systematic progression.

What stops you from taking small steps is the fog. You may be conditioned to desire and expect instant gratification, which makes you shy away from any committed effort to create change through many small steps. Or, you may be lost in the notion that if you can't see the whole path ahead of you with every step you need to take mapped out in advance, then there's no point in taking the first step at all.

You do not need to know what steps will be required tomorrow or next week or next month. You only need to consider what steps are available to you today. As you step forward, you will have greater sight of what is required next. Much like a car driving in the dark of night, the headlights only shine a few feet forward, but as the car moves ahead, more of the road is lit up, showing you where to go. Your steps today will help show you the steps for tomorrow, and those steps tomorrow will inform and open up the best steps for the following days and weeks.

It is this commitment to take small steps forward in alignment with your passions, inspirations and intuition, despite not knowing exactly what lies ahead, which fulfills your part in the co-creation process. Higher consciousness can't co-create with you, and give you divine guidance, if you won't play the game. The more you act, the more the path unfolds, the more new possibilities, people, things, opportunities and points of leverage have the chance to show up on your unfolding path. If you remain still, with no willingness to take a step, there is no unfolding. Your stagnation keeps possibilities, people, things, opportunities and points of leverage shrouded in darkness and off your radar.

## Truth #146—The World Gravitates to the Authentic You, Not to an Adapted Version

From within the fog, it is easy to get lost in believing that success looks a certain way, talks a certain way and walks a certain way. Success is portrayed to you through advertising, mass media and social media in a particular light. If you are not conscious to it, you may fall victim to a common trap—adapting yourself to fit what you perceive success looks like.

Your success, both internally in accordance with the New World model, and externally in the sense of all the tangible experiences and results you desire, will come fundamentally from one thing ... you being *you* in all your glory.

You being you, means you without the fog. It means expressing your uniqueness without inhibition, in all settings, with all people. It means not adapting yourself to try to be more of something or less of something, indeed trying to be something you are not.

There is zero value in attempting to present a mask, façade or adapted version of yourself, or to fit a mold of what you believe the world most values. It will suck the joy out of you and exhaust you, because being someone you are not does not come naturally. It is nothing but an exhausting process.

The world does not need you to be someone or something else. If it did, you would have been born as that already. You were not. You were born exactly as you are. Any time you deny yourself, and attempt to be something else, you rob the world of receiving what it needs—you. Do not rob the world. If you give the world what it needs, you support your own success in every way because you are moving with the natural flow just as it was intended to be.

With regards to being yourself and how this generates success, here is the key. Your entire life is an interaction with other people. Your success inside and out is a play between yourself and your external environment, which predominantly involves other people. No matter what people say and do, no matter what you are sold into believing, human beings are acutely aware of what authenticity looks like, smells like and feels like. Human beings resonate with authenticity. They want to be around it, they find it magnetic, they want to engage with it, be in relationship with it, buy from it, sell to it, commune with it, share with it, receive it and give to it. They can pick up on a mask, façade and inauthentic adapted you from a mile away. When you apply this truth to your relationships, career, business or any other vocational endeavor you engage in, you will begin to see shifts occur, both in the inner freedom you feel and in the external results you create.

## Truth #147—You Pay a Price for Defensive Walls

If you were conditioned to believe that being strong is the most important thing, and that showing weakness will limit your success in life, then it is likely you have built up high defensive walls around you.

When your walls are up, it is true that you keep out the potential for ridicule, misunderstanding and nonacceptance. But you also keep out the gifts. You keep out the nourishment of meaningful deep connection that occurs when you allow other souls to truly see your soul. You keep out the possibility of shifts in your paradigm when you refuse to let down your guard even for yourself to see what lies within you for resolution and healing. This is the price you pay.

To receive, give and feel love, you must bring down your walls. Yes, you will be vulnerable. You will be equally as open to pain as you will be to love. But rather to live with love and pain, than with isolation and pain alone.

To notice and receive synchronicities, miracles and joy, you must bring down your walls. You may feel uncertain, but uncertainty is all there is. You are not foregoing anything. You will be open to many new paths, some that serve you and some that don't. But better to live with many paths open to you and to have the choice to listen to your intuition than to live with no paths available, behind a solid high wall where you cannot harness possibilities.

To receive traction, leverage and support for your cause, passion, goals and dreams, you must bring down your walls. You will put yourself out there and speak your truth; you will be opening yourself up to life. You will open to success, and to mistakes. But rather to live with the opportunity to breathe, walk, talk, expand, act, react, respond, choose, move, live, love, create and evolve, than to die not knowing what you were really here to experience.

You cannot receive the gifts of life and the open hearts of others, if you continue to guard yourself within a well-protected fortress of your mind, unwilling to show the world who you really are.

## Truth #148—Blame Gives Your Power Away, Personal Accountability Reclaims and Retains Your Power

It is easy to acknowledge the role you play in producing positive outcomes in your life, by retrospectively seeing the actions you took that led you to particular results. You can celebrate this.

It takes far more self-awareness and courage to acknowledge your role in the tough times and to own any actions you took that led you there. You have freewill, and you exercised that freewill to end up where you are right now. It may not have gone the way you wanted it to, but nevertheless, you are personally accountable for wherever you are standing and you are also personally responsible for lifting yourself out of it.

If you don't focus on yourself and own your own actions, it is likely you will send your attention outside of yourself and seek to find external reasons why you are where you are. It is easy to fall into the trap of blaming—other people, things, situations, circumstances or life in general. That process of blame gives away all of your personal power. You victimize yourself to the external world. You are not an "outside in" creator. You are an "inside out" creator, and the external world cannot take your power from you, unless you freely give it away. Blame will do just that.

You reclaim and retain your power when you remember and live from the truth that you and you alone are accountable for your actions, no matter what the circumstances. You do the best you can in any given situation. At times you may end up in situations you could not predict and you do not prefer. There may well be other people involved, and they may well have acted in ways that contributed to you experiencing those circumstances. None of this stops you from living with personal accountability for where you stand, and thus living with personal power. The two go hand in hand.

No one else walks in your shoes. No one else lives in your skin. The absolute beauty of this is that no one else can tell you what to believe, what to think, how to feel or how to act. You were gifted freewill when you were born; it is your personal responsibility to be accountable for how you exercise it.

## Relationships

### Truth #149—Relationships are Life Classes

If life is your soul education, then relationships are the classes you take. The core of all your learning in this life will take place in relationship with, or in relation to, other people, be it family, friends, work, romance, acquaintances, perceived opponents or complete strangers. You do not need to be in an actual relationship with a person per se, to be "in relationship" with them from a soul perspective. Anyone you have any interaction with at all, crossing paths, means you are in relationship of some nature.

It is the energy, words and actions of other people that challenge and trigger you, or support and uplift you. Your energy, words and actions are constantly challenging and triggering, or supporting and uplifting other people as well. Every interaction is invaluable.

## Truth #150—Self-Love Leads to Loving Others Freely

No amount of love from another person will ever be enough to make you feel complete, if you do not love yourself and come to know your own inherent completeness first.

If you reconnect to the truth of who you are, the absolute miracle you are, and nurture your self-love, you come to feelings of wholeness within yourself. From there you will no longer seek to find love outside of yourself from a place of "need" in terms of filling a seeming void within, but rather from a healthy place of wishing to express love and connect.

That is the place where you can be the most fully and freely loving partner, parent, child, sibling or friend—when you love yourself as much as you love anyone or anything else.

## Truth #151—No Person Ever Projects Pain Unless They Are in Pain Themselves

As human beings are inside out creators, what is within always comes out. Where pain is projected, pain is within. Where love is projected, love is within.

Painful words and actions quite simply do not come out of a person who is living from their natural state of love. Whenever you are on the receiving end of someone else's negativity, remember that they are expressing their painful inner space. This does not endorse or excuse their words or actions. This also does not mean you pity them. You are not here to judge them or anything they do as "wrong," or to explain their problems to them.

You are called upon to be present and to respond from conscious loving awareness, in realizing the painful projection is not about *you*, but instead a mirror of their own issues. From that presence, you can then follow your intuition about what is best to do—whether to remove yourself from the situation, to remain but be nonresponsive, or to respond in word and actions from that conscious loving awareness.

## Truth #152—No One Needs You to Change Them

From within the fog, it is often a default position, and alluring to the ego, to focus on the problems other people have and to seemingly be able to identify with conviction what is "wrong" with them, their actions or their life.

This shows up for one of three primary reasons: (1) to make others wrong as a way of blaming them for what frustrates and upsets you, (2) to deflect attention off yourself and onto other people as a way of avoiding personal responsibility for your own life and (3) as a desire to help people resolve their inner issues or circumstances due to genuine compassion.

Fundamentally, no one is "wrong," and no one is broken, just as you are not wrong or broken. Everyone faces a journey of challenges in order to learn, for that growth to feed into contribution. We must each come to see our own fog, through the design for awakening. We must forge our own path, stumble in our own way, learn from our mistakes and come to do all of this uniquely in our own way. In essence, others don't need you to change them. You are not responsible for their growth; they are. You cannot force anyone to change; they must want to.

By all means, share your insights with them, without attachment to what the outcome will be when they hear you. Offer support to them, without judgment if they do not want support. Just as you operate with your own freewill and personal accountability for your actions, you must allow others in your life to operate from their own freewill. The fact is that some people are just not ready for the change that you want to see within them. That makes you uneasy and unhappy, but that is your inner experience to work through, not theirs.

Let your own conscious living, awareness, presence, choices and unconditional love be healing to all those you come into contact with. Role modeling the change that you wish to see in others is more powerful than trying to force that change on them.

## Truth #153—When You Relate to People as Their Full Potential, You Support Them to Unleash that Potential

If you relate to others based on their past, their mistakes, their challenges, their circumstances and the present level of their capability, then that is how they will continue to appear to you, because you are not looking for anything else from them or within them. You are instead unconsciously looking for evidence to support your existing perspective of them.

Unfortunately, others energetically pick up on this perspective you hold, whether you realize it or not. It is conveyed in your words, tone, facial expression, body language, actions and the overall energy vibration you emit. For them, this feels like the world is showing them their limitations. They will feel like their past is who they are, and that what you expect from them is more of the same.

While it is true that this is a perspective they can freely choose, and they have the power to live from and change their own beliefs, thoughts, feelings and actions at any time just as you do, it is also true that if you love them, then you can support their paradigm shift by relating to them not as their past or their circumstances, but relating to them as the full potential of their soul.

No matter how much darkness others may have been through, no matter the extent of their fog, if you choose to focus on the light within them, you create an opening for them to glimpse that flicker of light themselves. If you convey in your words, tone, facial expression, body language, actions and the overall energy vibration you emit that you believe in the love and good in them, and you believe they deserve every good thing that this life has to offer them, at the very least they will be curious about that possibility for themselves.

It may not be immediately apparent to you that you seeing their potential has unlocked anything within them. It may seem like your message, in word or in energy, has gone unheard. But you have planted a seed. And with ongoing reinforcement, you nurture that seed. Eventually, with enough support that seed can sprout. Someone has to plant the seed. That someone can be you.

## Truth #154—True Listening Has the Sole Purpose of Seeking to Understand

When someone speaks to you and you are not consciously present, but instead lost in your mind, without even realizing it, you won't be fully receiving what is being offered. Your mind may be silently passing commentary about the person or the words being spoken. Or, you may be thinking about something or someone else unrelated or related, preparing what to say next, or perhaps thinking of another topic altogether with the intention of changing the conversation as soon as you get the opportunity. If this is your train of thought, you can't possibly be offering your full attention, which means you are not fully listening, which means they are talking to themselves.

Everyone wants to feel seen and heard. If you are not present and attentively listening when others speak to you, they will either pick up on that consciously through visual cues or energetically they may feel like something isn't quite right. The bottom line is that this affects the quality and depth of your relationships.

Fully listening to another human being means offering your full attention and receiving the words shared with the sole intent of understanding them. Understanding does not mean agreeing; it means processing to make sense of both what has literally been said, as well as the energy behind the words. People convey energy and feelings through not only their words, but also with tone and body language, which you will pick up on if you are consciously aware—that is, completely present. From that place, you are then able to respond from a position of clarity. This is powerful.

Listening in this way is a practice. You don't have to agree with or like what others communicate to you or how they do it. But despite any conflict of values or perspective, you are always able to bring the intention to understand what they are seeking to express, and to convey that understanding before responding.

## Truth #155—You Have Soul Assignments with Certain People in Your Life

There are certain people in your life that you have specific soul assignments with. These are energetic soul agreements to intersect in each other's paths in this life for a reason, season or lifetime. You may have experienced other lifetimes with these souls, in different types of relationships with them, and now for the purposes of your soul evolution and their soul evolution, your souls have agreed to help each other in some way.

Do not mistake this help as a mission of love in the sense that you know it. Unconditional love is the basis of all soul agreements, from a higher perspective. However, it shows up in the human experience in many ways. Evolution requires us to balance our learning, to experience life from different angles, and at times to encounter challenging people, situations and circumstances in order grow and heal, and to expand our capability for understanding, compassion, forgiveness, acceptance, allowing, resilience, trust, love and an endless number of other traits and capacities. As you develop these, of course you share these traits and capacities with others you interact with, thus aiding every person you encounter going forward, and the planet as a collective because of your important place in creation. This is your soul's learning and contribution intersecting with another soul's learning and contribution process.

Those in your life, who support you unconditionally and stand by your side, may be in soul agreement with you. Those in your life who challenge you, hurt you and crack open wounds deep within you that call for healing, may also be in soul agreement with you. It does not matter what the soul agreements are, or whom they are with. Do not obsess over this, for you may never truly know the answer. The point is this—how can you know how to heal and be your natural state of love in the face of challenge, and thus let that energy flow on to others, if you are never able to experience and practice that for yourself. Every challenge is a gift and the ones who deliver you challenges may be doing you a soul favor. That doesn't mean staying in the vicinity of what and whom you do not like. It means noticing the gift in your challenges and then freely moving on as a wiser you.

### Truth #156—You Are Responsible for Defining How You Wish to Be Treated, but You Are Never Responsible for Any Mistreatment

When you understand your values, and you choose to live your life consciously anchored around those values, you become increasingly clear about what you wish to do, why you wish to do it, who you want to be with, why you want to be with them, how you want to live your life and how you want to feel; you will start to align your life around these foundations. This means you become values-based in everything you do.

This also means that you simultaneously become clear about what is *not* acceptable to you in terms of your relationships and how you wish to be treated. You can be the state of love in the face of any pain projected at you, but that does not mean you have to remain standing in firing range. Your freewill allows you to communicate your values, communicate how you wish to be treated and authentically express the possibilities you desire for your relationships. You do this in order to help other people in your life understand you more deeply, and to be clear with them about what being in relationship with you means. They then have the choice to listen to your needs and respect those, or not.

To express your values and needs is your responsibility. This is part of your journey. However, once you have done so, it is not your responsibility when people cross those values-based boundaries. That is their responsibility. You are never to blame for any ill treatment you receive from other people. You are not responsible for someone else's beliefs nor their thoughts or feelings, and most certainly not their actions.

While you set the stage for how you are received, valued and interacted with, there are many actors in the scene; all must choose how to play their role.

## Truth #157—Forgiveness Is a Gift You Give Yourself

You do not forgive yourself or others in order to remove responsibility. Forgiveness is not a process of exoneration or endorsement of what has occurred.

You forgive others in order to free yourself of the past. Similarly, you forgive yourself in order to free yourself of the past. You do this by first acknowledging what was or what is that causes you to feel upset. Then you focus on understanding your feelings about it, and you listen closely to the messages those feelings are giving you about what is important to you and what you can learn about others, life and yourself from this situation. You look at the gift within the challenge. Then you remember the truth—about the soul of the other person, about your own soul, about our interconnectedness, and about how the fog is at play in so many people's lives that they are completely disconnected from their own true nature, with uneasiness deep inside that easily projects outward at others. You then forgive the other person, situation and/or yourself from this higher perspective—not endorsing what occurred, not embracing what occurred, but simply making peace with the facts of the situation and the weaving of energy as it was or is, by saying, "I accept what was/is, and I choose to no longer carry this with me."

In forgiveness you energetically release your resistance to whatever factually occurred, and you energetically release yourself from anything or anyone you are experiencing negative emotions about and toward. Forgiveness might be literally communicated to another person, or it may simply be a silent declaration within you, purely for yourself.

Forgiveness is honoring the present moment by letting go of attachment to the past. For what is done is done and cannot be changed. Forgiveness is saying no to pain and suffering, for you. Forgiveness is a walk back into your natural state of love. It transmutes pain and creates the conditions for inner peace. That shifts your energy vibration, which reignites the natural flow of your energy and the unfolding of your life.

## Truth #158—You Cannot Be Everything to Everyone, nor Do You Need to Be

If your illusion is that you are not enough and that perfection is possible, then it is relatively easy to fall into the trap of believing that the more you do for others and the better you are at everything you do for them, the more enough and perfect you will be.

Societal conditioning would have you believe that success is "having it all together"—being a faultless parent, being a perfect partner, having a top career with no glitches, being in perfect shape physically, looking immaculate, being able to juggle one hundred things simultaneously and coming out the other side smiling and unshaken. Societal conditioning would have you believe that superman and superwoman are not only real, but actually necessary role models if you want to measure up to standards. What standards? The Old World model of success standards.

You are human. You cannot be faultless, because humans are beautifully imperfect beings by design. You also know that you have limited human energy to give into the world each day. Limited physical, mental and emotional energy means you have to make conscious choices about what you give that energy to. If you attempt to be everything to everyone, in order to align to an illusion of being superhuman, then you will personally come last in that equation. When you come last, you become physically, mentally and emotionally exhausted. You will then suffer and be in pain within. You will then no longer be able to sustain the façade of trying to be superman or superwoman. This will lead you to feel like there is something wrong with you. Nothing is wrong with you.

## Truth #159—People Can't Truly Know You, if You Don't Show You

When someone in your life doesn't seem to understand you, and it is a person whom you love, value and want to have in your life, then take the time to help him or her understand you. The people in your life are not mind readers; they only know what they see, hear and what you share. So take the time to share with them authentically—what you are about, what you value, what is important to you, why you do what you do and what you believe in.

Give people the chance to evolve with you. If you love them dearly, give them plenty of room to grow, and give them multiple opportunities to know the real you and make choices about what that means for them.

Having shown them who you really are, if they do not like it, and will not support, love and uplift you, then you have a choice to make. Your choice is about what type of relationship you have with them going forward.

You will intuitively know if and when it is time to release yourself from certain people in your life who do not accept you just as you are. However, you do not have to, and sometimes it quite simply isn't possible to, walk away from certain people who bring you down. If that is the case, you can define the type and frequency of interaction you are willing to have with them, and be conscious in those interactions to protect your own energy by not taking on their low vibration. In those interactions you can stay true to who you are and your values. Do not fall into alignment with their expectations of who you should be, how you should be and what you should be doing. Do not give them the power to chain you to old ways of being and old habits of doing that previously kept you stuck, just because that is their comfort zone and their preference. You are unleashing. Your life is too short to be shackled.

## Truth #160—Not Everyone Will Understand You or Like You, and There Is Nothing Wrong with That

When people do not like you or understand you, it has nothing to do with you or your likeability. The world is not designed for you to have seven billion friends and seven billion supporters.

Your values, drivers and unique expression will be vastly different to some people and, as such, who you are being and what you are doing may seem quite foreign to them. That has nothing to do with you, rather it has to do with how they perceive you from their unique paradigm.

Just as you will not be understood or liked by everyone, there will be many people in this world who you meet, see or hear that you do not understand or like either, simply because their values, drivers and unique expression don't resonate with you. That doesn't mean they are not likeable. It also doesn't mean that you dislike them; it simply means you don't naturally "gel" with them.

Your job is not to please everyone or be understood by everyone, even though it is a natural human urge to want to be understood and liked. The primary reasons you want people to understand you are because you want reassurance that who you are is okay, that what you want to do is the "right" thing, and you want people to trumpet that support around you to make you feel more secure on your path. You may want this, and most people do. But do not mistake want for need. You do not need it.

You can forge a path of truth, purpose, passion, inspiration, intuition, creativity, abundance and excitement, and live your full life and achieve your greatest potential and contribution into this world and not have one single person supporting you while you do so. It would not matter. What would matter is that you did what you were put on this planet to do. And yet, as divine order would have it, when you do what you were put on this planet to do in this way, you will always have the support you need show up when you need it, and sometimes that happens in the most unexpected of ways.

## Truth #161—Advice Can Come from Love and Fear at the Very Same Time

There will be people in your support network who give you advice and offer help at different points in your life journey. They will do so out of their love for you. Some of it will be deeply valuable to you. Some of it, however, will be completely misguided and have the power to sabotage you. Misguided advice will most likely come from the people who might seem to understand you personally but don't understand what you are doing or why you are doing it. They may not understand that you are led by your inner voice. They will want to protect you from yourself, from making mistakes and from suffering unnecessary "failure." They may become caught up in a rehearsal for disaster on your behalf, scenario planning the entire negative "what ifs" that could occur as you step out bravely in your life. Their love for you is what lies behind this advice, but what also lies behind this is their own fear. This is entirely driven out of their own paradigm. They are providing what they deem to be genuinely helpful advice, but based upon their own unique version of reality.

Their way is not your way. Their path is not your path. Their advice and opinions, whether given from their love for you, or from their fear, or both, remain just that ... advice and opinions. If it feels helpful, take it. If it does not feel helpful, then peacefully listen, express gratitude for their care and support, and then silently discard the advice as you continue walking your path forward.

No one else knows your passions firsthand, nor can they feel your inspirations or hear your intuition. No one else can tell you what is "right" for you to do. You alone must walk your path and make your decisions. There is freedom in this. You do not have to struggle to make sense of all the advice you get. You do not need to worry about who is right, about who to listen to, about who to follow or about who has all the answers. You must trust, instead, in your own inner compass. You were born with this built-in guidance and your journey is to come to know it more closely and develop your faith in it.

## Truth #162—You Don't Get to Dictate Where the Love and Support in Your Life Comes From

The truth that many people don't want to hear is that sometimes the people who don't understand you and support you might be members of your family, or your friends, and at times you may have to go beyond your normal community network to find "soul family"—like-minded people, people who understand your true nature and will support you in ways your family or existing friends can't.

This doesn't make your family wrong. It doesn't make your friends wrong. It doesn't make you right. It just means you are all different, perceiving each other and life from different paradigms.

Each person in your life has different skills, capacities and paths to walk. Each has a contribution to make to you, and vice versa, for a reason, season or lifetime. Some people (even your family) may simply not be equipped to be supportive of you for every step of the path you are walking. They may not have the tools they need. They may not have the consciousness. They may be lost in their own fog and unaware of it. They may be projecting their pain or fear and it has them in a grip. Remember—your job is not to change them. You can only communicate openly, honestly and compassionately what it is that you need and want, and you can invite that from them, but if they do not receive that request nor respond to it in the way you desire, then please remember ... the universe always puts people in your life to support you, but you don't always get to choose where that support comes from. Sometimes you have to go outside the ones you most love in order to find the love you need right now.

Once you surrender to this and open up in readiness to receive that love and support, you may find that new people naturally flow into your life (through synchronicity and coincidence) who are the exact type of people you wanted and needed. While it may be new friendships, or a companion, it may also be new career or business support; it may equally be a static source of new information that uplifts you, like a book or a movie that seems to speak to your heart in just the right way, at just the right time. It may be an animal that comes into your life and provides you with unconditional companionship and joy.

You don't get to dictate where the love and support comes from or what it looks like. What you do have control over is your own conscious awareness to recognize it when it shows up, and your own freewill to welcome it in.

## Truth #163—Never Ask of Someone More than They Can Give in That Moment

One of the most empowering and peaceful moments in a relationship arises when you realize that you are never going to get what you want just because you want it, rather you are going to get what the other person has to give you. What another has to offer is based entirely on his or her paradigm and capacity, which have nothing to do with you. If the other person is limited within, then there will be limits to what can be given to you.

If others are doing the best they know how, with the sum total of what they know, and you need something completely different from them, that is beyond their physical, mental or emotional capacity to give you, then you need to consider whether it is loving and fair of you to ask it of them.

At times, it means realizing that specific people in your life might never be equipped to give you certain support. At other times, it means realizing that while a certain person is normally equipped to help you, he or she may sometimes not have the energy and capacity to support you in the way you need in that particular moment, perhaps due to circumstances.

When you stop fighting this truth and give over trying to get blood from a stone, and instead love people just as they are, acknowledging their overall or circumstantial capacity to love and support you, then two new possibilities open up for you: (1) you will more easily notice what your loved one might need from you in that moment, not just what you need, giving you the chance to lift someone else up (2) you can turn your attention to your own path forward and focus on where you may otherwise find the love, support and understanding that you are seeking in that moment.

## Truth #164—Relationships Devolve or Evolve and This Is Natural

The way you can best be of service to yourself, the world and those who don't understand you is to simply carry forward on your path, not wavering in the face of challenges, opposition, questions and pain.

When you sense that no one is with you on your path, and you wish that you were understood or that you had people around you to wrap you in love … remember this: There is often a transition period that occurs when you step up to live as the real you, without the fog, without the defensive walls, as the soul you are, creating change and making new things happen from the inside out. In that transition period, as you step beyond the stories and limitations you once lived within, you may notice that the people you spent most of your time with before suddenly do not resonate with you or you do not resonate with them in the same way as you are used to. It can feel lonely. That is normal. As you transition, you will flow into the path of new people who resonate with you, and you will form new networks more aligned to your awakening consciousness and your authentic values.

This does not mean that your new connections *replace* your existing network of relationships. It means your network grows. You enrich your life with more love and more people. You will have those people who knew you before your awakening transition, who do not necessarily understand the emerging "new you." You will also have those people that have known you always and stayed with you on your path, embracing you in all stages of your evolution. And, you will have new people you meet on your journey of transformation.

Be a pioneer. Be a leader of your own life. Whoever comes with you on that journey is meant to. Whoever does not, was not.

## Truth #165—Staying Small to Appease Other People Will Suffocate Your Soul

If you realize some people in your network, be it family, friends, acquaintances or colleagues, don't understand you or support you, there is a moment when you are faced with two options.

Your fear and your need for superficial acceptance and a sense of normality would choose option one. Option one is this ... you play small. You stay quiet. You silence your voice. You ignore your knowing. You avoid standing out. You toe the line. You align your life to the expectations of others in order to keep the peace. You make other people's expectations the guiding force in your life. You do what it takes to not "rock the boat," to ensure acceptance and to stay with the crowd. You cling to the desire to be liked and supported (even if by people you don't need to be liked or supported by). You forgo your own needs in this option.

Your soul would choose option two. Option two is this ... you play a big game and walk this life in total alignment with your own inner voice and values. You lovingly express what you know to be true for you, with appropriate awareness and compassion for how other people perceive and feel. You realize that staying small would suffocate your soul and keep you from succeeding in your purpose in all ways, for being the full expression of who you are, for learning and for contribution. You realize that the price you pay for standing out and no longer fitting in with some parts of your existing familiar network of people is a small price to pay in order for you to live the life you were put here to live.

## Truth #166—New World Success Is Your Birthright

There is nothing at all preventing you from living within New World success. It is your birthright. All that you need lies within you.

You are the only one in control of your inner landscape. The transformation is yours for the taking. The power is in your soul, flowing into and through your mind and body. What you do with this wisdom now is up to you. The choice is yours. There is no right time. There is only now.

It is your paradigm shift by learning and living from the truths that will take you directly into the New World, as the new and real you, living in your entirely new reality. That is where your inner peace, freedom and success exist.

# PART II
# CLEAR THE FOG

## Apply the truth to let go and break free of your limiting paradigm

*"Respect yourself enough to walk away from anything that no longer serves you, grows you, or makes you happy."*

— Robert Tew

As you discover new truths in your life, that process of awakening to a new reality spells the beginning of the end for the fog. Just the light of your conscious awareness alone, when first reflected upon the darkness of limiting beliefs (the core toxicity of any fog), is enough to loosen their grip on you. Where once you may have totally identified with them as being who you are and as being the only reality available to you, the truths are enough to rattle and form cracks in that illusion.

While becoming aware of new truths is powerful in this way, it is your conscious, proactive and practical application of the truths to your daily life that cements them as your new paradigm and brings them to life with tangible impacts on your personal situation.

You must first and foremost commit to letting go of what obviously does not align to truth, whatever you know right now is limiting you. This is the next critical step in the process of dispelling the fog, in order to become a clear channel for your soul to express out into the world.

## Declaration

I invite you to write a Letter of Commitment to yourself—a tangible declaration that serves as a pivot point in your life. The letter will state what you are letting go of and what you are choosing as an alternative for your life. You may like to write your Letter of Commitment in your own heartfelt words, specific to your situation. Or, you may like to utilize the Letter of Commitment template below exactly as it is, or as a draft that you can edit and add to, in order to fit your situation.

Inner peace, a sense of freedom and success inside and out all arise and expand because you plant and water the seeds of them within yourself. When you make this declaration, you signal the dawning of a new era. A fresh beginning—the day you chose to clear the fog, to plant and begin to water the seeds of a new paradigm.

You make this choice and declaration today for no one else, just for yourself, just because you know a more peaceful, free and successful experience of life is possible. Just because you know it is your birthright to unleash your life.

## Letter of Commitment

*I choose to let go of all that no longer serves me.*

*I let go of all limiting beliefs, and the thoughts and feelings they have given rise to.*

*I let go of all limiting behavior that has previously flowed on as a result of my old paradigm.*

*I release all the negative energy I have been carrying that was associated with the old paradigm.*

*I commit to living my life in alignment with truth.*

*I commit to always reminding myself of my true nature.*

*I choose conscious living.*

*I choose to be aware in each moment of my life, and to use my mind and feeling systems as navigational tools,* harnessing their power to support my journey, not being overcome and owned by them.

I rise above the Old World model of success and today I declare myself to be a member of the New World community of consciously living people, operating in the New World model of success.

I choose inner peace.

I choose freedom.

I choose success from the inside out.

I choose every good thing that life and this world has to offer me.

I choose this as my birthright.

Nothing exists to prevent me from living in alignment with my new foundation of truths.

I give myself permission to live simply and peacefully through a moment-by-moment strategy.

I accept that learning and living from truth is a life journey, and that in every moment I do the best I can, and that this is always enough.

I am always enough.

I commit to living in balance—with my soul, mind and body operating in unison for my holistic well-being.

I commit to being personally accountable for all areas of my life, and to bringing the light of consciousness to whatever challenges I face.

I commit to using my creative power in alignment with my passions, inspirations and intuition.

I commit to trusting myself and trusting in the co-creative process with the universe.

This is my commitment to my life purpose, which is to be the full expression of who I am, without inhibition, without apology and without judgment.

*This is my commitment to myself. This is how I honor my life.*

NAME: _____

DATE: _____

To download a template of this letter, which you can print out, sign and keep stored in your journal or displayed where you will see it visually on a regular basis, please visit: www.PinchMeLiving.com/Unleash-Your-Life-Free-Resources

## Letting Go—Practical Exercises

Next, having made your declaration, it is time to proactively name exactly what you are letting go of, whatever no longer serves you, via a series of practical exercises. This means identifying and releasing anything that is a contradiction to your solid new foundation of truths.

While limiting beliefs are absolutely the core of any fog you have been living within, and you will be guided shortly to identify, let go of and replace those limiting beliefs with empowering new ones, first you will focus on letting go of several surface level layers of negative energy in the fog. You do this in order to clear the way into the core limiting beliefs that lie below. The surface layers of fog include:

- hurt, guilt, regret and resentment (baggage from previous moments)
- resistance (rejection of the present moment)
- painful reactions (to the present moment)
- external validation
- external "muting" habits
- excuses (blocking possibilities for coming moments)

Have a paper and pen ready to write down your responses for each exercise. The exercises are designed for you to simply purge all that you no longer need. Whatever arises from within you—download it, offload it, dump it out onto paper.

As you name the limiting ways of being and doing that are holding you back, you may begin to recognize the absurdity of them in relation to your new foundation of truths. You will see how they contradict the truth and how glaringly they do not reflect who you truly are. From that new perspective, you will no longer *want* to carry them with you. Your desire to let go of them will be greater than your desire to cling on.

To support this process of applying truth, letting go and breaking free, you will also find a "truth mantra" under each exercise, which you can read whenever you want to reinforce your new foundation of truths. You can also download all the mantras as free audios from: www.PinchMeLiving.com/Unleash-Your-Life-Free-Resources

## Let Go of Hurt, Guilt, Regret and Resentment

Carrying hurt, guilt, regret and resentment inside of yourself blocks the fullness of healing, inner peace, freedom and success available to you. These low vibration, painful emotions are due to you living outside the present moment, lost in your mind, living in memories of the past—be it the past one hour ago or the past ten years ago.

If these emotions and perspectives relate in any way to another person (who you hurt, who hurt you or who you link your feelings of guilt, regret or resentment to), please take a moment to realize that this other person is not affected by your choice to carry this pain. The person suffering is you. Hurt, guilt, regret and resentment are poisonous to you. They are toxic to your soul, mind and body. There is no evolution available to you, nor to any other person connected to you, through your choice to cling to these emotions and perspectives.

To let go is not to diminish what occurred in the past. To let go is not to pretend and plaster over what was once a real and painful previous moment in your life. To forgive yourself is not to absolve yourself or endorse your actions. To forgive others is not to absolve them or endorse their actions.

Letting go and forgiving is a gift you give yourself, to learn and move on, carrying your learning forward to feed into your contribution to the world. You cannot learn and contribute, nor can you be the full expression of who you are (your life purpose), if you are clinging to, and blocked by, toxic energy.

Life gives you challenges to aid your evolution. All hurt is a pathway to healing. All guilt is an opportunity to practice forgiveness and self-love. All regret is a calling into allowing, acceptance and an opening back into the present moment where your life is actually happening. All resentment is a trigger to forgive others and see the soul in them that mirrors the soul in you.

You are not asked to continue bearing hurt, guilt, regret or resentment as part of your life journey. You are not asked by your source to carry any burden. You are not required to pay a debt to anyone or anything, least of all your source, by punishing yourself through holding on tightly to what hurts you. Your job is not to punish anyone else. To fulfill your purpose, walk back into your natural state of love. Return to the truth of who you really are; live from that truth.

### Shine Light on the Fog

- Who or what triggered/triggers a hurt emotion within me?
- Why am I choosing to hold onto that hurt?
- What benefits are there, that positively serve me and all souls connected to me, from holding onto this hurt?
- What does it cost me to live within hurt?
- What do I feel guilty about?
- Why am I choosing to hold onto guilt?
- What benefits are there, that positively serve me and all souls connected to me, from holding onto this guilt?
- What does it cost me to live with this guilt?
- What do I regret?
- Why am I choosing to hold onto that regret?
- What benefits are there, that positively serve me and all souls connected to me, from holding onto this regret?

- What does it cost me to live with regret?
- What or who do I resent?
- Why am I choosing to hold onto that resentment?
- What benefits are there, that positively serve me and all souls connected to me, from holding onto this resentment?
- What does it cost me to live with resentment?
- What do I now choose to let go of?
- Whom do I now forgive?
- What do I now forgive myself for?
- Can I see the possible peace, freedom and success available to me if I come to a place of forgiveness and release within myself?

If you have anything to forgive yourself for, please now write a letter of forgiveness to yourself. Purge, release and let go of all that you carry; offer yourself the gift of forgiveness. This energetically untethers you from the pain of past moments.

If you have anything to forgive another person for, and you intuitively feel compelled to literally convey that forgiveness to them verbally or in writing, please go ahead and share that forgiveness. Be compassionate in your forgiveness. Release any need to put a caveat or conditions on your forgiveness. Forgive from your natural state of love, seeing the soul in the other person that lies deep below actions and any fog.

If you have anything to forgive another person for, but the person involved has passed away or the person involved is not someone you wish to have communication with now, you can still powerfully process your forgiveness and energetically untether yourself from the pain of past moments by writing a letter that is never sent. Your conscious choice and your act of writing the words is the energy of loving forgiveness coming through you, as the channel, into this world. You might choose to keep the letter or burn the letter as symbolic of release.

The truth mantra below will further support you to embed your new paradigm, having let go of all hurt, guilt, regret or resentment.

## Truth Mantra to Dispel the Fog

*I am at peace with myself. I am at peace with other people. I am at peace with all that has happened in my life.*

*I am free of hurt, pain and upset. I choose healing.*

*I forgive myself. I have love for myself. I always do the best I know how.*

*I forgive others. I recognize the soul in each person in my life, even when others can't recognize it in themselves. I acknowledge the journey they are on for their own learning.*

*I know pain only projects out when pain is within, and so all pain projected at me I peacefully witness and deflect. It does not attach to me; it does not impinge upon me. I am not a sponge for other people's pain. Their fog is theirs. I am capable of being love in the face of it. At times being love means I reach out in support and kindness. At times being love means I remain silent and walk away.*

*I choose compassion, from my natural state of love. Compassion for myself and compassion for others.*

*I see all the lessons that my challenges have given to me. I understand how powerful this education is for my journey forward. I know that every person and situation that has challenged me has helped me to evolve, and I acknowledge that the wisdom I have unlocked within myself as a result is now part of my gift to contribute into this world.*

*I will not be a slave to the illusion of the past, which lives only in memories.*

*I release the past. I live fully in the present moment.*

*This moment now is the only moment that is real; it is the only moment that is ever available to me. I will not forgo my precious life right now.*

To download a free audio of this mantra, which you can listen to as a ritual to apply the truth and let go of what no longer serves you, please visit: www.PinchMeLiving.com/Unleash-Your-Life-Free-Resources

## Let Go of Resistance

The resistance you have to anyone or anything is keeping you at arm's length from the inner peace, freedom and success you desire. It is futile to resist the facts of the present moment. They are facts.

When you resist the present moment, in whatever shape or form it takes, you essentially reject your life. You are pouring all of your energy into a fight against what is. That energy of resistance, avoidance, rejection and denial is low vibration and it blocks your ability to flow forward into a new reality.

Conscious acceptance and allowing of the now moment removes all of your focus from futile resistance, giving you the opportunity to reallocate all of that energy to creatively bringing about what you most desire. This reignites your natural flow.

## Shine Light on the Fog

- What am I currently resisting?
- Who am I currently feeling resistant about?
- What is it about my present life circumstance that I refuse to accept?
- Where am I denying an issue exists and hiding from addressing it?
- What in my present life do I feel just as strongly upset and frustrated about as I feel strongly passionate about changing?
- Where in my life am I trying to force change to happen because I don't like how it is at present?
- Who or what am I not able to be at peace with right now?
- Who or what in my life would I label unacceptable?
- Who or what am I trying hard to pressure, convince or coerce in a new direction?
- What benefits are there, that positively serve me and all souls connected to me, from resisting the present moment facts?
- What does resisting cost me?

- Can I see the possible peace, freedom and success available to me if I come to a place of acceptance and allowing of "what is," before I then go about shifting my attention and energy to creating positive change in my circumstances?

The truth mantra below will support you to embed your new paradigm, having let go of resistance to the present moment situation.

## Truth Mantra to Dispel the Fog

*I do not control life or other people. I control my own energy, and that is more than enough. I powerfully create my experience of life and influence it through my peaceful energy.*

*I accept that my present moment is what it is. I allow others to be just as they are. I acknowledge the facts of the situation. I know that resisting the facts only causes me pain, and so I release all resistance to people, things, situations and circumstances that I do not prefer. I peacefully witness life without denial or attachment. Other people, things, situations and my circumstance do not define me in any way. I am able to stand here in observance of it all and remember the truth of who I am.*

*I know my job is not to force, demand, push or pressure in order to experience the reality I desire. While I may not like all aspects of my present moment, and I do not need to embrace every aspect, I am at peace with their existence. I know that making peace with my here and now is what allows me to free up all of my energy to transform the present into a new reality, with each passing moment.*

*Where I experience challenges, I see they are gifts for my learning. I am grateful for whatever lessons are given to me. I let go of feeling that anything is wrong. I know from a bigger picture perspective that nothing is wrong, and that I am evolving and moving into a new reality. My nonresistance is the very energy that most expediently aids this process.*

*From a place of accepting and allowing, I choose now to focus enthusiastically on creative solutions for bringing about the change I desire.*

To download a free audio of this mantra, which you can listen to as a ritual to apply the truth and let go of what no longer serves you, please visit: www.PinchMeLiving.com/Unleash-Your-Life-Free-Resources

## Let Go of Painful Reactions

Any reaction to life challenges, big or small, that is not chosen from loving consciousness is going to create some level of pain for yourself and possibly for the people around you. Neither is going to serve you well.

You have a choice whenever you are triggered. Your choice is to remember that the external person, situation or thing is just a trigger, not the cause of your pain, and to acknowledge the cause of your pain lies within you, because of your paradigm. That doesn't diminish the fact that what is going on outside of you may not be your preference, but it does mean you are the only one in control of whether you feel pain in reaction or peace in response. Your choices define the quality of your life experience.

It is time to let go of painfully reacting to the day-to-day experiences in your life, no matter how significant or insignificant they may be. Your default painful reaction saps your energy and vitality. It blocks you from seeing solutions, and it delays your ability to move ahead into a preferred reality.

Peace is possible in all situations, from the inside out, based entirely on your chosen perspective. Your practice of peaceful responses will transform your life at all levels.

## Shine Light on the Fog

- What are my triggers? What people, behavior, words, opinions, beliefs, situations, things or experiences are guaranteed to generate a negative reaction from me?
- Why does that trigger me?
- What is my habitual negative reaction that has been holding me back? What pattern has been ingrained that I repeat? For example, do I erupt in anger, feel hurt, close down, fester, vent in unhealthy ways, complain, blame, or perhaps become aggressive?
- What are the immediate costs to me personally of this painful reactive behavior? How is my arising negative emotion impacting my overall attitude, how I feel immediately afterwards, my stress levels and my holistic health and well-being?
- What are the residual negative impacts for myself and others, well after the trigger situation has passed? How specifically is the negativity navigating a ripple effect to other people and into all areas of my life? Who among my loved ones is being affected by my painful reactions to situations? Who am I a role model to for whom I am currently demonstrating harmful, unconscious behavior? How is my mental and emotional stress showing up in my physical health?
- What benefits are there, that positively serve me and all souls connected to me, as a result of my painful reactions?
- Would I prefer to use my precious moments and energy on this planet in positive ways, beyond painful reactions?
- Can I see the possible peace, freedom and success available to me if I choose peaceful responses as a practice in the face of all the challenging moments still to come?

The truth mantra below will support you to embed your new paradigm of peaceful response in this moment and all coming moments, having let go of painful reaction as a pattern of the past.

## Truth Mantra to Dispel the Fog

*I always remember that whatever triggers a painful reaction within me is a gift, because it gives me the opportunity to practice peaceful response, helping my learning and evolution, which will feed my contribution to this world during this lifetime.*

*I acknowledge that the triggers in my life do not need to disappear in order for me to be at peace—my peace comes from within. Life is not about escaping my triggers. Life is about noticing what triggers me and letting life exist just as it is while choosing a peaceful response in the face of it.*

*This does not mean I must stay within the vicinity of what triggers me. I am empowered to move on and away from people, situations and things that I do not like. I apply my freewill to put myself in environments and situations that serve and uplift me.*

*I know that when I am peaceful in the face of a challenge, then from that peaceful place I have more energy, empowerment and clarity to see the best way to extricate myself.*

*I choose peace and inner freedom over pain. I recognize that I am the witnessing presence (the conscious awareness) that can observe the activity of my own mind, and the feelings I have. I thank my thoughts and feelings for the messages they deliver to me, showing me what I do like and what I do not like, showing me where my limiting beliefs exist, and offering me the opportunity to choose a new perspective, one based on truth—my new foundation for living.*

*I know that the only way to put a stop to painful reactions in the heat of a moment is to separate myself with conscious awareness from those old habitual reactions rising within, to notice them and to simply realize they are not reflective of who I truly am. In those moments, I remember I am love.*

*Whenever I feel a painful reaction rising inside of me, with my freewill I create a tiny gap within myself before letting my pain out into the world. I take a silent pause. I observe my mind as it runs any old negative thoughts on autopilot. I do not judge those thoughts. I simply let them flow and I watch them. I allow my feelings to rise up and notice that I do not prefer those types of painful feelings. I ask myself, "Is this a painful reaction or a peaceful response? What do I choose now in this moment?"*

*In the gap between being triggered and my response, I use my loving consciousness to choose peace. If I must say nothing to be at peace, I will say nothing. If I must walk away from a trigger to be at peace, I will walk away. If I must have time out, I will have time out. If I must be empathetic and understanding, I will do so. If all I can do to be at peace is to close my eyes and breathe deeply, I will do so knowing that is what the moment calls for.*

*Nothing and no one rules my inner landscape. Nothing and no one controls what I believe, what I think, how I feel and how I act. I am equipped with the tools to manage my own thoughts and emotions wisely. I am the captain of my ship.*

To download a free audio of this mantra, which you can listen to as a ritual to apply the truth and let go of what no longer serves you, please visit: www.PinchMeLiving.com/Unleash-Your-Life-Free-Resources

## Let Go of Validating Yourself Externally

Nothing external to you will ever validate who you are. You do not need validation. You are worthy, complete, whole, deserving, loved and enough, regardless of your actions, your achievements, your status, your possessions or any other external experience.

It is time now to look at what you may be linking your inherent worth as a human being to. Notice what you feel must be present in your life for you to feel comfortable with who you are and your place in society. Once you have greater awareness of how you have previously validated yourself with external people, things and situations, the light of that conscious awareness in your daily life allows you to break that validation link. Once that restricting link is broken, you can finally stand valid and miraculous just as you are. You are no longer tethered to external people, things or situations to validate your worth. You are free, from the inside out.

## Shine Light on the Fog

- Why do I do what I do in my work, career, business, vocation, and profession? What is my payback? How does it make me feel? Am I able to feel worthy and valuable as an individual without any of that in my life?
- Do I feel defined by my relationships?
- What do I believe I must have externally in my life experience in order for me to feel happy, successful and like a valuable human being?
- What people, situations or things in my life make me feel more important?
- What circumstances, commitments or activities do I have in my life right now that I don't actually enjoy, but I feel I cannot live without for fear that I will be a lesser person without them?
- When I feel most deflated in my life, what do I believe is missing?
- When I feel like I have no place, status, importance or value in this world, what do I believe would give me that desired sense of place, status, importance or value?
- What people, situations or things in my life do I feel show the world my worth, position, status and value in society?
- In what ways do I like to demonstrate to other people how good I am?
- What am I most proud of about myself in terms of my traits, gifts or achievements that I feel other people must know and understand about me?
- For me to feel more worthy, more valuable, more important, and for me to be noticed, recognized and

supported more in my personal network or in the wider community in general—what do I believe I would need to have, do or be?

- In relation to all of my answers above and the things I have identified that make me feel worthy, valid, important, happy, successful and complete as a person, do I believe I can be peaceful without any of them?
- What benefits are there to linking my sense of worthiness, and my desire for inner peace and happiness, to outer experiences?
- Would I prefer to feel worthy, valid and complete as a person, just for who I am, irrespective of what I do and have in this world?
- Can I see the possible peace, freedom and success available to me if I no longer use external experiences to try to validate myself, since I am already valuable and worthy to begin with?

The truth mantra below will support you to embed your new paradigm, having let go of the need to validate yourself with external experiences, and chosen to acknowledge your inherent value and worth.

### Truth Mantra to Dispel the Fog

*I am enough, just as I am. I can stand in this life without anything external (tangible or intangible), and I remain as worthy, valued and deserving as the day that I was born. I know that who I was when I was born, a spark of divinity, is who I am now; nothing has changed.*

*No thing defines who I am. Not one experience or achievement makes me more or less of a person. Being the full expression of who I am is all that I am called to do. There is nothing else I need to be, do or have in order to be more peaceful, fulfilled or happy right now.*

*I know my completeness and value is in my very being, not in my doing.*

*I do not need the external world to validate me. I do not need recognition from other people in order to recognize my own inherent worth. I do not need to be gratified, rewarded or even understood, liked or accepted by other people in order to know that I am enough.*

*People, things, positions, status, achievements, possessions and experiences can come and go from my life as free-flowing energy; I will stand confidently and unwavering in my value and worth.*

*I may stumble, and it has nothing to do with my value and worth. I simply fall forward into my success as a wiser version of myself. Any mistakes I may make fuel my learning, which fuels my contribution, which fulfills my soul's intention for being here.*

*I am able to aspire, dream, strive, act, create, express, deliver, excel, achieve, receive and thrive in this world in whatever I wish, and enjoy every single moment of it as a joyful blessing, without linking any of it to being worthy as a human being.*

*From knowing my inherent worth and completeness, I now act from pure passion, pure inspiration and pure intuition, channeling this soul language through me into everything I experience externally in this life. I be, do and have in alignment with truth, my new foundation.*

To download a free audio of this mantra, which you can listen to as a ritual to apply the truth and let go of what no longer serves you, please visit: www.PinchMeLiving.com/Unleash-Your-Life-Free-Resources

## Let Go of Muting Yourself

If you have previously experienced a sense of void within yourself, due to the fog, you have likely attempted to make yourself feel better. In those past moments you may not have known the truths to guide you to heal yourself with what your soul most needed, in which case you may have instead tried to avoid or suppress the uneasy feeling within yourself using external stimulus. For example, excessive alcohol, drugs, food, sex, shopping, work or entertainment. That avoidance or suppression is called muting. Like pressing the mute button on a remote control, you are attempting to mute your soul calling out to you. Muting is a common but misguided approach to resolving inner pain.

Muting is not the solution you need. While it might help you avoid or suppress unease within, temporarily quieting your inner voice calling out, it will not answer its questions nor stop that voice from speaking. It will not dissolve the root cause of your inner pain.

It is time to let go of muting yourself in this way, because from your new foundation of truths you are now empowered to apply sustainable solutions for healing from the inside out, to support your soul, mind and body with what they really need.

## Shine Light on the Fog

- What inner knowing am I avoiding, and in what ways am I avoiding it?
- How do I most often escape from feelings that I don't want to feel?
- Whenever I feel unhappy, uneasy, confused, anxious, fearful, hurt, frustrated, upset, depressed or any other array of low vibration emotions, what do I instinctively feel like doing or consuming?
- Do I try to escape the thoughts in my head by losing myself in a stimulating or distracting activity of any nature? Are those activities beneficial to me holistically in soul, mind and body? Are there any downsides to those activities?
- Do I work excessively in order to avoid anything going on in my personal life?
- Is the amount of time I spend working adversely affecting my physical, mental or emotional well-being,

or affecting any other aspect of my life including my relationships?
- Is food emotionally comforting to me?
- Do I eat to experience a type of positive feeling that certain foods give me?
- Do I often regret the type of food that I have put in my body?
- Do I feel a sense of companionship with alcohol?
- Do I drink alcohol in order to experience relief from any form of negative emotion, or to make myself feel relaxed or happier?
- Do I often regret drinking alcohol, or the volume of it, afterwards?
- Do I take drugs or other stimulants to make myself feel better when I am experiencing any form of inner numbness, void, lack of direction, lack of inspiration, lack of creativity or lack of joy? (Excluding those medically or alternatively prescribed, and consciously chosen for the improvement of my physical, mental and emotional health)
- Do I often regret taking drugs or stimulants in this way?
- Do I use my body, relationships or sex as a way to make myself feel better about who I am?
- Do I often feel worse about myself after engaging my body, heart and sexual nature with other people in this way?
- Do I spend money and/or obtain material possessions of any nature, online or in shops, because doing so makes me feel better about my life, or myself and/or because I feel like a happier person the more things I accumulate?
- Do I often experience buyer's remorse, feeling that my purchases were not necessary or didn't actually generate the improvement in emotions that I was seeking?
- Do I spend excessive time watching television, playing video games or phone games when I intuitively know that I would prefer to dedicate myself to well-being activities and rituals, exercise, sleep, relationships, or my passions and interests instead?

- In relation to any type of external stimulus that I have used to mute unease within myself, what benefits are there to me of stimulating myself in these ways?
- What am I missing out on in my life because of the ways I mute myself?
- What are the physical, mental, emotional and financial costs to me of how I mute myself?
- Do I believe I can be at peace, feel free, be successful inside and out, and have the happiness I desire if I continue muting myself?
- Do I believe that ceasing the muting, and instead engaging in true resolution of my inner unease through application of the truth, is a more effective pathway to my desired inner peace, sense of freedom and success in my life?

This truth mantra below will support you to embed your new paradigm, having let go of the need to mute yourself with external stimulus, and chosen to answer the unease within yourself through knowing and living the truths.

## Truth Mantra to Dispel the Fog

*I no longer mute myself with external stimulus as a way to hide from the messages that my thoughts and feelings are lovingly giving me. My thoughts and feelings are guidance systems that help me to navigate my life. I am not afraid of them. I am fully equipped at all times to look at any challenges going on within myself. I step forward in an empowered way to answer my inner voice, to feed my holistic self in soul, mind and body with what I really need in each moment, and to be a clear channel for my soul to express out into this world.*

*I know that I do not personally need to have all the answers right now about how to resist my old urges for external stimulus. I know that one of the bravest, wisest and strongest things I can do for myself is to reach out for help if and when I need it. I know there is nothing stopping me from accessing the support of my loved ones or the support of trained professionals, should I need that to help me withdraw from any addictive patterns that have been playing out in my life.*

*I know that any immediate high or short-term payback that I was getting from old ways of muting myself will never match up to the inner peace, freedom and success available to me when I shift my paradigm and act from truth.*

*I am consciously aware and capable of enjoying all the wonderful gifts of this world, without them owning me. I work, eat, drink, interact and entertain myself in ways that I enjoy, with balance and without physical, mental and emotional cost.*

*I feel vibrant and vital at all levels, physically, mentally and emotionally.*

*I have willpower. I am strong. I am capable. I am in control of my choices. I make empowered choices. I choose my well-being at every level. I choose to give my precious energy to ways of being and ways of doing that lift me up.*

To download a free audio of this mantra, which you can listen to as a ritual to apply the truth and let go of what no longer serves you, please visit: www.PinchMeLiving.com/Unleash-Your-Life-Free-Resources

## Let Go of Excuses

The reasons you have for not doing what is good for you, and for acting from fear not faith, are excuses. Those excuses keep you stuck. Those excuses do not help other people understand you or support you. Those excuses do not aid your cause in explaining yourself to anyone. Your excuses are simply your own way of trying to explain yourself to yourself, to help you justify why staying small is okay.

Repetitive excuses have built up a wall between yourself and the vision you have for your life. Breaking down your excuses breaks down the wall.

It is time to release your attachment to those excuses, to see clearly that they are a story that has limited you, and to build a new relationship with the endless possibilities that exist for you.

When you exhaust all of your excuses, and you see their absurdity in relation to the truths, they no longer have any power over you. You can then reallocate your energy to moving forward with creating whatever it is you have been blocking yourself from.

## Shine Light on the Fog

To begin, on a piece of paper brainstorm a list of all the aspects of your life that you deem to be negative or unsatisfactory, that you want to heal, overcome, change or leave behind.

For each item on that list, begin reflecting on why it is that you have not healed it, overcome it, changed it or left it behind yet. Consider what has kept you stuck and stopped you from breaking through.

Now for each item on the list, write down everything that comes to mind in response to the following "but" statements. Keep writing until you have completely exhausted the contents of your mind. Let the noise that cycles in your mind exit onto paper:

- But I'm not ...
- But I can't ...
- But I don't know how to ...
- But I don't have ...
- But it's not possible because ...
- But what if ...
- But I'm afraid ...

Next, on a piece of paper brainstorm a list of all the positive possibilities for your life that you want to create, expand into or further develop.

For each item on that list, begin reflecting on why it is that you have not created it, expanded into it or further developed it already. Consider what has stopped you from stepping up and what keeps you from experiencing that as your reality.

Now for each item on the list, write down everything that comes to mind in response to the following "but" statements. Keep writing until you have completely exhausted the contents of your mind. Let the noise that cycles in your mind exit onto paper:

- But I'm not ...
- But I can't ...
- But I don't know how to ...
- But I don't have ...
- But it's not possible because ...
- But what if ...
- But I'm afraid ...

This truth mantra below will support you to embed your new paradigm, having let go of all excuses, and chosen to live right now as your limitless self.

## Truth Mantra to Dispel the Fog

*I release all excuses from my life. They are gone and with them goes any associated negative energy.*

*I am everything I am meant to be. I am not missing anything. I am imbued with everything I need to succeed.*

*I am able to face any challenge in my life. I know how to navigate each decision I face powerfully using my intuition and logic together in unison.*

*I have every gift, talent and capability that will aid my success, to overcome challenges and to bring about exciting new creations. Every resource I need in this moment I have. Every resource I need in the next moment is available to me and can be created, found or flowed into as a result of my willingness to drop excuses and step forward in my life.*

*I can step forward without having all the answers. I know what I know, and that is more than enough right now. What I don't know I can find out. As I take small steps to discover more about myself and life, and to create my life proactively, I flow into the path of more information, more opportunities and more answers that help me.*

*Unseen helping hands are here to guide me and support me. As I step forward courageously, the universe celebrates and energy whirls in response synchronistically allowing people, things and situations to flow into my path to leverage both my learning and my contribution.*

*I have endless outcomes available to me. All scenarios lie before me for my choosing. I rehearse success as the scenario for my life. I imagine possibility, and I create it into my reality through action. Anything that hasn't occurred yet is just a wave of possibility waiting to be brought to fruition, from intangible energy to tangible experience in my life.*

*I live in the now moment and give life to the passions, inspirations and intuition channeling through me. I know this is the way my soul speaks through me, to give expression into the world, and these feelings always guide me well.*

*I know that within uncertainty lies all possibility. I am at peace with the uncertainty that I experience. I understand and accurately perceive risks and manage them effectively with what I know in this moment. I am courageous. The fear I feel in relation to any challenge or any new creation is simply an invitation to shift. I know fear is helping me to understand that great expansion is available to me in this moment.*

To download a free audio of this mantra, which you can listen to as a ritual to apply the truth and let go of what no longer serves you, please visit: www.PinchMeLiving.com/Unleash-Your-Life-Free-Resources

## Let Go of Limiting Beliefs

Having cleared away surface layers of negative energy that block you, it is time to focus now on the foundation of the fog.

You do not need to "fix" fear, expectations or societal conditioning. Instead, focus on transforming the foundation upon which all of this rests—your limiting beliefs.

When you identify and then transform your old limiting beliefs to new empowering beliefs that accurately reflect the truth of who you are, and the truth of life, then you will have the power within you to answer the invitation for a shift that your fear presents to you. You will no longer be trapped by expectations; instead, you will peacefully witness them and freely glide forward irrespective of them. You will no longer be a slave to societal conditioning; instead, you will observe it and live above and beyond it, as your soul freely, passionately, inspiringly, and intuitively speaks through you as a clear channel for it to create out into the world—as your unique expression.

While there are any number of beliefs that you might have about yourself, other people and life in general, every person typically has a small, strong, core set of beliefs about who they are, which speak to the root of their existence and the deeper meaning (or lack of deeper meaning) of that existence.

Those core beliefs, negative or positive, are like the foundation upon which all other beliefs rest.

While each person is unique, and is raised within a unique set of life experiences, all of which help to form their belief system, there is still a strong, common thread to the experience of being human no matter who you are, where you live or how you were raised. Further, societal conditioning occurs in similar ways across the planet, despite borders, ethnicity, culture and faith systems, and that pervasive conditioning gives rise to common beliefs.

The common core limiting beliefs which many people have, but may not consciously be aware of, include:

- I am not _____ enough (fill in the blank)
- I am not good enough
- I am not enough
- I am incomplete
- I am undeserving
- I am not worthy
- I am unsupported
- I am unsafe
- I am unloved
- I am alone
- I am nothing

It is time now to focus on identifying your specific personal limiting beliefs with the question and answer exercise below. Whatever you shine the light on, you can see clearly. What you can see clearly, you can name. By seeing clearly and naming, you can better understand. What you understand you can choose to let go of and powerfully replace with something more aligned to your true nature and preferred reality.

There is nothing at all to be concerned about, ashamed of or afraid of as you uncover the depth of your limiting beliefs. This is part of your journey, part of being human—to shed light onto darkness, as the pathway to your transformation. Give yourself permission to let whatever is within you rise up to the surface and out onto paper.

### Shine the Light on the Fog

- What limiting beliefs am I already consciously aware of that I have and that I do not want to live from any longer?
- What types of negative experiences/situations have I noticed seem to recur in my life over and over again? What do I believe about myself and life in relation to those negative patterns of the past?
- When I consider instigating positive change in my life or creating a way to achieve my highest priority goals

and aspirations, what are my predominant, recurring negative thoughts about that?

- If I could change anything about my mind-set, what would it be specifically?
- What emotional experiences am I tired of having and ready to let go of?
- What triggers those types of emotional experiences/reactions within me? What people, situations, things, circumstances and thoughts typically precede that emotional state?
- What do I generally believe/think about myself?
- What have I been told about myself by other people? By family, friends, intimate relationships, work colleagues, acquaintances or passing strangers?
- Considering the most traumatic moments of my life to date, what do I believe about myself and life in relation to those events?
- What do I dislike about myself?
- What immediately comes to mind about myself when I start a sentence with "I am ... "?
- What immediately comes to mind about myself when I start a sentence with "I'm not ... "?
- What do I believe my weaknesses or limiting traits are?
- What do I wish I could be more of or better at?
- What inside of me is holding me back in my life?
- How am I being and what am I doing that I know is sabotaging my progress?
- When facing challenges, what is my typical thought pattern about myself, and about life generally?
- What are my greatest fears in life?
- In what types of situations, or in relation to what types of ideas, do I most often notice that I have doubt or fear?
- When I am experiencing doubt or fear, what is my mind saying to me? What messages are running over and over in my head?
- What do I wish I could change about myself?
- Do I feel like there is something missing within me? What do I sense that might be?

- Do I feel like there is something fundamentally wrong with my life or me? If yes, what do I sense that might be?
- In moments when I don't feel love for myself, why is that?
- In moments when I don't feel like I'm good enough, why is that?
- Do I believe that I am good enough? If not, why not?
- Do I believe I am enough? If not, why not?
- Do I believe I am whole and complete? If not, why not?
- Do I believe I am deserving? If not, why not?
- Do I believe I am worthy? If not, why not?
- Do I believe I am supported? If not, why not?
- Do I feel safe? If not, why not?
- Do I believe I am loved? If not, why not?
- Do I believe I am loveable? If not, why not?
- Do I believe I am connected and understood? If not, why not?
- Do I believe I am a good person? If not, why not?
- Do I believe that my being alive in this world is meaningful and important? If not, why not?
- Other (include anything else that comes up in thought or feeling for you).

For each individual written answer you provided, look closely now at what you wrote down, and:

- Underline or highlight any obvious limitation, block or negative connotation within your written response.
- Notice what emotion was stirred up by each question and your answer. The more it triggered a negative emotion within you (such as upset, frustration, sadness, pessimism or pain), the more likely that it is a limiting belief or that it is directly pointing you to a limiting belief.

This means that you now have a written transcript that summarizes the core of the limiting beliefs that have been keeping you stuck, whether you were consciously aware of them or not. These are the beliefs that held the fog in place.

Without these, the fog cannot survive. To clear the fog, you clear the limiting beliefs.

## Choosing Your New Beliefs

To clear a limiting belief that holds you back, it is not possible to simply attempt to let it go. You must replace it with an empowering new belief, ingraining it to create an entirely new paradigm, which makes the old one obsolete.

These new beliefs you choose will positively resonate with you emotionally. They are the beliefs you have wished all your life to live from. Your new beliefs will form your new foundation for living. Your new beliefs will be aligned in every way to the truth, and will support your inner peace, freedom and success.

When choosing a new empowering belief to replace an old limiting belief, a simple, highly targeted and effective approach is to literally flip the statement—to choose the opposite of the limiting belief. For example, "I am not good enough" can become "I am good enough." "I am not deserving" can become "I am deserving." "I am anxious" can become "I am peaceful and calm." "I am a failure" can become "I am successful," and so on. Flipping belief statements like this is a starting point to help you define a more uplifting and truthful perspective for yourself. The new (opposite) belief will carry the necessary positive energy (high vibration) to counteract and dissolve the negative energy (low vibration) of the old belief.

Begin now to write a list of empowering new beliefs:

- For each limiting belief you identified in the earlier exercise, now choose and write down a positive new belief to replace it. Either flip the statement, or trust your intuition if it tells you what new belief you would prefer to live from.
- Write your beliefs as factual statements, in the present tense. This means using words such as am, is, do, have and now. It is helpful to omit words that reinforce a

sense of future projection, such as can, will, want, wish, hope and try. For examples of powerful belief statements, please see the list of affirmations provided further below.

- Phrase your beliefs in the positive wherever possible. Focus on what you do want, rather than stating what you do not want. Focus on what you are creating, rather than on what you are seeking to resolve. For example, "I move peacefully and powerfully through challenges" rather than "I am *not* held back by challenges." Or, "I am at peace with uncertainty" rather than "I do *not* fear uncertainty."

- While you can create just one new positive belief to counter one old limiting belief, you can also create additional new beliefs of any description. You are limitless. Let yourself create as many uplifting new beliefs as you desire for your new paradigm. Notice whatever rises up from within you as you write your new belief statements; let the positive perspectives flow out of you. Notice what you intuitively sense you would love to believe, think and feel about yourself and life. Write these positive statements down and keep writing until you exhaust all the desire within yourself. There is no limit to how long your list of new empowering beliefs can be.

## Embedding Your New Beliefs

How do you embed your new positive beliefs? In the same way your old limiting beliefs took a hold—through frequency and intensity. Beliefs are simply perspectives that have been reinforced so often (in word and thought) and so emotionally that they ingrain deeply to become the lens through which you see life.

The more often you absorb your new belief statements, the more positive emotion you put behind them as you absorb the words, the more air time you give the beliefs in terms of your conscious awareness and the more you have them at the forefront of your daily life, the more ingrained they become.

The old limiting beliefs will not survive long-term in the light of truth. It is your commitment to consistently feed yourself your new beliefs that brings about lasting transformation for you. There are three simple ways to ingrain your new beliefs with frequency and intensity:

- seeing them visually
- hearing them on audio
- expressing them verbally or in writing

You may like to use all three methods, or notice what you feel drawn to as a preference and trust your intuition that it is the best option for you.

Now take the list you wrote of all your preferred new positive beliefs, and you can begin to practically embed them:

**1) Seeing them**—Write down all the beliefs in a journal or on paper and strategically place that written list in clear sight in an area that you frequent on a daily basis in your home. It may be placed on your bedside table so that you notice the list every morning and night. It may be on your bulletin board or attached to the fridge. You may like to write the beliefs down on little notes and place them around your home or work area so that you are visually interacting with them in different places. If you wish to use electronic forms of visual reminder, you might consider pop-up reminders in your electronic calendar, or words on your computer screensaver or desktop background. Once you have displayed the beliefs visually, you will read them to yourself every day. Every time you see them, read them. Every time you read them, really feel the meaning of them. Take pause as you read each one; allow the empowerment of the statement to uplift you. Consciously smile as you read, or think of something joyful in your life as you read. That smile or visual image in your mind helps to shift your mood, and your positive mood puts high vibration energy behind the words you are reading.

**2) Hearing them**—Record yourself speaking the beliefs into any form of audio recording software, on your phone or other device. There are many free and simple recording tools, apps and software available online. Put a reminder in your calendar, or an alarm on your phone, to prompt you to listen to the recording on a daily basis. As you listen, be focused and present. Breathe deeply and allow your mind to fully absorb the words you are hearing. Consciously smile, or put an image in your mind of something joyful, as you listen. As above, this helps to shift your mood and that high vibration energy will support the words you are hearing. You can listen to the audio any time of the day, though there are four particularly powerful times to hear it. It is wonderful to listen upon waking, to set your mind to truth for the day ahead. It is helpful to listen before going to sleep, to clear your mind from the day and to send yourself into sleep state with inner peace and relaxation. Another optimal time to listen is while in nature, because the energy of nature is healing and free-flowing, and your energy is intersecting with that so you are in a greater state of peace, ease and receptiveness as a result. Finally, listening while you are exercising, if appropriate and safe, is also uplifting. As your body is in motion, your energy and vitality is up, your sense of well-being and confidence is up, and you are naturally in a higher vibration mood, which supports the beliefs statements you are hearing.

**3) Expressing them**—With the written list of your new beliefs, you can read them out loud to yourself, or you can journal them by copying them off your list, either one belief over and over again, to repeat and ingrain, or by copying the full list. Your mind will further absorb whatever you are concentrating on and repeating, verbally or in writing. If you choose to ingrain your beliefs through expressing them, you may enjoy supporting yourself further by listening to positive music at the same time, or being in an environment that you feel at peace, happy or inspired in. That puts high vibration energy behind the words you are expressing.

## Fade out the Old, Fade in the New

Consistency is key to embedding new beliefs. Practice the above techniques every day for at least thirty days, however, longer is better. These beliefs are the foundation of your life. There is absolutely no reason not to remind yourself of them every day of your life.

Beliefs of course give rise to thoughts and feelings, so you will notice new types of thoughts and feelings arise as the new beliefs take hold. However, you needn't be at all concerned if you still notice old limiting beliefs present (showing up as negative thoughts and feelings). Transforming your beliefs is like two songs overlapping as you switch between radio stations on different frequencies. This overlap happens for a period of time. The old melancholy song is being faded out, the volume decreasing, as the uplifting new song is being faded in, the volume increasing. There is always a transition where you can hear both songs playing. There is nothing wrong. Do not be concerned or discouraged. It is normal. How long that transition period is will be unique to you.

## Acting on Your New Beliefs

As you go about your day-to-day routine, you bring your new beliefs to life through your behavior. With each interaction you have, with each opportunity you see and with each challenge you face, you can consciously choose to look at life through the lens of your new beliefs. As you do so, you may witness the old negative thought and feeling patterns rise up within you. You simply acknowledge that old energy is still in the process of fading out and then you immediately begin to run your new belief statements over and over in your mind, proactively repeating them to yourself to shift your attention off the old and onto the new. You can then make conscious choices from that empowered space, to act in alignment with your new beliefs, taking actions that serve you. This cycle of behavior creates new results, materially impacting upon your circumstances and further embedding your new paradigm.

## 400 Positive Affirmations to
## Support Inner Peace & Sense of Freedom

To further support your new paradigm, here are over four hundred positive affirmation statements aligned to truth, which will uplift and empower you personally, bringing you to a place of inner peace, and providing you a sense of freedom to remember who you really are.

To download an audio of these affirmations, which you can listen to as a ritual to help embed your new paradigm, please visit: www.PinchMeLiving.com/Unleash-Your-Life-Free-Resources

*I am loved.*

*I am good enough.*

*I am more than enough.*

*I am enough.*

*I am whole and complete and always have been.*

*I am deserving of every good thing in life.*

*I am worthy.*

*I am supported.*

*I am connected.*

*I am surrounded by loving energy at all times.*

*I am already, always, unbreakably connected to and in touch with my source.*

*I am valid.*

*I am valued.*

*My life has meaning.*

*My being alive makes a difference.*

*I am cherished.*

*I embrace the way I look, talk, walk and express.*

*I create my own reality through my paradigm.*

*I love myself.*

*Every part of who I am is love.*

*I express myself openly from my heart.*

*My intuition is loud and clear.*

*When life is challenging I know it is just an opportunity for growth in disguise.*

*Every morning I wake up feeling more empowered and excited about life.*

*I am capable.*

*Life is a gift, which I am living fully.*

*My body is a temple of health and well-being.*

*I nourish my body with healthy food.*

*I am unconditionally loved.*

*I am infinitely connected to highest consciousness, the intelligent divine energy pervading all of creation.*

*I am unique.*

*All my goals and dreams are possible.*

*I always stay true to what I know in my heart is right for me.*

*I am confident.*

*I live my full expression every day.*

*I am grateful for my relationships.*

*The world I live in is abundant.*

*I am special.*

*Challenges forge me into a stronger and wiser person, like a diamond being molded under pressure.*

*I am empowered in every way.*

*I am wealthy.*

What I need comes to me when I need it.

I am provided for.

I am guided.

Every person I meet represents an opportunity to learn something.

I am beautiful.

Every step I take forward opens up more of my path in life.

I am healthy.

My life is unfolding in the best way for my soul.

Life has deep meaning; listening to my heart allows me to feel that meaning.

I am abundant.

I have all the answers to my own questions if I listen to my intuition.

I am giving.

I step outside of my comfort zone every day to expand myself.

I am courageous.

I am talented.

My beliefs create my reality so I only believe in my full potential.

I am successful.

My goals and aspirations are achievable; I am unstoppable.

I am responsible for my beliefs, thoughts and feelings.

I am responsible for my own actions.

I feel great, and my inner positive energy changes my outer experiences.

I offer my gifts into the world every day.

*I am uninhibited.*

*I act on all my inspirations.*

*I use my talents, skills and intellect every day.*

*I create stillness in my mind regularly, with presence, to allow space for passion, inspiration and intuition to flow through me.*

*I am a clear channel for my soul to express into the world.*

*I make no apology for who I truly am.*

*I forgive myself and others whenever the opportunity arises.*

*I am a creative being.*

*I am a soul.*

*I co-create my life journey with highest consciousness, the source from where I came and to which I infinitely belong.*

*My path in life is a reflection of my soul's intention.*

*I turn all challenges into bright light openings for change.*

*All breakdowns lead to breakthroughs.*

*I give love and love flows back to me one hundred times over.*

*I honor the planet and treat my environment as part of who I am.*

*I am empowered.*

*I live the life of my dreams.*

*I have within me all that I need right now to fly high in my life.*

*I am divine.*

*The entire universe, with all its wisdom, is reflected within me.*

*I am brave and step up whenever my heart calls me to act.*

*The actions I take move me forward in my life journey.*

*What I think about becomes my version of reality.*

*I freely share my gifts and resources, and what I need flows back to me one hundred times over.*

*I can change my reality any moment by perceiving others, the world and myself differently.*

*I choose to own my outcomes.*

*I go with the natural flow of life.*

*I allow my soul path to unfold.*

*I respect my body.*

*The past never dictates my present.*

*The past doesn't exist.*

*The present is the only moment and I savor it fully.*

*When I feel fear, I take action to expand into new territory.*

*My imperfections are perfectly allowing me to learn and grow in this life.*

*I courageously learn from all my blocks and expand my comfort zone every time I do.*

*I conquer fear.*

*My fear guides me to see my own resistance to the unknown.*

*I am blessed with love.*

*Opportunities knock on my door every day.*

*I am consciously aware each moment of my life.*

*My life is an adventure that I bravely embrace and cherish every day.*

*I am blessed.*

*I choose conscious living as my way of life.*

*Love is who I am.*

*Every day I am highly motivated to give of myself fully.*

*All that I need comes to me freely and easily.*

*I am a person of unlimited potential.*

*Success follows me wherever I go.*

*My life is an exciting adventure.*

*My abundance increases every day no matter what I do.*

*Whenever I need guidance, it shows up in my life.*

*I share my positivity with everyone around me.*

*Whenever I ask for support, it arrives just when I need it.*

*There is an abundance of all resources that I need.*

*I am a prosperous person.*

*My relationships are healthy, collaborative and loving.*

*I feel inspired every day.*

*I am positive.*

*My mind is a tool that I own and use for my benefit each day.*

*I have wisdom within me to guide every step of my life.*

*When I sit quietly in meditation, answers to my questions arise.*

*I love to honor my body by expressing my physical energy and keeping fit.*

*All the cells in my body are energized and working together for my greatest well-being.*

*People and things turn up in my life when I most need them.*

*Everywhere I turn there are paths opening up; I am blessed with choices.*

*Whenever I focus on what I need, I get shown ways to achieve my goals.*

*My gut instinct is loud and clear.*

*Money and other resources are energy; they flow freely into my life.*

*I am creative and inspired in all that I do.*

*I embrace fear as a natural reaction to stepping into unknown territory.*

*I step forward in my life even without having all the answers to my questions.*

*I make it my business to be compassionate to all those I encounter.*

*Nature is alive with fresh energy and I honor the natural environment around me.*

*I am grateful for all my blessings.*

*I am one with all of creation.*

*Each day I tell those that I love that I love them.*

*Everything I experience in life is connected to me.*

*Love exists in everything I see.*

*My greatest expansion occurs when I try something new.*

*I am committed to being who I am and doing what I love.*

*I choose joy.*

*I dissolve all doubt by stepping forward despite it.*

*I fuel my body with nutritious food and water.*

*Love and inner peace are my natural states of being.*

*Every day I am alive is a blessing.*

*I love to take action.*

*Every morning I burst out of bed with boundless energy.*

*I feel rejuvenated and energetic.*

*I bask in the sunshine.*

*Everything that I need exists here and now.*

*Being alive is exciting.*

*Each dawn brings promise of new opportunities.*

*The light of my consciousness, my choices and my courage dissolves fear.*

*I am here for a good reason.*

*Every day I wholeheartedly give my full expression to the world.*

*When I follow my heart I honor my soul.*

*My passion points me toward where I can most contribute in this world.*

*Source, the universe, divinity, God, highest consciousness—this is who I am, it is reflected in every aspect of my physical and nonphysical self.*

*My body heals when I sit peacefully in meditation.*

*I offer any sickness and imbalance within me the healing light of divine love.*

*I deserve abundance.*

*People who love and support me surround me.*

*Nothing that happens to me is a reflection of who I am.*

*Mistakes and adversity are the universe's way of helping me to learn deep wisdom firsthand.*

*When I sleep my thinking mind is quiet and deep wisdom floods in to connect with me, to feed and inspire my coming day.*

*The universe applauds my loving actions.*

*My awareness allows me to recognize signals and guidance that exist to support my path.*

*I trust myself.*

*I release all resentment freely and easily.*

*I hold only love in my heart for those who have challenged me.*

*I give thanks for all those who love me.*

*I am showered with gifts from the universe.*

*I am here to contribute to the world positively.*

*When I contribute, the universe flows all that I need back to me.*

*Telling people that I love them brings sunshine into the universe.*

*I am a magnet for all that I need to support my journey in life.*

*I choose to be a victor in my life.*

*I accept others as I find them.*

*I am committed to my personal growth.*

*I shine the light of my consciousness on my weaknesses in order to evolve.*

*I release all hurt from my mind, body and soul.*

*I was born creative.*

*No matter what happens outside of myself, I am safe and supported.*

*I am secure in who I am.*

*I know myself and show the true me to the world.*

*I am happy.*

*Actions create change in my life.*

*My mind-set is one of success.*

*Anything is possible.*

*Everything is available to me.*

*Endless roads open up to me when I step forward with an open mind and open heart.*

*I am fulfilled.*

*My life is a path filled with miracles.*

*Magic happens when I embrace my endless possibilities.*

*Dark times in my life are just doorways to the next level of my flourishing.*

*Every morning I burst into life with enthusiasm for the day ahead.*

*I'm a butterfly who just burst out of the cocoon; now I can fly.*

*I've got the capability to do whatever I set my mind to.*

*I am what I believe I am, what others think of me is irrelevant.*

*I trust my feelings.*

*I honor my feelings.*

*Life is a gift for expansion and I accept the challenges that aid my evolution.*

*Every moment I remember how divine I am.*

*Only love exists within my mind, body and soul.*

*I remember why I came into life.*

*I give my attention to what is meaningful and valuable in life.*

*I embrace all my quirks.*

*I release all regrets.*

*My focus is on the present moment.*

*The next coming moment of my life is being created by my beliefs, thoughts, feelings and actions in this moment.*

*I place my attention on wherever I want to direct all my creative energy.*

*I live in accordance with my truth.*

*I honor this energy-based world and let love energy flow through me.*

*Divinity's love heals my body when I invite it in.*

*My body is infinitely intelligent and has the answers to its own health.*

*My mind is powerful beyond measure.*

*Whenever I feel nervous or anxious, I breathe deeply into calm.*

*Fear is a signal that I am about to expand beyond what is familiar to me.*

*I am radical and courageous in how I express my love to the world.*

*When I am who I am and do what I love, the entire universe celebrates.*

*I am empathetic.*

*There are unseen helping hands supporting my life journey.*

*My soul is wise beyond my mind.*

*What other people think is none of my business.*

*I keep my mind, body and soul in balance, working as a trio in unison.*

*The sun is the universe shining on me.*

*The rain is an opportunity to wash away what doesn't work in my life.*

*I commit my energy to things and people that matter.*

*The only words to leave my mouth are ones of love and positivity.*

*I choose to place my focus on solutions.*

*My life experiences are as sweet and juicy as a ripe peach.*

*I move away from negative people and situations to embrace positivity instead.*

*When I need support, it shows up in miraculous ways.*

*The universe is designed to support my success.*

*Thriving in this life comes more freely and easily when I am who I am and do what I love.*

*I trust at all times that what I need will flow to me.*

*I lift off into my dreams like a 747 in full flight.*

*I am fulfilled in my work.*

*I hear my soul call to me with passion, inspiration and intuition.*

*Loving relationships evolve in my life because I exist as my full loving self.*

*Being present in each moment is healing to my soul.*

*I am whatever I say I am.*

*I am my own best friend.*

*I talk lovingly to myself at all times.*

*When I open my mind, paths open up before me.*

*I remind myself daily of how awesome I am.*

*My life rocks because I rock.*

*Mentors and guides show up in my life whenever I need them.*

*I honor myself.*

*The entire world benefits when I let my heart sing loud and clear.*

*I am here in life because I am needed.*

*Even though I don't know how to do something, the universe shows me the way.*

*I am surrounded by positive like-minded people.*

*I am a great listener.*

*I speak from my heart.*

*I embrace who I am no matter where I go or who I'm with.*

*I accept myself.*

*I am always right where I need to be.*

*I am articulate.*

*I trust my decision-making abilities.*

*I enjoy living life to the fullest.*

*I give myself fully to what I love to do.*

*If I notice hesitation, I take the time to understand why it exists and then walk ahead into action.*

*I believe I am powerful and so I am.*

*Whatever I believe is what I achieve.*

*I am a vibrant and bright person.*

*The world is a safe and loving place to be.*

*I see what I choose to see.*

*I am accountable for my life and everything I do.*

*I am quick-witted, smart and capable.*

*Loving myself unconditionally heals my mind, body and soul.*

*The more gratitude I express, the more reasons I have to be grateful.*

*I make choices that serve me well.*

*I have every talent and capability I need in order to bring life to my passions, inspirations and intuition.*

*I let go of all old habits and live by life-affirming rituals.*

*I am at peace.*

*I only need ask and I am shown the way forward.*

*I listen to my body when it sends me a message.*

*Inner peace, happiness and joy are my daily reality.*

*I see oneness in all things.*

*Nature calms and energizes me.*

My life is filled with pleasant surprises.

Challenging relationships prompt my inner growth.

Loving companionship is here for me right now.

I dwell only in positivity and rise above any upset.

There is no shortage of time; the universe dwells in timelessness as I create my life.

I do what I can and it is always enough.

There is nothing wrong with me, and everything is just as it is meant to be.

I'm the only person in the world with my unique offering.

The universe is programed to support my success.

Loving myself is key to knowing the fullness of what this life has to offer me.

I give freely of who I am and all I have to offer.

Integrity underpins all my interactions.

I step forward in my life even when I don't have all the answers.

Giving is the access to receiving.

I express my ideas effectively.

Synchronicities are the universe's way of helping me.

I act in alignment with my inner knowing, even when I am unsure of where it might lead me.

When my feelings are low, I instantly pick myself up.

I am courageous enough to look into any negative feelings and dissolve their source.

I carry around a suitcase of self-belief and say goodbye to the old backpack of baggage.

My confidence expands the more I act confidently.

My actions in the face of fear are what build my self-belief.

*I sleep when my body is tired.*

*My body is a vessel that carries me in life and I respect it.*

*I use my mind power for the good of all people.*

*When I succeed, everybody wins.*

*I have everything within me right now to flourish in this life.*

*Having big audacious goals is part of the adventure of life.*

*Every morning I express gratitude for the small things in life.*

*Letting my positive energy flow out of me is a service to the whole world.*

*I do all I can to leave a positive mark on the world each day.*

*I give 100 percent to my life and see results return one hundred times over.*

*I honor my word.*

*When I see a need, I step forward ready to contribute.*

*I take care of myself.*

*I know my mind, body and soul are always communicating with each other for my highest benefit.*

*Meditation is an essential part of resetting myself each day with inner stillness.*

*I love who I am.*

*I give thanks for being alive.*

*I take responsibility for creating my life experience.*

*I anticipate miracles.*

*I view myself as magical and abundant in all respects.*

*My life is an expression of my inherent divine nature.*

*It is my duty to follow my heart at all times.*

*I live an awesome life.*

*I own my experience of life and accept my creative nature.*

*Nothing and no one external to me defines who I am.*

*I instantly shift my experience of life through shifting my paradigm.*

*Breathing deeply brings fresh rejuvenating energy to all the cells of my body.*

*I sense divine guidance, tune into it and utilize it.*

*I am never alone because I am supported energetically by highest consciousness, to which I belong.*

*I am complete.*

*I give my full attention to whoever is talking to me.*

*My relationships add value to my life.*

*When I flourish, I help others flourish too.*

*The universe supports win-win outcomes whenever I follow my heart.*

*I treat others as I wish to be treated.*

*Invisible intelligent energy creates everything in my reality.*

*I am committed to my growth.*

*I bring passion to all that I do.*

*I am responsible for picking myself up whenever I feel down, and I have the tools to do so.*

*I bring awareness and focus to each moment of my day.*

*I respect other people.*

*I see every other person as a soul here on its own journey.*

*Laughter makes my body sing.*

*Every day alive is a gift that I wake up to unwrap and marvel at.*

*I am a success irrespective of any external experience in life.*

*Failure is a mind-set and I prefer to set my mind in the direction of success.*

*I always give my full attention and effort to whatever I am doing or whomever I am with.*

*My behavior aligns to my values.*

*Shining brightly like a star is what I do best.*

*I need no validation from anyone, I love myself fully regardless.*

*There is more than enough of everything I need.*

*In the face of adversity, I remember the truth that my paradigm creates my version of reality.*

*I watch and read positive material, and consciously choose to absorb only content that uplifts me.*

*I dedicate time to relaxation and understand its importance in fuelling my action time.*

*My body is alive with energy.*

*I smile at every person I see as a way to share bright light love with them.*

*Before I go to sleep I dwell on my blessings.*

*I reach out for support when I need it.*

*I am surrounded by people who lift me up.*

*I am wrapped in warmth every day.*

*Whatever I believe, I create.*

*I've got wings and I'm going to use them to fly.*

*I soak up every good thing in this life.*

*I'm ready and rearing to love, live and give every day.*

*I live each day like it's my only day.*

*I let go of trying to control external events and people and trust in the overall flow of life.*

*I influence the world through my positive energy, and accept responsibility for my important place on this planet.*

*The truth is that I am beloved, connected and always guided.*

*The peace within me emanates outwards.*

*My life starts within myself and mirrors into my external reality.*

*Tiny shifts in my thinking create mammoth shifts in my reality.*

*Little steps forward consistently are all that is required to bring about radical change.*

*Whenever I am confused about what to do, I listen to my heart.*

*I ask for help when I get stuck.*

*Nourishing and caring for my body is a high priority in my life, as it is the vehicle that allows my soul to experience this world.*

*I treat my environment with the same respect I treat myself.*

*When I feel down, I smile at myself in the mirror until I can't help but smile back.*

*Love surrounds me.*

*I know how to get back into my flow whenever I feel stuck.*

*I play every day with childlike wonder.*

*I was born with everything I need within me.*

*Abundance starts with my mind-set.*

*My energy levels are high, and I'm ready to rock and roll.*

*I feel vibrant.*

*I'm surrounded by loving people.*

*Whenever I notice negativity in my environment, I understand it does not belong to me and that my job is to be love in the face of it.*

*I take action daily toward my goals and aspirations.*

*My actions support my desires.*

*My body is energized and all the cells are working together collaboratively.*

*I show up every day with the intention of living my greatness.*

*My imperfections are part of my humanity, as they are for all people, and I embrace all of who I am.*

*Universal wisdom resides within every cell of my body.*

*I'm whole, complete and miraculous just as I am.*

*My thoughts and feelings are powerful navigational tools.*

*I'm wondrous and I don't need anyone or anything to show me this in order to truly know this.*

*Every day I'm surrounded by guidance, tangibly and intangibly.*

*The world is filled with endless opportunities, experiences, possibilities and adventures, all of which are available to me even when I cannot see how.*

*I apply my intellect for the creation of good in this world.*

*Positivity is my natural state.*

*Every person I encounter has something to share; I listen with the intent of learning.*

*I open myself to life and release all resistance.*

*Pure life force energy flows through my body as I breathe in and out each moment.*

*I am always exactly where I need to be.*

*I am wise beyond my years.*

*My body has the capacity to heal itself when I get my soul and mind into alignment.*

*When life is tough, I relish the lessons available to me.*

*In every darkness, I know there is a light switch available to me.*

*I express who I am openly and freely, with courage, and with compassion for whoever is listening.*

*Everything I am creating is available to me now.*

*I notice all my hunches, nudges and inner whispers and I focus in on them for guidance.*

*I am needed.*

*My being in the world makes a valuable difference.*

*Just by being who I really am, I contribute massively to the world.*

*Doing what I love helps me shine like the bright light I am.*

*I walk my talk.*

*My beliefs, thoughts, feelings and actions align to my own goals and aspirations, which are a service to the world.*

*I care for myself as a priority.*

*I am cherished.*

## 300 Power Affirmations to Support Career/Professional Success

If you are engaged in a job, career, vocation, business, community endeavor or voluntary contribution, here are over three hundred power affirmations aligned to the truths to further embed an empowering new paradigm, supporting you to unleash your success from the inside out.

To download an audio of these power affirmations, which you can listen to as a ritual to embed and support your new paradigm, please visit: www.PinchMeLiving.com/Unleash-Your-Life-Free-Resources

*I operate from my intuition.*

*I have an endless well of creativity.*

*My professional life is thriving.*

*The work I do is fulfilling and meaningful.*

*Abundance flows from my career.*

*I impact people's lives in a positive way.*

*I create value, give value and receive value back.*

*Giving my gifts and talents into the world is what I am here to do.*

*I express myself fully through my professional path.*

*I live my life in balance, personally and professionally.*

*I am consciously aware in my day-to-day work life.*

*I bring empathy to my workplace and listen compassionately to all those I encounter.*

*I role model empowerment, inner peace, inner freedom and success at all levels.*

*My work life is an energy exchange—my gifts, talents, time and energy, for fulfillment, achievement, connection and reward.*

*I navigate my professional decisions with clarity and precision.*

*No matter what challenges I face at work, I am always in tune with the best way forward for all parties involved.*

*I am emotionally intelligent and draw upon this capability to help myself, and others, thrive at work.*

*My professional purpose is always evolving.*

*I build strong, healthy, mutually beneficial relationships.*

*I listen to people when they speak to me.*

*I am present in my daily work life, and enjoy the moments of my day.*

*No challenge is too great for me to manage.*

*The vision I have for my professional life is entirely possible.*

*Even though I don't always know how to create my professional success, I know having the vision and intent is enough to move forward with.*

*My actions every day stem from integrity.*

*I hold myself accountable for how I behave.*

*I behave in alignment with my values at all times.*

*I speak truth and honor myself and others in the way I communicate.*

*When I feel upset or notice frustration rise within the workplace, I breathe deeply and choose peaceful response over painful reaction.*

*Every person I encounter through my work is of value to me—for me to learn something from and for me to share something with.*

*I am a powerful communicator.*

*I solve problems with ease.*

*I express inspired ideas, solutions and possibilities.*

*I am calm in the face of adversity.*

*I hear my inner knowing loud and clear.*

*I own my mistakes and learn from them.*

*I choose to represent authenticity in all that I am and in all that I do.*

*I enjoy solving problems.*

*I fill an important place on this planet, and my gifts and talents are needed.*

*My professional potential is unlimited.*

*I am capable of much more than I realize, and I eagerly enter each new day with the intention of extending myself.*

*I believe in my abilities.*

*I embrace my areas for growth and development.*

*My strengths are a platform for me to leverage myself forward from.*

*When I notice I am blocking myself, I instantly remember I am also the solution to that block.*

*I recognize that all I desire professionally always remains possible, no matter what challenges I may face.*

*I leverage my time and energy.*

*I am a clever and compassionate negotiator.*

*Everything I do is for the betterment of myself, my loved ones, my work community of contacts and society as a whole.*

*My life is in balance and this helps me to be on my A Game at work.*

*I am relaxed.*

*My passion is my soul speaking through me; my job is to notice this and bring it to life.*

*Stress has no place in my life.*

*I respect myself enough to walk away from people, situations and professional positions that no longer serve me.*

*I trust my instincts.*

*I have genuine interest in the uniqueness of each person I meet.*

*I nourish my talents by continuously exercising them.*

*I am committed to my professional development.*

*I focus on being my fully expressed self.*

*I honor my inspirations.*

*I embrace opportunities when they are presented to me.*

*I am grateful for my skills.*

*I breathe deeply through any difficult situations.*

*I am optimistic about what I am creating professionally.*

*I trust that there is a professional path for me that is meaningful and abundant.*

*I listen to my body and take breaks frequently when I need to recharge.*

*Every day I am present to the now moment.*

*I remember that not everyone may understand me or like me, and that is okay, because my job is to be my authentic unique expression.*

*When I feel fear, I acknowledge personal expansion is available if I step into the uncertainty.*

*My creativity flows into my work.*

*Success follows me wherever I go.*

*My success stems from my way of being and what I believe, which influences how I behave and the results I generate.*

*I am grateful for the work I do, for all that it teaches me and allows me to contribute.*

*I am energized and ready to give 100 percent to each day.*

*I greet all work situations with an open mind.*

*I walk with my head held high, proud of who I am and humble in my attitude.*

*I am openhearted and willing to be vulnerable in my work relationships, to foster deeper connections and meaningful work experiences.*

*I am grounded and balanced in how I view all situations, taking a bigger picture perspective before diving in.*

*I am grateful for my professional path to date and for all that lies ahead.*

*I know that my full potential is unleashed when I live from my own self-belief and in alignment with my values.*

*I release any need to achieve Old World standards of success at the expense of my well-being.*

*I know that the New World model of success is all about thriving from the inside out.*

*The paradigm I live from is anchored in self-love, self-assurance and self-confidence.*

*I only have so much physical, mental and emotional energy to give the world each day; I manage that precious energy wisely.*

*I operate proactively and am powerful in the way I manage my reactions to unexpected demands and crises.*

*I role model a conscious, healthy and thriving life, personally and professionally, for all those in my life whom I care deeply about.*

*I am clear about my vision, goals and dreams for my professional life.*

*I am supported in the work I do and have an abundance of resources to work with.*

*What I need shows up in my professional life synchronistically when I need it.*

*I am tuned into what my work community needs from me.*

*I frequently take breaks to allow my mind to go into "off mode" to rejuvenate myself for peak performance.*

*Every time I experience success and fly high in my work, I celebrate it and remember that there is so much more to come.*

*I release any resistance to what isn't working well for me in my professional endeavors, and let myself flow into the solutions that serve me best.*

*My mind is powerful beyond measure and I get the best from it.*

*Often I resonate with something as truth at a deeper level, beyond my thinking mind, and I tune into that.*

*I treat other people with respect and compassion, just as I would want to be treated.*

*I bring fun and lightheartedness to my work.*

*I step outside of my comfort zone professionally, in order to continually develop my skills and experience new horizons.*

*I know how to effectively switch off from my work, to have me time and family/friend time.*

*I sleep well every night, no matter what is going on at work, and return each morning refreshed and ready to create new ways forward.*

*I attract opportunities.*

*I am recognized and rewarded for my contribution.*

*My professional life thrives in equal order to the amount of authentic effort I bring to it.*

*I make decisions day to day wisely and effortlessly.*

*Every day I am alive is an opportunity to express my talents for the joy of it.*

*I stand peacefully and powerfully in my values.*

*I have a multitude of high vibration, mutually beneficial relationships.*

*People come into my path and leverage me forward professionally.*

*My professional life grows in alignment with my vision.*

*I give my time and energy to things that matter and do so with enthusiasm.*

*I understand how to say no to things that don't serve me.*

*I know how to strategically create the opportunities that leverage me forward.*

*I confidently present myself to others.*

*I speak from my heart and am received by whoever is listening.*

*I openly and authentically share who I really am in my workplace.*

*I manage my energy at work effectively, bringing presence, patience and understanding to all that I do.*

*I operate with precision, on target and channeling my gifts directly into the results I desire.*

*My success has everything to do with operating in balance, with presence and from intuition.*

*I live in complete alignment with my values and focus on things that make my heart sing.*

*Whenever I need help at work, I openly ask for it.*

*I have mentors who guide me and show me how to expand my professional capabilities.*

*I am excellent at navigating my way through challenging conversations.*

*I do all that I can and give 100 percent of myself, and that is always more than enough.*

*I release perfection and the illusion it is; I only care for progress and inner fulfillment.*

*I live my life with inner peace and freedom; this helps me to enjoy and flow in my work.*

*I am successful at all levels of my life—as defined by standards of importance to me.*

*I live my professional life to meet my heart's desires, and release any need to meet the expectations of others.*

*I am a magnetic person.*

*Everything I do stems from conscious choices.*

*I own my work and outcomes.*

*I display accountability and responsibility for everything I do.*

*Opportunities keep knocking down my door.*

*I am unattached to what others say about me, good or bad; I simply live in alignment with my truth.*

*I believe I achieve whatever I want, and that belief fuels my success.*

*I see my work as a service to the world, making a positive contribution to others.*

*I am trustworthy.*

*I have many gifts, skills and talents; the older I get, the more they become apparent to me.*

*I have everything that my mind, body and soul need.*

*I was born with the exact combination of gifts and challenges that I needed to thrive and learn in this life, both personally and professionally.*

*I deserve every good thing this life has to offer me.*

*I have integrity and honor my word.*

*Professionally I make a profound impact every day, no matter whether I see that firsthand.*

*I know the difference between genuine foreboding and pointless fear when I am faced with work decisions.*

*I know how to network with flair.*

*I enjoy meeting new people and forming relationships.*

*Positivity drives my professional life.*

*I am talented.*

*I am agile and able to dynamically move with changing environments.*

*I anticipate my own success in every way.*

*I am empowered.*

*I am skilled.*

*My talents are endless; I have only scratched the surface of what I can do and offer.*

*I am a quick learner.*

*For every person who tells me I can't, there are more who tell me I can.*

*My professional life is soaring.*

*I respect myself.*

*I am committed to my development at all levels.*

*I bear no grudges or resentment in my work life. It is toxic energy, and I release it instantly.*

*I build my confidence each day through being present, remembering my true nature and then giving wholeheartedly, without judgment, to whatever I am doing.*

*I remember that what other people say and do is not about me; it is a projection of their own inner space.*

*I am self-assured and carry myself with confidence.*

*When things veer off plan at work, I breathe deeply and remember that every day is a fresh new start.*

*I am at peace with what is, and I remember that there is a flow to life and out of every challenge comes something valuable.*

*Every day I learn new things.*

*I offer my support to others if I see that they need help.*

*I am open to feedback and actively seek to grow as a person.*

*I see mistakes as opportunities to become even better at what I do.*

*I notice other people thriving and celebrate their success and learn from them.*

*I love my work.*

*My energy is positive and I bring it to my work each day, even in the face of challenges.*

*Everything is just as it should be, always.*

*I have every talent I need in order to fulfill my life purpose.*

*I behave beyond reproach.*

*I appreciate and value the people around me.*

*I am committed to making a valuable contribution in my work.*

*When I notice my passion for what I do has gone, I proactively reconsider my path.*

*When I thrive, everyone around me benefits.*

*I focus on letting go of habits that block my success.*

*I practice rituals every day that support my well-being.*

*When I notice fear or anxiety in relation to my work, I take the time to understand what the thoughts and feelings are telling me.*

*The world needs the gifts I have to offer.*

*My success at work is a joyful part of expressing myself, but it never defines my worth or value as a person.*

*Unique passions and inspirations come through me, and they exist to be expressed; I honor that and act upon them.*

*Challenges are gifts for growth dressed up as problems.*

*I breathe deeply into calm whenever I feel stress arise.*

*I am peaceful in the face of other people's upset.*

*My health is a priority; it supports the delivery of my professional passions, and so I take care of my body every day.*

*I take time to celebrate my wins.*

*I know when to block out distractions and focus on the task at hand.*

I understand that relationship building is about personal connections, letting people see the true me and desiring to see the true them.

If I feel out of my depth, I put my hand up for help, rather than waiting to sink down.

Vulnerability is a strength, it is the truthful center of who I am and I proudly show it.

I am worthy and complete as a person, and seek no validation from anyone.

I march to the beat of my own drum, and never suffocate my soul for the sake of anyone.

My imperfections are perfectly designed to help me grow, and that growth further feeds my professional success.

My professional success is simply the culmination of a series of moments. I make heart-led choices moment by moment, and that is all that is required.

The way I eat and drink while working aligns to what my body needs in order to be in high vibration and healthy energy, ready for peak performance.

I am respectful of others and make the effort to listen compassionately and understand their perspective, even when I don't agree with them.

Despite hierarchy, no other person is above or below me; I treat everyone as my equal.

Worry is wasted energy and I release attachment to anything I cannot change.

I focus on solutions.

I visualize the outcomes I want at work and then act in alignment with that vision.

I make good strategic choices that serve me well now and in all my coming moments.

I am disciplined.

I am financially abundant.

*I intuitively know when a workplace relationship is open for improvement and when I need to shift away from toxicity.*

*I proactively reevaluate my professional life each year and consciously stay aligned to what is most important to me.*

*I say no thank you to societal conditioning of what I'm told I should be, what I should do and what I should have, and instead I say yes to what my heart tells me.*

*I am clear on my purpose.*

*I understand my drivers, motivation and where I am going with my work life, and it fuels me every day.*

*I do what I know is right to do.*

*I am self-motivated.*

*I am savvy.*

*I say what I know is honest and appropriate for the situation, always delivering my messages with compassion.*

*I am highly organized.*

*I am acutely aware of how to interact with other people to get the best out of them and the situation.*

*I manage my time effectively.*

*I notice how synchronicity plays out in my career, when I remain focused on what I most desire with honest intent.*

*I feel free in my work.*

*I am respected and treated well.*

*I am grateful for all aspects of my professional life.*

*I dream big and give everything I have.*

*I plan for my success and act upon my plan to make it happen.*

*I am intelligent.*

*I am great at delegating, leveraging and leading.*

*I have tenacity and it serves me well.*

*I deal well with ambiguity.*

*I am excellent with all types of people.*

*My self-awareness is my greatest asset.*

*I am hungry to create a difference in this world.*

*I have a trusted team of people who support my career and give me solid advice.*

*My vision for my life evolves the more that I learn and grow, and I enjoy that fluidity as it keeps me open to all possibilities.*

*My inner voice is loud and clear, and adds immense value to my work outcomes.*

*The universe supports my professional path.*

*I understand that I do not know everything and am open to receiving knowledge, ideas and input from all those around me.*

*I am resourceful.*

*Collaboration with other people is fulfilling.*

*I am diligent.*

*I am a talented multitasker.*

*I wholeheartedly act upon my aspirations.*

*I am able to tune out what doesn't serve me to focus in on what is most important in any moment.*

*I am a sponge for wisdom.*

*I realize that I am a leader no matter what position I hold; others always witness my behavior and take something from it.*

*I am attentive when being communicated to.*

*I am honest.*

*I treat people as the unique, valuable individuals they are.*

*I know how to express my emotions in an open, healthy and balanced way in the workplace.*

*My professional life is engaging, interesting, challenging and fulfilling.*

*I act in alignment with my word.*

*I take action to rectify any mistakes I make.*

*I present myself in a way that shows I respect who I am and the work that I do.*

*I am always on time, and understand that this shows people I care and respect them.*

*At work I am the full expression of myself.*

*I bring joy and gratitude to the work I do every day.*

*I thank and acknowledge everyone who adds value to my work life.*

*My work pays me back one hundred times the effort I put in.*

*I am decisive and quick witted.*

*I live from a victor mind-set.*

*I am empathetic in the face of dysfunction.*

*I bring consciousness to all that I do.*

*My workspace is vibrant and enjoyable to be in.*

*I am a "make it happen" person.*

*I am committed to continuous improvement.*

*Work is one way I channel my full creative expression into the world.*

*I refuse to delve into complaining, blaming and other limiting habits; I rise above it all to a place of effecting powerful change from a peaceful perspective.*

*I am building new skills every day.*

*I am resilient.*

*I do all that I am asked to with 100 percent commitment.*

*Surrounded by inspirers, every day I see the opportunity to fly at my full potential.*

*The messages in my head are supportive and lift me up; I'm my own cheerleader.*

*I appreciate everything I have.*

*I know what I focus on is what I get.*

*Excellence is the name of my game.*

*I manage my schedule and priorities effectively.*

*I say no to things that don't serve me and consciously say yes to opportunities that carry me forward.*

*If exhausted, I know how to stop and allow my body and mind to rest.*

*I know collaboration mind-set is the New World answer to thriving.*

*I shed light on anything that isn't working well for the pure purpose of improving it.*

*I live from my deeply held values in all situations.*

*I am here in life for good reason and my professional life is a key part of my journey.*

*I do things with great care and love.*

*I welcome opportunities even if I'm not exactly sure how to execute them, as I have the capability to unfold into them and learn what I need as I go.*

*I give thanks for my blessings and they multiply.*

*There are always people helping me when I need help.*

*I have more than enough resources, talents and skills right now to achieve my purpose in this moment.*

*I am thoughtful.*

*I am considerate in my approach.*

*I invest in my professional growth.*

*It is the small things in my daily life where the most meaning exists.*

*I have already made a difference in the lives of people through the work I do, in ways I might never know or truly understand.*

*I trust my judgment.*

*No problem is irresolvable.*

*I relish new tasks and projects.*

*I open myself up to change and invite the learning and opportunities that come with it.*

*Even in the face of complete uncertainty, I stand proud and empowered, ready for whatever life brings me.*

*I focus on what is important and eliminate noisy nothingness from my focus.*

*I am a deep well of strength.*

*My success is supported by my willingness to learn from all those around me.*

*I choose to work as a conscious being.*

*I am committed to helping all those around me in my professional circles to thrive in what they do.*

*There is unlimited possibility and abundance for everyone.*

*I am creative with the resources I have and creative with how I generate and access new resources.*

*I put my focus on any things, people and situations that uplift me.*

*My perspective of my work creates my work reality.*

*I choose beliefs, thoughts and feelings that work in my favor.*

*No one is coming to save me, I am the person I am waiting for—and I choose to stand up and own my professional life powerfully.*

*Regardless of what others believe, I know that what I believe for myself is real, and that my goals and dreams are available to me.*

*I am reliable.*

*When there is pressure in my work, I remain calm and anchored within myself.*

*I make smart choices about what I focus my effort and attention on.*

*I choose to step into uncertainty rather than stay in the familiar discomfort that holds me back.*

*There are many ways to reach the professional success I desire; whenever one door closes, another opens up.*

## 166 Truths as Affirmations to Embed Your Unleashed Paradigm

To support you to live from the New World model of success, with an unleashed paradigm, here are the one hundred and sixty six truths from Part I as short positive affirmation statements.

To download an audio of these affirmations, which you can listen to as a ritual to embed your new paradigm, please visit: www.PinchMeLiving.com/Unleash-Your-Life-Free-Resources

*Everything is energy.*

*Everything is energetically connected.*

*Shifts in energy in "one place" have influential ripple effects.*

*I have a unique energy vibration.*

*I am committed to my energy vibrating positively.*

*My energy vibration influences the types of actions I take.*

*I adjust my energy vibration positively, thus adjusting the core of my creative power.*

*I resolve any negative energy as soon as it arises within me, ceasing the yo-yo cycle and bringing me to an even ebb and flow.*

*My energy constantly creates my life.*

*Where my attention goes my energy flows.*

*I have unlimited divine energy.*

*I have limited human energy and I use it wisely.*

*I am fully responsible for my energy expenditure.*

*I control my own energy, and that is always enough.*

*I know that pent-up unexpressed energy becomes destructive, so I am always expressing my energy in healthy ways to support my physical, mental and emotional balance.*

*Opportunities and synchronicities are the natural flow of energy.*

*Every interaction is an energy exchange.*

*I have the capacity to protect myself from low vibration energy.*

*Everything beyond source energy and soul-level is impermanent.*

*Source energy nourishes me.*

*My connection to my source is constant and unbreakable.*

*Love is my natural state.*

*My life is a journey into love.*

*Love is remembrance of the soul in me and the soul in all others.*

*There is no lack of love.*

*Love uplifts all my actions.*

*Loving consciousness heals.*

*I choose to embody love.*

*I am infinitely loved, supported and never alone.*

*I already completely love myself and choose to remember this every day.*

*My relationship with myself is the most important love to nurture.*

*There is enough for everyone.*

*Collaboration is more powerful than competition mindset.*

*I uplift humanity when I am willing to be of service.*

*How I give is more important than what I give.*

*Giving and getting is a circular flow of energy.*

*Healing myself comes before healing humanity.*

*I am a reflection of divinity.*

*My soul is expansive.*

*I am soul first, body second.*

*Due to being more soul than body, I must nourish myself accordingly.*

*Spiritual is who I am.*

*There is a design for my awakening and I trust in it.*

*My soul may travel numerous lifetimes; I have much wisdom within me.*

*I have soul shadow and soul light, and both are beautifully designed for me to thrive in my learning and contribution in this life. My soul learning and contribution feed each other.*

*I have unique soul lessons to learn in this lifetime.*

*There is information available to me about my unique life path and soul lessons.*

*The recurring patterns in my life point me to the lessons I am here to learn.*

*My purpose in life is to be the full expression of who I am.*

*I was born with everything I need to achieve my purpose.*

*I honor my purpose by acting upon my soul language of passion, inspiration and intuition.*

*My soul asks that my mind not judge or block my unique expression.*

*My full expression unlocks the potential in others.*

*I am, and always have been, enough.*

*I am co-creating my life.*

*Divine signals help me to navigate my life and I am tuned in to them.*

*I take two journeys simultaneously, internal and external.*

*The universe always lovingly gives me what I need to grow.*

*My soul intention and my human freewill occur in unison.*

*What my soul needs and what my mind/body want may differ; I always trust in the flow of my life, however it unfolds, and willingly accept each moment for what it is.*

*There exists divine order and divine timing, which support my soul journey.*

*Dead ends are never truly dead ends.*

*I intuitively resonate with higher wisdom.*

*I am fully present to receive guidance.*

*I follow my intuition and do what is heart-led; this is never selfish.*

*My life is a process of undoing and removing layers that no longer serve me, to uncover my true nature.*

*As long as I am breathing, my work here continues; I wholeheartedly embrace the dawning of each new day.*

*Consciousness is my greatest tool.*

*Conscious living is my choice and a moment-by-moment practice.*

*Enlightenment is an ongoing process within my life journey.*

*My beliefs, thoughts, feelings and actions are a creation equation.*

*My beliefs are the internal code that runs me.*

*Limiting beliefs are the core foundation of any fog, and as I see them, I transform them to empowering new beliefs.*

*I acknowledge the power of both my conscious beliefs and my subconscious beliefs.*

*My beliefs are created and cemented due to frequency and/or intensity, and I actively reinforce my positive beliefs in this way.*

*My beliefs can be of this lifetime or energy carrying over from other lifetimes, and, regardless of their origin, I know they trigger me or aid me in my journey for inward growth and external expression, for learning and contribution.*

*Limiting beliefs do not belong to me and I willingly release them.*

*Limiting beliefs are signposts to my success.*

*Limiting beliefs can be changed, and I know exactly how to do that effectively.*

*I act from my new empowering beliefs and they come to life in my external reality.*

*My mind and feeling systems are navigational tools, which I use wisely.*

*My mind is never bad, it may simply be off on a tangent; I bring conscious awareness to each moment in order to provide leadership to this aspect of myself.*

*The majority of inner pain and inner peace stems from my perspective. I am empowered to own my painful reactions and I know how to create and respond from inner peace.*

*Learning and living from truth is a lifetime's work.*

*I am living in natural cycles of expansion and contraction, and I flow fluidly with these cycles.*

*I am willing to let go of the life I have in order to experience the life I know is possible. My willingness is a powerful attitude and energy.*

*My entire reality is unique.*

*There are countless versions of reality occurring at one time.*

*While every person is in a different reality, there is common ground for love and understanding.*

*I always find evidence to support my perspective of reality; I choose a perspective that serves me well.*

*Miracles are everywhere, every day.*

*Time is not real, now is what matters.*

*The past is a memory and the future is a mental projection. I dwell in the present and am free of both of these.*

*Time cannot run out. My life is naturally unfolding.*

*There is no right time. Now is always the moment I choose my inner peace, freedom and success.*

*Challenges are a natural part of my life experience and I see the gifts within them.*

*Drama and chaos dissolve. I choose a peaceful perspective.*

*I am never given more than I can cope with. I have great reserves of strength within me.*

*Loss leads to learning and creates a clearing, which I peacefully acknowledge.*

*The more challenges I face, the more I have within me to contribute to others.*

*My capacity to cope with challenges at any given time may vary depending on what else I am facing; I am kind to myself whenever feeling overwhelmed.*

*Being at peace and being successful doesn't mean challenges disappear. From my current inner peace and success, I know new challenges arising are simply forging me further on my soul's path for learning and contribution.*

*My possibilities exist irrespective of any challenge. All possibilities remain possible, always.*

*I accept my unique path and release the urge to compare myself to others. I keep challenges in perspective and remember that others face challenges on their own unique paths.*

*Challenges unlock the deeper meaning and true value of my life.*

*Solution identification and learning are the only reasons I dive into or dwell in challenges.*

*Challenges are the making of me.*

*While some situations may not be conducive to happiness, it is entirely possible for me to be at peace in all moments and that is what I choose.*

*Being at peace consistently comes with practice, a practice that I am committed to.*

*Peace as a practice returns me to my natural state of love.*

*No one else is responsible for my inner peace, ever. I am totally empowered to create and hold my inner peace irrespective of anything or anyone.*

*I accept the present as it is and this provides the doorway into inner peace.*

*I accept the present by simply acknowledging the facts of the situation.*

*Giving over is essential for both inner peace and effective change.*

*There is no destination I have to get to, only a journey.*

*Practicing peace in the present helps me to reduce any fear that I feel.*

*My physical, mental and emotional well-being supports my inner peace.*

*I act in alignment with my values, and this supports my consistent and sustainable experience of inner peace.*

*The most important freedom to me is the freedom I now have to live outside the fog of warped perspective. I am deeply grateful for my empowering new paradigm based upon truth.*

*My true "home" is a state of being. I am at home wherever I am, when I remember my true nature.*

*My value and place in this world are inherent in who I am.*

*Freedom is expressing myself for the joy of it.*

*Perfection is an illusion. I embrace all of my imperfections as they are part of my soul journey to aid my learning and contribution, and they are a part of my humanity.*

*I expand beyond my circumstances in every way.*

*The core motivator behind my desire for external success is to feel happiness, inner peace and love. All of these feelings are available to me right now. I have the power to create them from shifting my perspective and returning to my true nature.*

*The New World model of success is about living as a conscious being from the inside out.*

*Success is first my way of being, before it is an outcome of what I do.*

*I am committed to both my way of being and my way of doing, which together create my external results.*

*There are many paths to any desired result.*

*Mistakes and stumbles are part of the journey and I embrace what I learn from them.*

*I openly ask for help when I need it, knowing it denotes my wisdom and strength.*

*I never truly fail, I hold a success mind-set.*

*I choose to rehearse for success.*

*The way I go about creating external success in my life is always in alignment with my values.*

*There are no sacrifices for success in my life, only empowered choices.*

*My dominant state is what matters most, and I choose positivity.*

*I need very little in order to thrive, and so I see that what I have right now is abundant in every way and that abundance grows each day.*

*Things, including money, are simply energy.*

*I came with nothing and I will leave with nothing—I have no need nor desire to grip on to anything.*

*I understand that there is nothing but uncertainty and I feel liberated by this.*

*Uncertainty is the breeding ground for all great possibilities.*

*Creating my goals and dreams may not always to be easy, but it is exciting and worth every step of the journey.*

*No one is coming to save me; I am totally supported to save myself. This is my path and I own it wholeheartedly.*

*Fear is an invitation to shift, either in my inner perspective or in my outer action, and I accept the invitation every time.*

*I needn't literally leap in order to make leaps. Small steps are the key.*

*The world gravitates to the authentic me.*

*I let down my walls and open myself in every way to life.*

*My personal accountability reclaims and retains my power in any given moment.*

*Relationships are life classes and I embrace the education I receive.*

*My deep self-love supports me loving others freely.*

*No person ever projects pain at me unless they are in pain themselves, so I have empathy in all such situations.*

*Others do not need me to change them.*

*When I relate to people as their full potential, I support them to unleash that potential.*

*I actively listen, knowing that true listening has the sole purpose of seeking to understand.*

*I have soul assignments with certain people in my life and I acknowledge these connections exist.*

*I am responsible for defining how I wish to be treated, but I am never responsible for any mistreatment.*

*Forgiveness is a gift I give myself.*

*I cannot be everything to everyone, nor do I need to be.*

*I show my true self to others, so that they may have the chance to know who I really am.*

*Not everyone will understand me or like me, and I am at peace with this.*

*Advice can come from love and fear at the very same time, and I know how to tell the difference. I am able to peacefully be with the advice of others and intuitively take onboard what serves me, while silently discarding what does not.*

*I trust that the love and support I need always show up in the best ways for me.*

*I am attuned to where other people are at, and never ask more of someone than they can give in any moment.*

*Relationships devolve or evolve and this is natural. I trust in this flow.*

*I choose to live from my soul, clear of the fog, channeling that full expression of who I am powerfully out into the world.*

*New World success is my birthright.*

# PART III
# CREATE & BLOSSOM
## Redefine your life to live with clear vision and inspired actions

*"There are no extra pieces in the universe. Everyone is here because he or she has a place to fill, and every piece must fit itself into the big jigsaw puzzle."*

— Deepak Chopra

In Part I and Part II, we primarily focused on transforming your inner experience of life, your paradigm—shifting your way of being by considering new perspectives of life and transforming your beliefs, which flow into your thoughts and feelings. Now we are going to focus on transforming your outer experience of life with a practical action plan—shifting your way of doing.

While the practical actions you decide upon and implement are vital to creating shifts in your circumstances, please never forget that your energy underpins and drives everything you do and create. Your energy is founded within your way of being (your beliefs, thoughts and feelings), and that feeds into and drastically influences your way of doing (your actions). The fact that you have already transformed your paradigm, choosing to live life from a solid new foundation of truths, means your energy has shifted, and that energy is already influencing your life experience (inside and out). The transformation is well under way, even if you have not seen shifts in your external circumstances yet. The formation of a practical action plan, aligned to your true nature and heartfelt desires, only adds further momentum and power to the unleashing that is already taking place.

## Your Purpose

Having cleared the fog, there is nothing left to block you from living your purpose, the full expression of who you are, and sharing that uniqueness with the world—without inhibition, without apology and without judgment. You are a clear channel for your soul to reach out and touch the world.

You might feel a little caught up in the notion that your purpose should be something that you "do" out in the world. You might ask, "Shouldn't my life purpose be a specific job, activity or contribution?"

Your purpose is to be your unique expression; it's an inner state of being flowing out into your doing. It is absolutely true that you do go out into the world and give life to your unique expression through your actions; in this way, it does become what you do. It is also your relationships, your career or business and your hobbies. It is what you say, create and offer this world tangibly. In this way your purpose may well shine out in a specific type of job, activity or contribution that you feel drawn to and deeply compelled to do. Yet, any of these actions are just avenues for you to give life to your unique expression. Fundamentally, all of that starts within you as soul language—passions, inspirations and intuition wanting to be expressed. Purpose always starts in your being, flowing into your doing.

As you journey onward in life, growing, becoming wiser and coming to understand yourself more, you may notice new points of passion, inspiration and intuition arise within you and want to emerge through you. Existing points of passion, inspiration and intuition may deepen. This is the continuing unfolding of you on your soul journey, from the inside out. Your outer doing changes over your lifetime, to stay in alignment with that inner unfolding. You might not, therefore, have *one* specific job, profession, vocation, business or career as your lifetime "purpose." Outward actions will shift to stay aligned to your true purpose.

## Your Clean Slate

After living a lifetime trapped by the fog, at first it can feel daunting to stand free of it. All of a sudden you realize that truly anything is possible. You not only *remember* your true nature, before all the limiting beliefs, fear, expectation and societal conditioning, but you *feel* that true nature. It can be an almost shocking experience to meet your true self for the first time!

You now have a clean slate—an opportunity to design your life with clear vision and to create your physical reality through inspired being and doing, and to blossom as you do so. It is a transformational turnaround to go from living your life from an "outside in" reactionary model of reality, to living your life from an "inside out" creative model of reality.

You might immediately start to consider what it is that you want to create. You might start to wonder how you will know what the best vision is for your life. You might feel concern arise over the best path to take, or how to get started. Let the questions rise up, because the answers will come through you ...

## Your Soul Speaks to You

You needn't struggle, try hard or push to figure out what to create or how to blossom. Simply tune into and act upon your soul language in the small moments of your daily life. Honoring your passion, inspiration and intuition is honoring your purpose. Your soul offers you intangible energy, which becomes tangible creations through you. When you live in alignment with your passions, inspirations and intuition—noticing them, trusting them and acting upon them—your life flows in a natural unfolding. Inner peace, freedom and success are all consequences of living this way.

## Soul Language Guides You in Every Aspect of Your Life

Passion is not just for your work or for your relationships. Inspiration is not just for creativity in your pastimes, work or business. Intuition is not just for problem solving.

You can notice passions in relation to any area of your life. Inspiration can spark new insights, ideas and perspectives without limit. Intuition is your partner in relation to every single waking moment of your life, no matter where you are, what you are doing or whom you are with.

Your physical, mental and emotional well-being, your personal and professional education and development, your career or business, your relationships at home and at work, your finances, your lifestyle ... are all guided by your passion, inspiration and intuition, which exist to help you navigate your journey, for learning and for contribution.

## Transforming Current Circumstances and Navigating Forward

Your soul expression is powerful for two reasons: (1) it helps you transform your current circumstances by guiding you on the types of adjustments you need to make in order to progress into the life you know is possible and (2) having created that life, it will help you navigate each moment so that you can maintain and deepen that meaningful life.

Let's work through each of the three ways your soul speaks to you, so you can better understand how to live a soul-led life.

## Giving Expression to Your Passion

There are certain aspects of life that you may notice seem to compel you, intrigue you, light you up, bring you joy, create a sense of drive within and prompt a sense of possibility, hope, happiness, lightness, fun and vitality. You are naturally drawn to these aspects of life.

Your soul guides you to recognize the value of these uplifting worldly experiences through the feeling of passion. Whatever you feel passion for, is where you are being called to step into. Giving life to your passion through expression and action will support your inner peace, freedom and success, from the inside out.

You don't have to find passion. It is not outside of you. It exists as soul energy and comes through you as feeling; your job is to notice whenever you feel passion arising within you, notice what it is in relation to and honor and give life to it by expressing that passion outward, into whatever the external experience is. Having said that, just because passion comes through you as a feeling, and is not something to "find" but rather to feel and act upon, doesn't mean you can't go out into the world in your day-to-day life and investigate, test, experience and develop your sense of understanding about what passions you naturally have. You're an interactive, expanding being and you're living in relationship with the entire world, not independent of it or separate from it. Exploration invites you to discover more about yourself and about life, and to develop a greater understanding of how and when passion arises for you.

Follow your curiosities, notice what makes you feel good; play with life and give yourself permission to try things out. For example, you might investigate new career paths, meet new people or explore places and activities you've been intrigued by but have never made time for. As you do so, notice what that sparks within you. Where is passion present? When is passion present? In relation to what is passion firing up?

## Why does your soul speak to you through the feeling of passion?

There is no mistaking what you are passionate about. It is designed. What you have passion for is uniquely set up to support your journey in life. Your soul helps you understand, through the language of feeling, what aspects of life you are most naturally aligned to and what aspects of life you will gain the most benefit from. Your soul compels you in order to *optimize* your experience of life.

The benefits of your passions are key. What lights you up brings you joy, makes you feel calm, offers you a sense of freedom and leads you to feel your best self. Giving life to your passions helps bring you closer in alignment with your true nature, letting your soul express through you out into the world. Acting on passions generates the most desired human feeling experiences of happiness, inner peace and love. As a result, it supports your physical, mental and emotional well-being.

All of this lifts your energy vibration and, lest we forget, your energy connects with the fabric of universal energy to which you belong, and continuously influences the creation of your life and magnetizes you for similar vibration energy (for example, people, things, situations, experiences, opportunities and synchronicities).

## Why must you listen to and act upon your passion?

You must give airtime to your passions. No matter how busy you are, no matter how little time you feel you have, no matter how many challenges you have on your plate to deal with—all of those circumstances are just further evidence that you must listen to your passions.

You listen and act on passion because doing so allows you to fulfill your purpose. Your passions are unique to you. While it is true that there are many people on this planet who are passionate about similar things, this in no way diminishes the beauty and uniqueness of what lights you up, and how magnetic and magical you are as an energy being when you are lit up. The combination of passions you feel stem from your soul in terms of what you specifically need to experience in this life in order to be most balanced, happy and healthy. The passion feelings guide you like an inner compass pointing to true north, showing you how to navigate into your most successful experience of human life.

If you don't allow yourself to listen to and act upon your passion feelings, you block your own energy. You get in your own way. You suppress yourself, and don't let your energy flow naturally in the course it seeks to move.

## What gets in the way of your passion expressing out into the world?

The only thing that could have stopped you from having this wonderful experience of passion being expressed was the fog. That would previously have given rise to you not trusting yourself, judging your passions, prioritizing less meaningful things, or worrying that you might not be good enough at something and thus giving up before giving it a go. It would have kept you thinking that passions were only for expressing if you could make a lot of money from them, receive recognition, make a career of it, or any other various illusionary reasons and excuses not to listen to your soul speaking through you. None of which are valid, and none of which are part of your paradigm any longer. You are clear and open.

You don't need to foretell what payback you might get as a result of expressing your passions, or whether it will be worth your while, or what others might think of you or if you'll be good enough at whatever you are passionate about doing. Trust your soul. That is, trust yourself. You express passion because passion exists to be expressed. Period.

## How can you tune into and give life to your passions?

To begin to tune into your passion:

- Pay attention to your curiosities.
- Pay attention to your positive compulsions.
- Pay attention to anything that sparks a fire within you, particularly anything that you feel driven to stand up for, to share, to support, to grow or to make a difference with.

- Pay attention to what you get really excited by.
- Pay attention to what you have natural enthusiasm for.
- Pay attention to what you wish you could spend most of your time doing, where you would love to spend most of your time being, or the people you would like to spend most of your time with.
- Write down in what situations, when and with whom you have your most passionate feelings come through you.
- Write down what you may have been passionate about in the past, but may have given away, ignored or never tried because of the fog.
- Notice where expectations might have led you down one path when your passions might have been pointing down another path.
- Notice where fear has previously kept you stuck, instead of acting upon your passions.
- What would you do and try and experience if you took any fear you felt as an invitation to shift?
- What would you do if you weren't living within society's standards of what "success" and "normal" are supposedly meant to look like?
- From your new limitless paradigm of empowering truths and positive beliefs, what passions do you now sense?

Passion feelings do not exist to be ignored, suppressed or judged. Listen to passion. Let it flow through you. Give it airtime. Be willing to act upon it.

## Where will your passion lead you?

Passion will lead you into New World success—the inner success of peace, freedom, fulfillment, happiness, joy, balance and well-being. In these inner states, all the outer success you desire can more easily flow as a natural consequence.

When you begin to act upon your passion, you will be surprised by what you discover about yourself, what new learning you have, what you contribute, the new people you meet, which opportunities arise and what synchronicities occur. However, remember that you do not act upon your passion as a means to an end, to get these flow-on experiences. You act upon your passions because it is what you are here in life to do. The bonus is that since expressed passion supports the natural unfolding of your life, then all of these other magical things can occur as a result of your free-flowing high vibration energy.

## Acting Upon Your Inspirations

There are moments in your day-to-day life when you notice a sudden insight, new perspective, possibility or creative idea arise in your awareness. These can often appear "out of the blue," as unexpected sensations. They are often described as little lightning bolt strikes, where you can be occupied doing something completely unrelated with your mind or body, and all of a sudden you are struck by something you hadn't thought of before.

It grabs your attention momentarily because of the accompanying inspiration feeling (you might notice excitement, enthusiasm, intrigue or hope). The inspiration plants a seed of possibility in your mind and your powerful thinking mind is then able to take that seed and formulate it into something you can intellectually grasp, build upon, analyze and prepare for whatever action you decide to take to bring that inspiration into the world.

Inspiration might be a solution to a problem you face or an answer to a question you've been pondering. Inspirations might be brand new creative ideas that seemingly arise from nowhere. An inspiration might be something you could or need to do for your work, your health, your relationships, your finances or any other area of your life.

Inspiration it is not something you sit down with a pen and paper and decide to force out of you. That would be your thinking mind trying to squeeze out a logical, rational thought that will help you. And here is the most important thing you need to understand about inspiration ... it is not coming from your thinking mind. While the energy wave of inspiration may trigger a thought, ultimately, inspiration is soul language at its source.

While your mind is undoubtedly an extraordinarily powerful tool, which you use to harness inspiration and bring it to life through action, it is not the creator of those inspirations. Inspiration is born in the highest consciousness of the universe that you belong to. Your soul language is what allows you to tap into and receive that intelligence and wisdom. You are a receptor for your soul and highest consciousness—you receive the wave of energy that is soul language coming through you, and your job is to harness that and give expression to it.

## Why does your soul speak to you through inspiration?

You are a creative being. Your consciousness is a creative power that you were born to use.

When you receive inspiration and give all of your energy to it to bring it to life, a partnership occurs—the pairing of divine wisdom and your human capability. Inspiration is the input, which is processed through you as the channel, to produce outcomes. Inspiration is a way that divinity creates through you.

## Why is it so important to listen to your inspiration?

Inspiration exists as an intangible energy—be it an idea or a solution desiring to come into creation through you, to help you, your loved ones, your community or the world. It exists as a wave of possibility that is being given to you to harness. It cannot be made manifest into the world without you. You are the vehicle for that wave of possibility to come into life. If you suppress inspiration, there is nowhere and no way for that wave of possibility to come to shore. It is being given to you specifically. It is you who must receive it and use it.

If you're here in life to be your full unique expression, to learn and to contribute as you do so, then inspiration is part of what fuels this journey. If you don't listen to it, you block it. If you block it, you block your own energy and your own natural unfolding.

## What stops you from noticing and acting upon your inspirations?

Many people are so lost in their noisy automatic thought processes and their doing-ness that they unconsciously tune out inspiration. Alternatively, they may have a split-second recognition of inspiration arising, but they do not shine their full attention onto it, and their incessant autopilot thinking resumes as they continue doing whatever they were doing.

When inspirations strike, they typically momentarily break through that monologue of thinking and then disappear as quickly as they arrived. It's quite common for people to notice an inspiration and then hardly recall what it was just a few minutes or hours later. While inspiration will *seem* to fleetingly come into your consciousness and then go, it doesn't occur this way because you're only allowed a limited amount of inspiration, or a limited amount of time to capture it. There is no rule or trick occurring. This is simply about learning to tune in to higher consciousness. You are so solidly associated with and anchored in your physical body and your mind as being who you are, that you simply aren't used to tapping this soul aspect of yourself. It is like you have been listening to one radio station for a long time and another station is just one bandwidth away; sometimes you notice it trying to break into your chosen frequency, but you have to pay closer attention and choose to listen to it if you want to pick up on it more often and more clearly. You have to give inspiration airtime.

Even if you are consciously aware, noticing and capturing your inspiration, you still have to consciously choose to take your inspiration and do something with it. Many people are caught in judging their soul language, particularly when inspiration strikes. They judge its validity, its worth, whether it warrants their time and effort, where it might lead them, and if it will give them enough payback, money or validation in the world from acting upon it. They judge themselves in relation to their ability to act upon it. They diminish and ridicule the quality of the inspiration. Essentially, they squash their inspiration before it even has a chance to come to life. Inspiration wants to come out and create in the world. This occurs most effectively when you get out of your own way and allow yourself to be the full expression of who you are—uninhibited, unapologetic and without judgment.

## How do you harness and live from that inspiration?

If you want to live an inspired life, if you want to create out of inspiration, if you want to access wisdom and solutions that are expansive and in your best interests, beyond what your thinking mind can produce, then you might begin with these recommended practices:

- Practice presence in the small moments of your daily life. Bring conscious awareness to whatever you do and how you do it. This level of awareness makes you much more open and receptive to inspiration when it arises.
- Reduce the noise in your mind that stops you from noticing inspiration. Meditation is one way to do this, and meditation is simply anything that allows you to quiet your mind. It may be stillness and breathing techniques, or it might be peaceful walking in, and witnessing of, nature. Anything that promotes you simply being, without getting lost in thinking, breaks your identification with the thinking process and creates more space within your awareness. Creating space in your awareness is powerful—inspiration loves space because there is more room to be noticed and to flow through you. However, this doesn't mean that while you are in the practice of meditation that you will have an inspiration arise at that specific moment; you may, but the point is that you meditate to clear space and you take that space with you into all the coming moments of your daily life. Then, while you are busy in

your daily routine and work, there is a little more space, and all of a sudden a new idea arises, a solution pops into your head, or a creative notion grabs your attention.

- Warmly welcome inspiration. If you want a solution to a problem, if you want creative ideas to feed your work, if you want ways to help you expand your relationships and network, then literally ask for inspiration. Meditate and invite new insight to spark into your awareness. When it comes, be ready to receive it. You open yourself by taking pause and noting down your inspiration—in writing, in your calendar, by leaving yourself a voice memo on your phone or in any way that works for you while you are busy working, with your family or with other commitments. If you don't take note of your inspiration, your mind will likely forget and move on.

- Surrender to the divine order and timing of when inspiration will come. It won't arrive on command. Inspiration isn't born in your thinking mind, rather it arises from your soul and highest consciousness; you can't dictate when it will appear.

Now consider:

- What ideas do I have that have been percolating for some time?
- What insights have I had that surprised me?
- What has struck me lately that I've been thinking of acting upon?

When you begin to notice and write your inspirations down, and to even simply *consider* acting upon them, let alone actually acting upon them, then you attune more to your soul and the highest consciousness with whom you are co-creating. The fabric of energy to which you belong picks up on this shift in your awareness. As a result of giving those inspirations an outlet (even if simply onto paper), you open the floodgates to that part of yourself. When those floodgates open, more inspiration can flow.

## Where will your inspirations lead you?

Your soul language will not lead you astray. Your inspirations exist to help you unfold in your life. Maybe they will lead you into learning, or maybe into contribution to your life or someone else's life. Maybe inspiration leads you into a challenge that you need to experience in order to unlock something valuable inside of yourself, to help you evolve. Maybe it will lead you into greater external success and financial abundance, better health or new relationships.

What you can rely upon is that if your soul speaks to you, then you need to listen. Wherever it will lead you is part of your unfolding soul journey.

## Following Your Intuition

Intuition is called many things including inner knowing, inner voice and instinct. These are all the same thing. It is a knowingness that goes well beyond your mind. It is not rational or analytical thinking. It is not thinking period. It is your soul speaking through you with feeling.

Intuition can often feel like a leaning toward something, an inclination to be, do or move in a certain way or direction. Or, it may feel like a nagging within, asking you to pay attention to, or act upon, something. You have the ability to push your mind to the back burner and *feel* the best option before you.

At times your intuition may feel like it defies logic. It won't necessarily line up to what your mind tells you is best or true. In most cases, especially if the fog of your mind has previously trapped you, this can be a good thing. Remember, your soul is the master, and your mind is a servant, not the other way around. Your intuitive knowing is equally if not more important than what goes on in your mind.

## Why does your soul speak to you through intuition?

The intuition feeling arising within allows you to *sense* your way forward with whatever situation you face, with any decision you make or whatever path you take. Your soul is feeding you wisdom from the most expansive view, beyond the narrow perspective of your mind, to help you navigate effectively.

## Why must you listen to your intuition?

You are soul, mind and body. If you navigate life with your mind alone, you are not harnessing the fullness of your navigational capabilities. Your mind cannot conceive of all possibilities and does not have access to all the wisdom that is available to you.

Being mind-driven is like being in a maze with high walls all around you blocking your view of all available paths. From that narrow perspective, you still try to navigate your way out of the maze toward your destination in the most effective way; however, from where you stand, you simply can't see the most expedient and efficient way to get from where you are now to where you want to go. You operate blind to the bigger picture.

Imagine that your soul and the wisdom of highest consciousness hover above the maze in a helicopter, able to look down and clearly see all the paths and possibilities, and how you can best move forward with the least amount of effort and stress. Your soul seeks to give you that guidance through intuition feeling, so that down in the maze of your life, from the perspective of your thinking mind alone, you can make optimal moves for the unfolding of your soul journey.

Intuition is not necessarily about navigating out of a problem or confusion, or figuring your way through a "maze" in life but rather it is your navigational tool into learning, contribution, better health, new relationships, career and business advancement, greater prosperity and new possibilities that best serve you holistically.

Once you realize there is a higher perspective to your life, and you can't tap into it with your thinking mind alone, you will likely feel compelled to tap into it through your intuition.

## What stops you from listening to and acting upon your intuition?

What stops you from listening to your intuition, and what led you to ignore it in the first place, is that you don't trust it. You don't want to trust a subtle sense, as you are used to trusting fact, evidence, opinions and the advice of others, all over and above your own feelings of intuition.

It was easy in the past, from within the fog, to claim that feelings weren't valid, and that they shouldn't be elevated above more familiar and supposedly reliable decision-making tools like rational thinking. But clear of the fog, this is no longer the case for you.

## How can you tune into and harness your intuition?

Noticing your intuition requires presence, simply being in the present moment with awareness. Once you notice your intuitive knowing, then it is a case of acting upon that with trust and faith. If you don't trust it, then the best thing you can do is actually give yourself permission to act upon it a few times as an experiment, and witness the results. The results will build your confidence in your intuition.

Start to utilize your intuition now:

- If you are facing any type of decision in your life, big or small, write down everything that your mind has been telling you about it—questions, possibilities, scenarios, pros, cons, concerns, worries and fears.
- Now close your eyes and sit quietly while holding the decision point in your mind. Allow yourself to fully focus on feeling, rather than thinking. Do this for at least five minutes. When you open your eyes, write down what you feel—notice what insights you've had, what nudges you felt, what the nagging sense within you says.
- Does your head say one thing and your heart another? Meaning, is your thinking mind scanning for the best solution based on a narrow factual perspective while your intuition sings out for a different path?

- What decision would you make if you were trusting and confident in your inner voice?
- What decision would you make if you had no fear?

## Where will your intuition lead you?

Intuition leads you in the best possible direction for your life, no matter how seemingly insignificant the point of intuition is. Your intuition is never wrong. You will still face challenges as they are inherent to your life experience, and while life may not pan out exactly as your thinking mind plotted that it would, remember that you are always getting the exact experience your soul needs when it needs it.

## Creating Your Personal *Unleash Your Life* Action Plan

Part of unleashing your life means to have a clear vision for your life and to act upon that vision with inspired action. It's time to establish what that vision is, and what those actions are, by crafting your own *Unleash Your Life* Action Plan.

Your action plan sets the scene for how you will operate moving forward. You will feed your passions, inspirations and intuitive nudges directly into this plan—to formulate actions that are in complete alignment with your soul.

Here is what we will cover and what you will include in your *Unleash Your Life* Action Plan:

- Your values
- Your life anchors
- A map of the life you want to live, broken down into eight core life areas
- A prioritized list of actions, leading you to create and blossom into that life you want to live

To download your free copy of a simple *Unleash Your Life* Action Plan template, please visit: www.PinchMeLiving.com/Unleash-Your-Life-Free-Resources

## Defining Your Values

When you stop living your life in alignment with the fog, you can instead live it in alignment with your own values. You may not have taken pause to consider what your values are, or you may know your values but not yet be living fully in alignment with them.

No matter what you do in life, if you do not live in alignment with your values, you will feel uneasy. Inner peace is not possible when you ignore your values. A sense of freedom is also not possible when you sidestep your values to fit a situation or appease other people. True success in the New World means knowing your values, standing for your values and imbuing all your words and actions with those values.

Values are your chosen standards or principals, of what is most important to you regarding human behavior, personal conduct and the way in which you live your life. You might refer to them as ethical or moral guides. Your values underpin the tapestry of your life experience; they transcend any particular situation, outcome or interaction. They align to your positive new empowering beliefs, and they motivate you from the core of your soul flowing out into the world. This means they resonate deeply with you and are emotionally compelling. Your values are also the basis from which you commonly measure (consciously or unconsciously) other people's behavior and the way in which you weigh options for your own behavior.

Your values will not be the same as someone else's values. No one else gets to say what your values are. You get to choose your own values, and you get to exercise freewill in living those values. The living of your values will lift you up, energize you and lead you to a true sense of inside out freedom, no matter what your circumstances are.

Write down answers to the following questions to help you brainstorm what your values are:

- What standards of behavior do I want to live by?

- What is most important to me about the way I live my life, in how I carry myself through my daily interactions?
- What characteristics or traits in other people do I most admire and value?
- What do I want other people to say about my nature?
- If I have or could imagine having children, what traits would I want to role model for them, and to have them to embody in their own lives?
- In relationships, what traits, morals and standards do I look for, appreciate and need in other people?
- If I could invite every person in the world to behave in certain ways that I think would make this planet a happier, more peaceful place for the thriving of everyone, what would those behaviors be?

If you struggle to answer the above questions, below is a list of example values. This list is by no means complete, but rather a prompt to help you brainstorm your own values list:

trust, loyalty, acceptance, allowing, awareness, patience, faith, belief, love, wisdom, courage, integrity, authenticity, compassion, cooperation, collaboration, empathy, honesty, respect, calmness, diligence, dedication, flair, fun, individuality, generosity, kindness, gratitude, boldness, ambition, wholeheartedness, maturity, joyfulness, oneness, lightheartedness, self-expression, adventure, commitment, balance, stability, tolerance, understanding, resilience, justice, humility, appreciation, accountability, responsibility, reliability, peace, open-mindedness, adaptability, sustainability, equality, freedom, humor, harmony, positivity, perseverance, quality, simplicity, truth, well-being

Look through your answers to the above questions and identify the values they hold. Compose a succinct list of values, along with any additional values from the example list above that strongly resonate with you. If you have a long list of values, consider prioritizing the list with those that are most important to you at the top. For each value, write a short description next to it regarding *why* it is important to you.

This newly defined set of values is the first section of your *Unleash Your Life* Action Plan.

You can now use your defined values as a guide in your life, aligning your behavior to your values, to help you authentically navigate day to day. You can refer back to these values anytime you face challenges or feel uneasy about how you might manage a situation or circumstance, to help you stay true to what is meaningful and important to you.

## Defining Your Life Anchors

Whereas values are principals you hold and live from, life anchors are consciously selected and recurring things you do and experiences you have, which form the foundation of your day-to-day *lifestyle* in order for you to be as healthy, balanced and peaceful as possible, irrespective of what is going on around you in your life. Life anchors secure you to a sense of inner stillness in this busy and noisy external world we live in, by inviting you to take pause. When life becomes chaotic and stormy, they tie you to what is real and important by keeping you present, focused and in perspective. And, they keep you grounded when you might otherwise get lost in your head or consumed by your ego, thus helping you to avoid becoming disconnected from your values and soul language.

Life anchors can be considered rituals. Rituals by their very nature are for frequent and repetitive use in your daily life to support your thriving. They are not just go-to activities when you are feeling depleted, exhausted and at your wit's end. If you focus on ritualistic living day to day, anchoring yourself by choice on a regular basis, then you will not end up in those depleted, exhausted states in the first place.

As things you do or experiences you have, life anchors help to either stimulate, or provide the conditions for experiencing, the much needed positive emotions within you of happiness, inner peace or love. They are reliable access points for you to experience those emotions or similar vibration emotions.

Yet, it is actually neither the anchor (the things you do or experiences you have), nor the resulting emotion that is truly key. It is the fact that the anchors and resulting emotions help you to remember the core of who you really are, and connect you to the deeper meaning of your life.

Life anchors commonly include, but are not limited to:

- Interaction with beloved family and friends
- Interaction with beloved pets
- Interaction with nature
- Activities, experiences or rituals that support physical health, fitness, relaxation and stress relief
- Activities, experiences or rituals that support a calming and quieting of the mind and promote presence
- Activities, experiences or rituals that support a balancing of the emotional state
- Activities, experiences or rituals that allow for self-expression, giving life to passions

The issue many people face is that they don't know what their life anchors are, and/or they do not prioritize their life anchors. Your life anchors need to be the foundation of your life experience; they need you to give them time, focus and energy so that you can derive the most benefit from them. If you prioritize your life anchors, they will offer you healing at the physical, mental and emotional levels. They nourish your soul, and they refuel, replenish and energize you regularly so that you are ready to give your full self to life. Remember that life is a process of expansion to express and contraction to refuel. You need time off or "anchor time" as a contrast to the busyness and demands of life, in order to refuel.

Many people live life out of order, giving most of their time, focus and energy to non-priorities, and reverting to their life anchors in desperation, to recoup a sense of meaning and balance, instead of prioritizing their life anchors and letting those fuel them for all the other endeavors and commitments in their life.

You might be choosing an overcommitment to work above family or other key relationships. You might be choosing addiction (food, alcohol or drugs) over health. You might be defaulting to mindless, numbing pastimes over your passions. When I say, "choosing," what I really mean is not consciously choosing, but defaulting—habitually or accidentally swaying too far, away from your anchors. No one in his or her right mind would consciously, happily, wholeheartedly and passionately choose, on purpose, to create an imbalanced life where, from a bigger picture perspective, less meaningful things take priority over life anchors.

Begin now to consider what your life *currently* revolves around, even if unconsciously:

- What are you giving most of your time and/or energy to? Does it uplift you? Is it creating balance or imbalance in your life?
- Who are you giving most of your time and/or energy to? Do they uplift you in any way? Is that creating balance or imbalance in your life?
- Is your general daily and weekly routine centered on activities and experiences that you deem to be at all negative, limiting, draining and/or not your preference? If yes, what are they and why are you engaging in them?
- Do you find yourself going for long periods of time feeling depleted and out of balance, holding out for a chance to regain a sense of meaning and control in your life?
- Is your general daily and weekly routine anchored around activities and experiences that you deem to be positive, uplifting and aligned to your preferred reality? If yes, what are they?
- Do you feel refueled, revitalized, rejuvenated and energized on a regular basis?
- Do you feel balanced or imbalanced physically?
- Do you feel balanced or imbalanced mentally?
- Do you feel balanced or imbalanced emotionally?

It may be that you are already orienting your daily and weekly routine around your life anchors. Alternatively, it may be that adjustments need to be made.

Now, using the questions below, begin to define what your consciously chosen life anchors are. Use your intuition to sense what will anchor you, and how often you need to be engaged with that life anchor in order for it to be beneficial for you, meaning it is able to do its job of grounding and balancing you.

Each person is unique and faces different life circumstances, challenges and demands. Each person has a different physical, mental and emotional constitution, and therefore a different combination of what is needed in order to feel balanced. So your anchors, their place in your priority list and the frequency you engage with them, will be completely and utterly unique to you.

- Who are your most loved family members?
- How do you like to interact with those loved family members?
- How often would you ideally like to be seeing them, speaking to them or engaging with them in some way?
- Who are your most cherished friends?
- How do you like to interact with those friends?
- How often would you like to be in connection with these companions?
- What beloved pets do you have?
- How do you like to spend time with those pets?
- How often are you able to engage with these creatures that love you unconditionally?
- In what ways do you enjoy interacting with nature?
- Where do you currently like to go to be in nature, or where do you think you might like to go to be in nature?
- How often would you like to be in nature as a healthy balance to the other aspects and environments of your life?
- What physical fitness activities do you find enjoyable and/or nourishing for your health, or what new physical fitness activities do you feel drawn to take up to support your health?

- How often do you need to be engaged in physical fitness activities to ensure you honor your body to keep in balance?
- What health rituals of any nature do you know of that uplift you and care for your physical body? Consider what you choose to consume, what you do, any health practitioners you visit, or health information you listen to or read about to support your well-being.
- How often do you sense you need to be doing those things in order to feel at your optimum?
- What positive activities and experiences do you find are most relaxing?
- What positive activities and experiences do you find most conducive to stress relief?
- What types of new activities and experiences do you feel drawn to incorporating into your life as possible relaxation and stress relief support?
- How often do you need to proactively engage in those relaxation and stress relief activities and experiences in order to keep balanced?
- What have you noticed is most calming to your state of mind, quieting your thoughts and bringing you a sense of inner peace?
- What positive activities and experiences make you feel most free and in the "now" moment, where you forget about the past and the future and are able to enjoy the vitality of yourself and your life in the present?
- How often do you feel you need to be engaged in those mind-calming and presence-promoting rituals in order to ensure you maintain a grounded, healthy day-to-day life experience?
- What do you find the most balancing for your emotional state in terms of what helps you feel calm and/or uplifted?
- How often do you sense you need to be caring for your emotional state in that way in order to remain balanced?
- What hobbies, pastimes, interests and curiosities do you love to engage in?

- What activities and experiences make you feel most passionate and self-expressed, and bring you a sense of joy and happiness when immersed in them?
- How often do you sense you need to be engaged in those types of passion-led activities and experiences in order to feel fully self-expressed?

Your answers are your life anchors.

While all of them are important and valuable, some are more critical to you than others. As you only have so much physical, mental and emotional energy in any given day and week, and you also have a busy life with many commitments to attend to, you have to make choices about where and how to expend your energy in order to live a happy, healthy, balanced and fulfilled life.

Right now, noticing whatever imbalance you are experiencing in life, and intuitively sensing what is most important for your well-being at present, you can prioritize your life anchors from most critical to least critical. This order of priority may shift and evolve over time as the seasons of your life change.

Consciously choose, prioritize and create space in your routine for these life anchors. They play an invaluable role in keeping you connected to your true self and the deeper meaning in your life. They can only serve you if you let them.

You don't need your life anchors to take up all your time or resources. You don't need to make your entire life about your anchors. You do, however, need your life anchors to be just that ... anchors that form the foundation and focal point around which the rest of your life dances. Most often when people get busy and overwhelmed, their life anchors are the first things they let go of. If you turn *away* from them, you put yourself on a pathway to imbalance. An unanchored boat in a stormy sea gets battered. Instead, when you get busy and overwhelmed, turn *toward* your anchors. With anchors solidly in place, they will help to steady you.

Write down your prioritized list of life anchors as the second section of your *Unleash Your Life* Action Plan.

## 9 Recommended Holistic Well-being Rituals

Having completed the life anchors exercise, you may still feel unsure about what rituals, activities or experiences you want to use to anchor yourself, or you might want to introduce additional rituals to enhance the current life anchors you do have.

Here are nine types of rituals that you can choose to incorporate into your life if you wish, specifically designed to holistically support physical, mental and emotional well-being.

### Presence Rituals

An effective way to immerse yourself in the present moment, instead of being immersed in your mind, is through physical sensation. When you place your attention on and in your body, you are able to tune out the noise in your mind momentarily. This may only happen for fleeting seconds initially, but the more you practice the more you widen that moment of presence.

Pick only one of the following four physical sensations to practice with at a time, to give your full focus to that one part of yourself. This can be a daily practice, for as little as five minutes, to begin or end your day:

**1) Hearing**—Close your eyes and tune into your hearing sense. Focus on all the different sounds that you receive. Notice the layers of sound—near, distant, loud, quiet, nature sounds, wind, animals, people, vehicles and machines. Notice how you fully receive the present when you observe sound so consciously in this way.

**2) Sight**—Tune into what you see around you. Focus on all the different objects, colors, textures and contrasts that you perceive. Notice the vibrancy, the miracles of shape, form and life in both animate and inanimate objects. Notice how you fully receive the present when you observe your environment so consciously in this way.

**3) Breathing**—Close your eyes and tune into your breathing. Focus on the air flowing in through your nose, down into your lungs, and follow it back out of your body as you exhale. Notice the life-giving quality of the air you breathe, and notice how your entire physical presence is supported by this breathing process. Notice how you fully receive the present when you consciously breathe in this way.

**4) Inner energy**—Close your eyes and tune into the sense of aliveness within your body. Your heart is beating, your blood is pumping, and there is energy within each part of your body that can be felt as a gentle, tingling and alive sensation. Put your full focus on your hands or your feet. Sense the subtle energy feeling in those body parts. Notice how you fully receive the present when you consciously tune into your inner energy in this way.

## Conscious Breathing Rituals

You don't need to be consciously aware to breathe. It already happens as an instinctive process. However, there is a vital difference between ordinary, unconscious, instinctive breathing and what we will call conscious breathing.

Conscious breathing means to choose with your awareness to focus all of your attention on your breathing and to breathe in particular ways—consciously controlling, deepening and lengthening your breath, to support your holistic well-being.

Most people spend their day-to-day life in shallow breath. This means short breath cycles, which do not fully tap the power of their breathing capacity. One of the results of short and shallow breathing is that you feel trapped in your ribcage, experiencing a sense of tightness, restriction, limitation and tension in your torso. This leads to feeling less vitality in your body.

What is most important to understand about breathing is that you are utilizing both your lungs and your diaphragm in each breath. Your diaphragm is the muscle located between the chest cavity and abdominal cavity. As air enters your lungs, your diaphragm contracts, and your belly gently rises. As air exits your lungs, your diaphragm relaxes and your belly gently falls. With the sensation of shallow breathing, you do not exercise the full capacity and power of your lungs and diaphragm, to give you the most empowered breathing experience. What it *feels* like, but what you may not notice without conscious attention, is that you are using the top half of your torso to breathe, rather than using your entire chest and abdominal area.

Conscious breathing is about utilizing both your lungs and your diaphragm in their fullness, in order to maximize the benefits of each breath. This is known as deep breathing, diaphragmatic breathing, abdominal breathing or belly breathing. The focus is on relaxing your abdomen and letting your belly rise and fall with the movement of your breath. If you pay close attention to the subtle movement of your body as the air moves into your lungs, you will notice your belly expand first, then your lower rib cage and then your upper chest—the fullness of one breath is like a balloon being inflated from down in your abdomen up to the top of your lungs. If you've ever watched a baby breathing, you will notice this belly rise and fall motion occur naturally. You can practice conscious breathing at any time, to take you back to that optimal, natural state.

There are many benefits of conscious breathing, including optimizing various body functions for physical health. One powerful benefit for holistic physical, mental and emotional support is that conscious breathing triggers the brain/body to switch into relaxation response mode (instead of fight or flight response), which makes conscious breathing highly effective for countering the effects of stress, fear and anxiety.

Here are seven different ways you can practice conscious breathing in your daily life, many of which are common yoga breathing practices. To begin with, pick one to master, and then enjoy exploring the others for variety and fun. Practice for at least five minutes every day.

**1) Standard belly breathing**—Standing, sitting or lying flat on your back, place both your hands gently on your belly so that you can easily feel your belly moving. Relax your belly. You may practice this with eyes open or eyes closed. Close your mouth and inhale through your nose slowly and deeply; allow your belly to gently rise as you do so. Exhale through your nose slowly and deeply; allow your belly to gently fall as you do so. You can breathe this way for as long you wish to bring yourself to a state of physical relaxation, mental and emotional calm, and even a sense of overall vitality. The beauty of belly breathing is that you can do it anywhere, any time. It is an always accessible, effective and reliable tool to employ whenever you feel negative emotions.

**2) Lengthening breathing**—Utilizing the standard belly breathing technique above, once you feel comfortable with the natural motion of your belly rising and falling, focus now on inhaling slowly and deeply to the count of three, and exhaling slowly and deeply to the count of three. Repeat this ten times. Next, focus on inhaling slowly and deeply to the count of four, and exhaling slowly and deeply to the count of four. Repeat this ten times. Then, focus on inhaling slowly and deeply to the count of five, and exhaling slowly and deeply to the count of five. Repeat this ten times. Finally, focus on inhaling slowly and deeply to the count of six, and exhaling slowly and deeply to the count of six. If you wish to make this a more meditative practice, you can close your eyes while breathing and counting. However, you can effectively practice this lengthening breathing in any environment, at any time.

**3) Ocean breathing**—Utilizing the standard belly breathing technique, focus on drawing the air against the back of your nasal cavity and throat along the airway into the lungs as you slowly and deeply inhale and exhale, to make a noticeable sound as you breathe. It is the sound you might imagine hearing if you put a seashell to your ear, hence the name ocean breathing. It is also the sound you might imagine hearing from someone who is breathing loudly while asleep. As you relax your belly, letting it rise and fall with your inhales and exhales, place all of your attention on the sound of your breathing. This can be a meditative practice with your eyes closed.

**4) Countdown breathing**—Utilizing the standard belly breathing technique, focus on counting your breathing, starting at one hundred, counting down to one. Each inhale is one count, each exhale is one count. Breathe in one hundred, breathe out ninety-nine, breathe in ninety-eight, breathe out ninety-seven, breathe in ninety-six, breathe out ninety-five and so on. This is a meditative practice best done with your eyes closed, either lying flat or sitting. The counting allows you to keep your mind focused, and the challenge of counting backwards keeps your attention keenly on your mind/body connection.

**5) Energizing breathing**—This technique is energizing and relieves tension, and is best practiced in a seated position. Sit up straight, place your hands in your lap and close your mouth to begin. Completely relax your belly so that it naturally rises and falls in sync with your breathing. Your inward breath will be four short, sharp inhales through the nose, and your outward breath will be one long, loud and empowered "ha" sounding breath out of your mouth to empty your lungs. This can be practiced for whatever length of time feels comfortable. You may notice yourself feeling light-headed with the increased oxygen from short, sharp, consecutive inhales. You can stop the breathing at any time if you feel dizzy, and remain sitting in a relaxed seated position until that sensation dissipates. Do not practice this technique if you already feel light-headed, nor if you have any health conditions that may be adversely affected by it.

**6) Alternate nostril breathing**—This technique is best practiced sitting. Rest your left hand on your left upper leg, and raise your right hand up to your forehead. Place the tips of both your index and middle fingers together between your eyebrows. Now rest your thumb on your right nostril, and rest both your ring and little fingers on your left nostril. You will use these fingers to open and close the nostrils during this breathing technique, keeping your mouth closed the entire time. To begin, press your thumb down on your right nostril to close it and exhale fully out of your left nostril. Inhale slowly and deeply through your left nostril, and at the peak of your inhale press your ring and little finger down on the left nostril to close it and release your thumb from the right nostril, then exhale out slowly and deeply through the right nostril. Now, inhale slowly and deeply through your right nostril, and at the peak of your inhale press your thumb down on the right nostril to close it and release your ring and little finger from the left nostril, then exhale out slowly and deeply through the left nostril. Repeat this process, breathing out and in one nostril, and then switching to breathe out and in the alternate nostril. Whenever you exhale out one nostril, you always inhale through that same nostril, before switching. This technique, once you are familiar with the instructions, is best practiced with your eyes closed.

7) **Mantra breathing**—Utilizing the standard belly breathing technique, your conscious awareness can be placed on a life-affirming and empowering mantra. You may wish to create a mantra from the affirmations provided in Part II of this book. Write down two short, simple and positive statements that reinforce the way you want to feel. For example, "I am relaxed" and "I am confident." As you inhale through your nose, silently state your first affirmation to yourself. As you exhale through your nose, silently state your second affirmation to yourself. For example, breathe in "I am relaxed" and breathe out "I am confident." Repeat this over and over again for as long as you wish. This connects soul, mind and body.

## Meditation Rituals

Meditation is any technique that supports you to reduce, slow or quiet the thoughts that automatically run through your mind.

Meditation is not about eradicating thinking completely, but rather a practice to create and benefit from small gaps in that incessant thinking we are prone to. Those small gaps can literally be fleeting seconds, or perhaps longer periods with practice.

In those small gaps of "no thinking," you access a sense of inner peace because you get momentary relief from the automatic thoughts in your mind. In those small gaps you also have a direct experience of your true nature—because your conscious awareness and soul essence is always there beyond thoughts, but not always experienced by you because of the noise in your mind.

Meditation comes in many, varied forms. There is no one type of meditation, or right way to do it. There are meditations practiced across countries, cultures, faiths, religions and consciousness movements. Below are four types of simple meditation rituals. You can pick any one to practice. Even ten minutes on a daily basis, as a consistent ritual, will provide benefit.

Before you begin your practice, please understand that there is no optimal state of meditation you are trying to create. You are simply allowing this ritual to be a part of your daily life, and whatever you experience is what you experience. How you feel that day is how you feel. How active your mind is that day, is just what it is. If you enter each meditation with no expectation, other than a commitment to allow yourself this gift of practice and time away, you will be more open to receive whatever experience is available to you.

**1) Letting go meditation**—This meditation can be practiced seated or lying down. It is important that you are comfortable and that you are physically supported, in case you accidentally fall asleep. With your eyes closed, begin by taking five deep, cleansing breaths. Continue breathing gently and rhythmically throughout this meditation. Now focus all of your attention on the space between your eyebrows. In the quiet, stillness and darkness, train your mind to keep focused on that space. As each thought comes into your mind, it will feel like it has entered this space between your eyebrows. Notice the thought and immediately let it go by imagining it literally leaving the space. Return your focus to the space between your eyebrows. As another thought comes into your mind it will again feel like it has entered this space between your eyebrows. Notice it and immediately let it go by imagining it literally leaving the space. Return your focus to the space between your eyebrows. Continue to repeat this process for any thoughts that arise. Each time you return your focus to the space between your eyebrows, you will have a small space without thought.

**2) Breathing meditation**—This meditation can be practiced seated or lying down, but seated is optimal. With your eyes closed, you focus all of your attention on your breathing. You simply follow the air moving in and out of your body. Any time that thoughts arise and you notice yourself caught in the thinking, simply refocus your attention on witnessing your breath. The breath is what takes you away from the thinking. This will also support small moments without thought.

**3) Nature meditation**—This meditation is ideally practiced outdoors in nature, but can be practiced indoors with a live specimen of nature—a plant or an animal. You can be standing, seated or lying down. You will choose an aspect of nature to observe and with full alertness and eyes open, you will focus all of your attention on that part of nature. The reason this meditation is so powerful is because nature is alive with miraculous, uninterrupted, natural, positive energy just as highest consciousness created it to be—free flowing. You may choose to lie on the ground and observe the sky, sun, clouds, moon, stars or a tree canopy. You may choose to sit or stand while observing flowers, plants, trees, a river, an ocean, a pond, a lake, a stream or a waterfall. You may choose to observe an animal—a pet or wildlife. Take five conscious breaths, releasing any body tension with each exhale. Continue breathing peacefully, slowly and deeply. Relax your entire face, let go of tension in your forehead and jaw. Now soften your gaze by relaxing your eyelids and with that soft gaze focus all of your attention on your chosen aspect of nature and simply observe it. Observe its beauty—without analyzing it, without labeling it, without questioning it. Let yourself get lost in its wonder. Allow yourself to immerse into its positive, life-affirming and love vibration energy. In that immersion, you will again experience moments without thought.

**4) Guided meditation**—Another way to put yourself into a deep state of peace where your thinking mind gives over to moments of silence, is through meditation via guided visualization. There are many free audio resources available online, where you can listen to someone guide you into a relaxed physical, mental and emotional state, and during the guided meditation there may be periods of silence on the audio, which may allow you to experience a break from thinking. The gaps occur when the words you hear on the audio cease momentarily and your mind is left in silence awaiting the next instruction. To download such a free guided meditation audio, which will carry you into a deep state of peace and relaxation, followed by a one minute gap of silence, please visit: www.PinchMeLiving.com/Unleash-Your-Life-Free-Resources

### Affirmations Rituals

Just as physical substances can be toxic to your physical body, there is a toxicity to negative written words, negative spoken words, negative stories, negative news, negative media and negative visual imagery. All of this is an assault on your mental and emotional well-being, and can drastically affect you without your realizing it. If you are not consciously aware, you are like a sponge for the external stimulus around you.

It is entirely possible and incredibly empowering to reduce the amount of negative input you absorb on a day-to-day basis through conscious awareness of what you give your time and energy to—what you choose to watch, read or listen to. However, you are still living in an interconnected world with over seven billion people, a world filled with mixed energy and mixed messaging. Therefore you will never entirely eradicate negative external stimulus from your life. More importantly, you don't need to. Rather, once you have proactively minimized whatever toxic content you can from your life, there are two powerful ways in which you can strengthen your immunity to any remaining negativity that you may encounter.

Firstly, your conscious awareness to declare, "I am not a robot. I am awake to what I observe in the world around me. I do not take on board what I do not want and need. I choose not to absorb and buy into negativity that I witness. It does not belong to me."

Secondly, you can counterbalance any negativity that arises by proactively plugging in positive messaging. The easiest and most effective way to do this is with audio affirmations. In Part II you may have created a personalized audio of your own new, empowering beliefs as affirmation statements for listening to on a daily basis. If not, you can download several free audios containing a total of over seven hundred uplifting positive affirmation statements by visiting: www.PinchMeLiving.com/Unleash-Your-Life-Free-Resources

There are two particularly vital times of the day when listening to positive affirmations as a ritual will make a radical difference to your mental and emotional state—early morning when you first rouse out of deep sleep, and at night just before you go to sleep.

**1) Morning: Wake with wonder**—When you first wake in the morning, before your eyes are open and you are fully alert, your sleep state gives way to your thinking mind. When this transition occurs, your mind begins its busy job of automatic thinking. For many people, when that transition occurs, the nature of the thoughts running through their mind is negative. This is often when fear-based thoughts arise, when most past moment recollection and future moment projection takes place. Many people will spend this transition period, before being fully alert and ready to get up, unconsciously ensnared in plotting, planning, worrying and strategizing about what has happened or what is about to happen. Given that you are technically awake and able to have full-blown emotional reactions to these thoughts, but not fully alert in terms of actively interrupting unwanted thoughts with your conscious awareness, you are incredibly receptive to their negativity. That low vibration energy takes over your mental and emotional state before you have even gotten out of bed. That energy then sets the tone for the coming day. This waking transition is, therefore, an important period of time to receive positive messaging. Your task is to own your mind and interrupt this negative process before it takes a hold of you. A ritual you can use, based on affirmations, is called "Wake with Wonder." This ritual simply requires that the moment you come into conscious awareness out of the sleep state, even if you are lying in bed with your eyes still closed, you start repeating positive statements to yourself over and over again. You can use any affirmations that you conjure up on the spot. Your positive beliefs are excellent statements to use as this further embeds them as your new paradigm. Alternatively, you can have an audio of general positive affirmations next to your bed and start playing them as soon as you wake.

**2) Evening: Feed your sleeping self**—When you go to bed at night, a shift takes place again, in reverse this time. You transition out of your busy thinking mind and into deep sleep when another aspect of mind is most alert—your subconscious mind. What you most need to understand about your subconscious mind is that it is open to suggestion and obedient to instruction. It is incredibly receptive to whatever messages you give it. It plays an important role in the acceptance and ingraining of any form of messages, including affirmations. The issue that many people face is that when they lay down in bed it is their first moment of stillness and quiet that they have experienced all day, and as they settle in for sleep, their thinking minds become quite active in drifting off to replay things that didn't go well during the day and dwelling on concerns about the next day. Then, with that negative mental and emotional state in place, you drift into sleep and the transition occurs, from alert and awake with your busy thinking mind focused on all that negativity, into sleep state where your receptive subconscious soaks up whatever you were thinking about just before going to sleep. Your subconscious then feeds on and swirls in that negative energy throughout the night as you sleep. A powerful ritual to address this is called "Feed Your Sleeping Self," where you proactively plug in positive messages in the five minutes before going to sleep. You can either say positive messages to yourself before going to bed, or you can listen to affirmations before sleep or literally while going to sleep.

## Self-Celebration Ritual

It's all too easy to be your own toughest critic, focusing on the areas in your life that you want to change, or the parts of yourself you want to evolve beyond. That can be a healthy, reflective and progressive attitude, but it easily borders on self-flagellation.

To counter this, you can put your focus squarely on your strengths, achievements, positive traits and growth to date, as a self-celebration ritual. This involves either writing a list, or creatively mapping with color, words and images, all that there is to celebrate about you. Focus on your entire life, from childhood to the present day, or focus on this year, this month, or the past week.

Include what there is to celebrate about your inner self, followed by what there is to celebrate about your contribution outwardly. This is a refreshing reminder of how wondrous you are, and how much there is to love about yourself, regardless of what else you want to progress with on your internal and external journey.

This ritual is helpful to revisit if you notice unease, lack of confidence, low self-esteem or doubt creep in. It is also an empowering exercise to do with the changing of the seasons, at the end of the year, start of a new year, or on your birthday.

## Gratitude Ritual

There are multiple benefits for you when you express gratitude. It places all of your attention on the good in others, the good in the world, the beauty of life and the blessings you already have. That shift in awareness automatically creates positive thoughts and feelings. You lift your energy vibration. You return to your natural state of love.

Having a ritual in place that puts you in a regular gratitude attitude also helps to keep your challenges in perspective. Often challenges take the limelight and suck up all your attention, such that you miss what is already working in your life at the expense of seeing all that is seemingly not working.

Gratitude as an energy is also a manifestation process, or prayer process, in that you tell the fabric of universal energy to which you belong, exactly what it is that you value, exactly what makes you feel great, and therefore exactly what you wish to experience more of or similar to.

Gratitude rituals can vary from verbal gratitude, meditative giving of thanks or journaling your thanks. If you live with other people, be it friends or family, you may like to introduce daily evening gratitude around the dinner table, where each person shares one gratitude from the day.

## Stillness Ritual

Your life is one of intense motion. You have many demands placed upon you and commitments to which you must attend. Every day you might be active from the moment you wake until the moment you sleep. In modern society across many cultures and countries, it is uncommon to have waking stillness for any length of time.

Stillness is powerful. Stillness in itself is like a meditation. You are awake, alert and you simply sit in complete stillness, observing and feeling life within you and around you. You allow yourself stillness in order to tune into the energy and aliveness of life.

Stillness can be practiced in silence and solitude, or it can be practiced in a busy and noisy environment, such as while waiting for a bus, train or flight, or during your lunch break at work. Even ten minutes practice on a daily basis will add immense value to your inner peace. Your entire focus in this ritual is just to be still. You can cease interacting, moving and talking, and simply be. In a world dominated by doing, this is a rare gift.

## Solitude Ritual

Most people spend their daily life in constant interaction with others, either in person or via technology. There are few, if any, days in a year when you could say you were in complete solitude. Being alone is a powerfully reflective ritual. Without the energy of other people to feed on, be drawn into, affected by or stimulated by, and without the constant interactive process of speaking, listening, absorbing and being in action, you are left with nothing to do but simply be.

In modern society, many people are completely overstimulated, which causes their minds to operate on high speed, and it makes it even more challenging for them to be present and peaceful. Being completely alone means you cease the incessant stimulation and allow yourself to rebalance. No noise, no people, no media, no social media, no technology or external stimulation of any nature, period. Just you and your environment. A solitude ritual does not need to be a huge commitment; even one hour of solitude makes a refreshing difference to how you feel.

## Pampering Ritual

With all that you do in your life for other people, be it delivering upon your work commitments, or supporting your family and friends, it is critical that you take time to care for yourself for the joy of doing so. A pampering ritual allows you to do just that. This type of ritual is simply where you create and frequently engage in an activity/experience that supports your physical, mental and/or emotional well-being, *and* sparks joy within you. Ideally it would be at least once a fortnight, preferably weekly, and the type of pampering activity/experience will be something you naturally feel drawn to.

A pampering ritual may be a bubble bath with a candle lit and your favorite music playing. Or, it may be going to the market to buy fresh produce and make your favorite green juice/smoothie to nourish yourself. A pampering ritual may be having fresh herbal tea, using your favorite teapot and teacup, and savoring aromatherapy while you drink your tea in the morning sun. It could be cutting fresh flowers from your garden, or purchasing some, putting them next to your favorite reading space in your home, and then reading your favorite type of book or magazine. Maybe it's going to yoga, walking or jogging, and then preparing your favorite type of nourishing meal, made with love to refuel yourself.

### Your Life Map—The Life You Want to Live

We have already established the first two, and most important, inclusions for your *Unleash Your Life* Action Plan—your values (the principles that guide you) and your life anchors (activities, experiences and rituals you require as the foundation of your life in order for you to be healthy, happy and balanced). Everything else you desire to be, do and have in your life is built upon this existing clarity.

Now you are going to begin literally mapping out a clear vision of the life you want to live, bringing it out of your imagination into tangible form as a Life Map, with your values and life anchors solidly underpinning everything. The Life Map is the third section of your *Unleash Your Life* Action Plan.

You may choose to create your Life Map on sheets of paper, on a large canvas or vision board, on the computer or in a writing journal. You might enjoy using sticky Post-it notes that you can write on and attach to a board, which you can move around as you plot out your ideal life experience. This is a fun and creative brainstorming activity, so give yourself permission to play with it—use colored pens and paper if you wish. If you are a visual person, you may enjoy printing out images, or cutting out pictures from magazines and newspapers that inspire you, for including in your Life Map.

You will need to set up your Life Map with eight segments or eight lists, one for each of the eight areas of life, as outlined below. If you wish to add other areas of life, do whatever resonates most with you. This is simply a guide as a beginning structure for you to work from. Please allow your passion, inspiration and intuition to flow. There are no rules.

If you are unsure what format you want to use for your Life Map, you will find a simple template inside the overarching *Unleash Your Life* Action Plan template for free download at: www.PinchMeLiving.com/Unleash-Your-Life-Free-Resources

**1) Well-being**—Physical, mental and emotional health and well-being

**2) Soul**—Spirituality, faith, religion, rituals and customs

**3) Relationships**—Family, companionship, intimacy, friends, colleagues, acquaintances, community, networking, supporters, inspirers, mentors, advisors, experts and ... pets!

**4) Learning**—Education, professional development, training, personal growth, self-help, intellectual stimulation and mind expansion

**5) Career**—Job, profession, vocation, business, contribution, community engagement and voluntary activities

**6) Lifestyle**—Location, home environment, work environment, natural environment, vacations, travel and lifestyle choices

**7) Interests**—Activities, pastimes, hobbies and passions

**8) Resources**—Money, investments, assets and any other resources that support your life

## Tips for Creating Your Life Map

As you define the type of life you want to live, remember these tips to guide you:

- Be true to the values that you wrote down in the earlier exercise. Remember that inner peace is not possible in a sustainable way unless your actions, lifestyle and successes align to your values.
- Remember to make your life anchors the foundation of your Life Map. Take the anchors you identified in the earlier exercise and make them the first things you put into your Life Map (allocating them into the eight life areas) so that all the other aspects of the life you want to live will orient to those focal points. If you want to enrich your life anchors with additional rituals, you may like to select from the nine recommended holistic well-being rituals.
- Create this Life Map from the expansiveness of all possibility, not as a projection of what your mind thinks is attainable or not attainable based on your current circumstances. To support this ...
- Listen to and incorporate your soul language as you do this exercise. Your passion, inspiration and intuition will guide you to create a Life Map that truly speaks to the heart of what you most need and want in order to live a healthy, balanced and happy life.
- Remain aware of the fact that all success you want in life (inward and outward) is motivated by one thing—your desire to feel a certain way. At the root of everything you put in this new Life Map, will be the motivation to experience inner peace, happiness and/or love. You may have many other motivators as well, but underlying it all is this fundamental human need to experience these feelings.

- In this Life Map you can orient your vision around the type of day-to-day lifestyle you want to experience, or around specific projects, goals and milestones you want to achieve, or both.
- Some of the areas in your Life Map will cross over, depending on your unique situation. That is completely fine; it does not have to be black and white. For example, sport may be an interest, your preferred physical well-being activity, and your career. Or you may want to change career paths, and need to link your financial resources and your education areas together in order to support that path. Or you may be passionate about hiking as a pastime, and it feeds your physical, mental and emotional well-being, and puts you into nature, which is a key part of your lifestyle in terms of environments and energy you love to be in. Or you may love architecture and environmental sustainability, and you may have goals relating to these passions spanning across your education and career, as well as interests and lifestyle. You will start to see these threads weave together across all areas of your Life Map. Do not be concerned about which of the eight areas of the Life Map to write your goals and desires under; simply having them in the map is the key.
- You don't have to know exactly what your ideal life looks like. If you are not sure exactly what you want to create or do, it is completely fine to write in your Life Map *how you want to feel*. Just knowing the overall feeling, flow and sense of the life you desire is enough to open the co-creation pathways going forward, to invite into your life that which will align with your underlying motivator to feel a certain way.

Begin now to populate your Life Map, as the third section of your overall *Unleash Your Life* Action Plan. To support you in doing so, below is a list of questions designed to prompt you for each of the eight areas.

## General

- What passions do I have that need to be expressed?
- What inspired ideas have I had that need to be acted upon?
- What has my intuition been telling me I need to follow through with?
- What or who do I have in my life right now that I am 100 percent certain I don't want or need in my life any longer? With that available space and energy opening up, what else might be possible for me?
- What decisions do I know I need to make that I have been putting off?
- What actions am I currently taking in my life that I already know are NOT good for me?
- What am I certain I do need (more of, or new) in my life as soon as possible?
- What actions do I already know I need to be taking in my life that will make a positive difference?
- When I was a child or young adult, what sort of life did I dream of having?
- If all my current challenges were gone, and I had whatever resources I needed, what decisions would I make?
- What are my goals and dreams?

Notice your responses to these questions. Expand upon them. Brainstorm. Notice what lights you up. Allow yourself to imagine the possibilities that most inspire you. Feel what you intuitively know you most need and want your life to be like.

Now articulate that, being as specific as possible with clear vision, writing your answers into whichever areas of your Life Map are appropriate.

## Well-being

- Am I currently treating myself as a priority?
- Do I have dedicated time in my weekly schedule for reflection, quiet time, slow time, off-line time, alone time or time to just enjoy being without doing?
- Am I physically healthy?
- Am I physically fit and strong?
- What has my body been telling me that I need?
- What do I intuitively sense I need to do for my body in order to be energetic and vibrant? Where, how and from whom might I seek out information and support in this area?
- Do I like to do my fitness/exercise activities indoors or outdoors?
- What types of fitness, exercise, sport, solo or group physical activities do I most enjoy?
- What types of physical activities/exercise have I always wanted to try, or am I curious about?
- Do I need to make adjustments to my nutrition?
- Is my body getting the fuel and support it needs in order to carry me through life?
- Am I getting sufficient sleep? What could I do to improve my sleep patterns?
- Do I need the support of medical, health, healing or therapy practitioners, mainstream or alternative practices, for any aspect of my physical, mental or emotional well-being?
- Is there anything about my physical, mental or emotional well-being that I am resisting addressing or afraid to reach out for help with?
- What do I need to do for my mental and emotional well-being to be as present, calm, balanced and positive as possible? Where, how and from whom might I seek out information and support in this area?
- Am I interested in practicing any martial arts, tai chi, yoga or meditation to foster greater conscious awareness and to support present moment practice,

focus, discipline, empowered mind-set, and to improve my soul, mind and body connection?

- Am I feeding myself positive content to uplift my thoughts and feelings? If not, what could I do to address this?
- What negative messaging do I notice in my daily life that I am ready to cut out?
- Am I getting enough off-line time regularly, to turn my attention off of my work, commitments and challenges, allowing myself to rejuvenate and refuel?
- Am I practicing conscious breathing regularly? Is that something I sense could uplift me?
- Would I like to introduce daily or weekly rituals into my life that directly support my unique physical, mental and emotional well-being needs?
- What might those rituals be?
- Have I given up on myself in relation to any area of my holistic well-being? If so, what specifically have I given up on, and what actions do I know I could take right now to regain control, to feel empowered and to commence shifts in that area?
- What areas of my well-being am I most interested in better understanding? What intuitively would I like to research more about, read more about and empower myself to be accountable for?
- What goals and dreams do I have for my well-being?

Notice your responses to these questions. Expand upon them. Brainstorm. Notice what lights you up. Allow yourself to imagine the possibilities that most inspire you. Feel what you intuitively know you most need and want your life to be like in terms of well-being.

Now articulate the life you want in terms of well-being, being as specific as possible with clear vision. Write your answers into the well-being area of your Life Map.

## Soul

- What, if any, spiritual, faith or religious practices hold deep meaning for me and add value to my life?
- What spiritual, faith or religious practices intrigue me?
- Are there any ways in which I wish to experiment with or deepen my spirituality, faith or religion?
- Is spirituality, faith or religion a personal and private matter for me, or is it something I like to be outwardly expressive about or within a community for?
- Are there any people, groups, networks or information sources that I would like to connect with to explore spirituality, faith or religion further?
- Am I interested in supporting, contributing to, collaborating or sharing with others in my spiritual, faith or religious community and if so how might I do that?
- How, when, where and how often do I want to put my energy and focus specifically onto soul-based practices?
- How can I integrate my soul-based practices into my day-to-day life and routine in a way that lifts me up?
- When I feel most deflated and lost in terms of the deeper meaning of my life, in what ways could I practically use spiritual, faith-based or religious practices to reconnect me back to that deeper meaning?
- What goals and dreams do I have for living a soul-based life?

Notice your responses to these questions. Expand upon them. Brainstorm. Notice what lights you up. Allow yourself to imagine the possibilities that most inspire you. Feel what you intuitively know you most need and want your life to be like in terms of nourishing your soul.

Now articulate the life you want in terms of soul-based living, being as specific as possible with clear vision. Write your answers into the soul area of your Life Map.

## Relationships

- Who are my important family relationships with and, for each one of them, are those relationships healthy and happy?
- Who are my important friendships with and, for each one of them, are those relationships healthy and happy?
- Where do I need to be more giving and loving in those relationships?
- Who do I want to spend more time with or give more attention to?
- What relationships are toxic and dragging me down?
- Where do I need to set better boundaries in my current relationships?
- What conversations do I need to be having with people in my life in terms of making adjustments to relationships, to grow them or to pull myself back from them?
- What do I intuitively sense is possible in terms of healing challenging relationships in order to lift myself up?
- What relationships do I need to walk away from?
- Who are the people in my life that always leave me feeling great about myself and my possibilities?
- Who would I consider to be the supporters in my life?
- Who do I feel compelled to be supportive of in my network, personally or professionally?
- Who inspires me?
- What types of new relationships do I want to invite into my life?
- What type of people do I want to spend more time with? What might their traits, values and types of interests be? Where might I meet people like that?
- Am I putting myself into situations where I might meet new people, and am I being open-minded and open-hearted when in those situations in order to foster new connections forming?

- What mentors, leaders and trailblazers are there in my existing personal or professional network that I can align with and learn from?
- Where can I meet more inspirers, mentors and supportive people, personally or professionally? What type of people are they and where might they be spending their time?
- Do I love animals?
- Do I currently have pets or interact with animals as part of my daily life?
- Am I interested in being around the free-flowing energy and unconditional loving nature of animals more frequently?
- What goals and dreams do I have for myself in terms of relationships?

Notice your responses to these questions. Expand upon them. Brainstorm. Notice what lights you up. Allow yourself to imagine the possibilities that most inspire you. Feel what you intuitively know you most need and want your life to be like in terms of relationships.

Now articulate the life you want in terms of relationships, being as specific as possible with clear vision. Write your answers into the relationships area of your Life Map.

## Learning

- What do I most want to learn, discover, expand my knowledge in or absorb wisdom about?
- What am I curious about, compelled by and eager to explore?
- What type of formal education or specific professional development do I need in order to support my success in other areas of my life, including my career, profession, business, vocation, voluntary contribution or passions?
- What have I always wanted to attend classes in or improve my proficiency at, just for the fun and joy of it?

- Am I interested in expanding my understanding of, and personal competency in, soft skills such as communication, relationship management and issue resolution?
- Do I want to go back to school (of any nature) for formal education?
- Do I want to go to community classes, evening classes or experiment with informal methods of learning to explore my passions?
- What topics do I most love to talk about, listen to others talk about, or engage in conversation about?
- Would I like to informally and/or experientially learn, research, read or discuss in these topic areas further? How might I do that?
- Would it benefit me to have a mentor in my specific areas of interest in terms of furthering my learning, be it for my personal life or professional life? Where might I find a mentor like that, or who might know how I can connect with such mentors?
- What goals and dreams do I have for my learning?

Notice your responses to these questions. Expand upon them. Brainstorm. Notice what lights you up. Allow yourself to imagine the possibilities that most inspire you. Feel what you intuitively know you most need and want your life to be like in terms of learning.

Now articulate the life you want in terms of learning, being as specific as possible with clear vision. Write your answers into the learning area of your Life Map.

### Career

- Am I fulfilled in the work I am currently doing for myself or for other people?
- Am I growing, learning and feeling stimulated and creative in my current work?
- Do I enjoy the people I am surrounded by in my work environment?

- Does my physical environment at work sufficiently meet my physical, mental and emotional needs?
- If I could make any changes at all to my current work situation, what would those changes be?
- Do I need to slightly adjust the trajectory of my work, staying where I am but doing something slightly different?
- Do I want to continue doing the type of work I am doing, but in a better environment?
- Do I want a complete change of scene, a new challenge, a brand new path, and a brand-new environment?
- What type of tasks do I most enjoy doing?
- What are the competencies and skills that I can offer to any type of work I do?
- What type of people do I most enjoy working with?
- What difference do I want to make in this world?
- What industries, fields or professions have always intrigued me?
- What subject areas light me up?
- What environments make me feel most creative, alive, inspired and energized?
- Do I enjoy solving problems/creating solutions? If so, what types of problems/solutions and who would I be most interested in helping in that way?
- If there were specific jobs or businesses that I could do just for one day to see if I enjoyed it, or to shadow someone who has that type of job or business for a day, what would those jobs or businesses be?
- What did I used to dream of doing as a job/career when I grew up? Is there any spark left in that childhood dream?
- Irrespective of my current skills, experience and education, what is my dream job or business?
- Does the idea of self-employment appeal to me?
- If I ran my own business, what immediately comes to mind as a vision in terms of what that business might be and look like, and how my days might feel as a business owner?

- Do any of these words light a fire within me— entrepreneurial, creative, growth, start-up or new venture?
- Have I bought, or would I ever consider buying, an existing business, either independent or franchised?
- Have I or would I ever consider going into business with another like-minded person who complements my skill set?
- How would I like to contribute myself to the community, other people and the world?
- Might there be any volunteering that I would find fulfilling and meaningful, aligned to my natural passions?
- If I could imagine having the best day ever at work, what would it look like? Where am I? What happens? Who else is there? What am I doing? How do I feel?
- What goals and dreams do I have for my career?

Notice your responses to these questions. Expand upon them. Brainstorm. Notice what lights you up. Allow yourself to imagine the possibilities that most inspire you. Feel what you intuitively know you most need and want your life to be like in terms of career.

Now articulate the life you want in terms of career, being as specific as possible with clear vision. Write your answers into the career area of your Life Map.

### Lifestyle

- What types of environments do I most love to be in?
- What landscapes do I feel most comfortable in?
- What types of physical building environments do I most like to be in?
- What temperatures do I feel most at ease and vibrant in?
- What visual aesthetics make me feel happy and/or peaceful?

- What is the ideal type of ambience in an environment for me?
- Within the home I live in, what is important in terms of the environment to ensure it supports my health and happiness?
- Within the place I work, what is important in terms of the environment to ensure it supports my health and happiness?
- Do I love the outdoors?
- Do I enjoy being out and about, at home, or a balance of both?
- Do I enjoy being in quiet, natural or rural areas, or do I enjoy being in busy, built-up city areas, or a combination of both?
- In terms of what I use, see, hear, touch, taste, smell, feel, breathe, absorb, am stimulated by—do my current environments lift me up? If not, what adjustments do I want to make?
- Am I a morning person or a night owl? Is the way I live my life currently oriented well around those times of day when I am naturally at my peak of energy, vibrancy and creativity?
- Where do I want to live?
- Do I want to move?
- Where do I want to visit?
- When and where do I want to take vacations?
- What type of lifestyle choices do I want to make?
- Environmentally, socially, politically, physically, mentally, emotionally—what do I stand for? How do I reflect that in my current lifestyle choices?
- How do I want to role model my values in terms of my lifestyle?
- Does my current lifestyle primarily support or hinder me?
- Am I happy about and/or proud of my current lifestyle?
- If I could change anything about my current lifestyle, what would it be?

- Do I have the balance I want in my life? If not, what adjustments can I make to the various areas of my life in order to support a healthier overall lifestyle balance?
- If I could design my lifestyle from scratch, what would it be?
- What goals and dreams do I have for my lifestyle?

Notice your responses to these questions. Expand upon them. Brainstorm. Notice what lights you up. Allow yourself to imagine the possibilities that most inspire you. Feel what you intuitively know you most need and want your life to be like in terms of lifestyle.

Now articulate that lifestyle, being as specific as possible with clear vision. Write your answers into the lifestyle area of your Life Map.

## Interests

- What interests, activities, hobbies, pastimes, passions or projects do I enjoy or am I curious about?
- What did I used to love doing but have stopped? Why did I stop? Am I ready to start again?
- Do I want to increase my participation in or compete in any physical activity, sports, hobbies, creative endeavors or passion projects of any nature?
- Do I want to take up a new group or solo sport?
- Do I enjoy land-based activities, water-based activities and/or air-based activities? What specific activities under each category do I love or have I always wanted to try?
- What types of technology and entertainment engages me and helps me to feel alive, excited, inspired or relaxed?
- What events have I been thinking of attending?
- When I feel most magically carried away mentally and emotionally from my perceived problems, what is it that takes me there? What prompts me to go into my imagination, my sense of possibility and helps me to forget about any blocks/pain that I carry?

- What projects have I previously thought about starting?
- What is intellectually stimulating for me and provides a sense of challenge and expansion?
- Which of the following forms of external stimulation tends to spark the most positive emotions within me—spoken words, written words, static visual imagery, moving visual imagery, objects, music or other sound, light contrasts, ambience, smells or other forms of sensory experience?
- Do I like to build, fix, tinker with, invent, test, or experiment?
- What types of creative, craft or art activities, displays or opportunities do I feel drawn to?
- Am I a collector, curator or connoisseur of anything, or would I like to be? If so, in what area?
- Do I enjoy exploring, discovering, being spontaneous and adventurous, searching or researching?
- Do I enjoy games, real time or online, with myself or with other people, that allow me to navigate, strategize or compete?
- Am I interested in history, culture, fashion, reading, writing, arts, design, music, theatre, languages, cuisine, architecture or travel? If so, how might I further my interest in these areas?
- Am I interested in health, healing, fitness, sport, psychology, technology, business, politics, world affairs, science, self-help, spirituality, gardening, nature, social activism or environmental sustainability? If so, how might I further my interest in these areas?
- In my community, what would I love to get more involved with?
- In my community, do I notice any passions, insights or creative urges within me in terms of what needs to be done, what I could create or how I could contribute and where I could provide input, support, time, energy or leadership—for my own enjoyment and for the betterment of others?
- When alone, how do I best enjoy spending that time?

- When with other people, what types of activities do I most enjoy doing collaboratively?
- If I were not afraid, I knew I would not stumble, and I felt supported and comforted by someone I love by my side—what passions, interests, projects, pastimes or hobbies would I dive into?
- Do I realize that I can do those things without any help or support, by realizing that my passion is enough to carry me through?
- What goals and dreams do I have for a passion-led, interest-filled and satisfying life?

Notice your responses to these questions. Expand upon them. Brainstorm. Notice what lights you up. Allow yourself to imagine the possibilities that most inspire you. Feel what you intuitively know you most need and want your life to be like in terms of interests.

Now articulate those interests, being as specific as possible with clear vision. Write your answers into the interests area of your Life Map.

## Resources

- Am I currently making the most of my potential in terms of generating resources to support my life?
- Am I being fairly remunerated for the work I do or for the investments I have made?
- How might I leverage my time, skills, money, financial assets, intellect or intellectual property in different ways to generate more resources to support my goals and dreams?
- Do I know how to leverage my resources to live the life I desire? If not, am I willing to research or reach out for help from experts to help me do so?
- Am I managing my money effectively?
- Do I need to set or adjust my financial goals?
- Do I need to start or adjust my savings and/or investment plans?

- Am I properly managing my assets and investments, or do I need expert input?
- Do I need to review my spending habits and reflect on how those may or may not be supporting the other areas of my life?
- Do I need to set up a debt repayment plan?
- Am I currently spending beyond my means?
- Would I benefit from expert help in getting my finances in order?
- Am I afraid to reach out for help to get my resources (financial or otherwise) sorted out or leveraged?
- What abundance and wealth am I intending to create?
- What is my mind-set about resources?
- Is my desire for abundance and wealth reflected in the way I earn actively or passively, in the way I spend, in the way I save, in the way I invest and in the way I behave in relation to all my resources, including money?
- What goals and dreams do I have for the creation and management of resources to support my life?

Notice your responses to these questions. Expand upon them. Brainstorm. Notice what lights you up. Allow yourself to imagine the possibilities that most inspire you. Feel what you intuitively know you most need and want your life to be like in terms of resources.

Now articulate the life you want in terms of resources, being as specific as possible with clear vision. Write your answers into the resources area of your Life Map.

## Gap Identification

Having mapped the life you want to live in all eight areas, you are now invited to reflect upon your *current* circumstances, choices, actions and trajectory in life, and to contrast that to your new Life Map. By contrasting the two in this way, you will notice gaps—seeing exactly where your existing experience of life *does not* match up against what you have just mapped out as your preferred reality.

## Chart Your Actions to Close the Gaps

To have the life you want, you have to make adjustments—to align your choices, behavior, actions and trajectory in life with what you say you want, as detailed in your Life Map.

Essentially, you have to close the gaps you identified between what your experience is now and the experience you desire.

You do not need to be concerned about *all* the steps needed to close every gap, how to achieve every goal completely, or how to fully transition yourself from where you are now into the life you desire. You needn't be concerned if you do not currently have all the knowledge, resources or answers to take you forward into the fullness of your new Life Map.

Instead, you simply need to plot the *first phase* of action that you know is required to start the process, and then act in alignment with those initial steps. Your energy shift into higher vibration starts by living consciously from your New World paradigm, with your soul-driven beliefs steering you, choosing to practice presence, and deciding on this new Life Map as your preferred reality—even if only on paper to begin with. The act of reflecting upon the gaps and charting an initial course of action to close those gaps is a powerful shift forward. Most importantly, that is the exact energy and momentum that will give rise to:

- increased recognition of soul language (passion, inspiration and intuition)
- increased awareness of co-creative support—unseen helping hands, guidance, synchronicities, coincidences, what you need when you need it and divine signals
- answers to your existing questions flowing into your life, plus new questions arising from within, which guide you to seek new information that, in turn, unlocks new insights and expansion within you

All of the above help with the natural unfolding of your soul journey. If you feel any fear or hesitation, relax. It is completely normal. Remember that within the inherent uncertainty of life exists all possibility as well. To bring any wave of new possibility into your reality (for you to tangibly experience and enjoy it), you have to be willing to step beyond your comfort zone into unknown territory. Courageously having redefined your life, with clear vision and prepared to take inspired action, you are fulfilling your purpose—to be fully expressed, to learn and to contribute.

You are now going to detail an action plan, for each of the eight areas of your life, regarding what new behavior, choices and actions you need to make and take in order to commence the initial first phase shift to the life you want to live.

For every item you wrote in your Life Map, under all eight areas, now write a list of initial actions next to each one, actions that will start to close those gaps so that you can begin to experience the life you want to live. Below are questions designed to prompt you to consider what those actions might be:

- What needs adjusting?
- What needs resolving, cleaning up or completion?
- What actions are required?
- What will I stop doing?
- What will I start doing?
- What conversations need to be had?
- What extra information is needed?
- What research is required?
- Who do I need to contact?
- What support do I need?
- What commitments do I need to make?
- What commitments do I need to reevaluate?
- What questions do I need to answer for each action?
- What resources, if any, might I need for each action?

## Prioritizing and Effectively Managing Your Energy

Your Life Map *does not* represent a destination you are trying to get to. Instead, it depicts the consciously chosen and exciting journey you are on. A journey you wake each day to dive into with the fullness of who you are, giving 100 percent of yourself to each gifted moment of your life. The journey never ends. You are journeying until the moment you pass over at the end of this life. There is no rush. There is no race. This is not a sprint. This is not about getting away from where you are as quickly as possible. It is about the small moments of each day, relishing the ability to be the conscious creator that you are and knowing that those small moments are exactly where the miracle of your life exists ... now, not somewhere "out there" that you project in your mind as a place to get to. Your Life Map simply provides a structure to guide you to live your present moment in the most full, expressive and conscious way possible.

Your Life Map is a statement that you are not at the whim of life. It tells the universe you are a creative visionary, one who is consciously awake and part of the New World. It gives the co-creative intelligent energy to which you belong a clear indication of what you desire.

No matter how extensive and detailed your Life Map is and regardless of how many gaps exist between your current experience of life and the life you desire, the process to take you where you want to go is always the same:

- Make conscious choices day to day about where you expend your physical, mental and emotional energy; completely align your choices to your Life Map.
- Prioritize your actions, completely aligning them to your Life Map, focusing on the most important ones first.
- Take small steps consistently.
- Say yes to what serves you.
- Say no to what does not serve you.

For each required action that you wrote down, begin to reflect upon *when* that action is needed. Prioritize your actions for all eight areas of your life into:

1) Urgent (immediate)

2) Short-term (next three months)

3) Medium-term (three to twelve months)

4) Long-term (twelve or more months)

Simply write 1, 2, 3 or 4 next to each action item as an indication of their priority. Then circle every item that you marked as 1 (urgent) across all eight areas of your Life Map; the 1s are where your new journey begins.

## Remain Completely Open to how Life May Unfold

There is one vital thing to remember now that you have mapped a clear vision and a list of prioritized inspired actions. Pay close attention ... because this is vitally important.

Your Life Map is *representative* of the life you want to live. The way your life plays out may not be exactly as you envision. It can happen in even more expedient, magical, unexpected, surprising, powerful and joyous ways. You are motivated, ultimately, by your desire to feel a certain way—to feel happiness, inner peace and/or love. Ultimately, if the feelings are what you most want, then the specifics of *how* you experience those feelings are secondary.

Remember that from the narrow perspective of your mind, you can't see all the possibilities in terms of what lies ahead, nor the best way for your path to unfold so that you experience your optimal learning, contribution and access the happiness, inner peace and love available to you. That is why co-creation occurs throughout your life.

The most important things to do are:

a) set a clear vision;

b) take inspired action; and

c) remain completely open to how your life may unfold.

How do you remain completely open?

Stay alert to anything interesting, outside of the vision you hold, that comes across your path. And, totally detach from mandating that life look exactly like your Life Map. It is your mind that always wants to attach. It is your soul that wants to flow.

If your soul, and the infinite wisdom of highest consciousness, knows a better, more expansive set of outcomes or paths for you, trust that you will be guided toward them. You can only access that guidance if you remain open-minded and openhearted.

## 7 Strategies for Slippage

All effective plans for change require an acknowledgement that no path of transformation or achievement of any goal comes without its obstacles and stumbles. When you acknowledge that this is likely to happen because of your human nature, and because of the uncertainty and unpredictability of life, then you can be proactive about creating a strategy to deal with any such slippage.

No matter what may cause you to stumble on your path, be it due to the "fade-out and fade-in" transition between old and new beliefs, which means you waver on your journey from time to time, or whether it is a moment of being unable to implement and live from your new paradigm in terms of your choices and actions, or perhaps an external event, person or situation beyond your control throws a curve ball your way—there are only two core adjustments you need to make. You either adjust your way of being (your beliefs, thoughts and feelings) and/or you adjust your way of doing (your actions).

Here are seven suggested ways to make those adjustments, to lift you up if you feel like you have stumbled:

1) Letter of interruption

2) Soul language mantra

3) Speak to Your Soul guided meditation

4) Affirmations to uplift your thoughts and feelings

5) Reminding yourself of the one hundred and sixty six truths

6) Continuing to let go of newly discovered blocks

7) Revisiting your Life Map

## Letter of Interruption

There are times every person in life loses sight of one's true nature in such a way that results in a complete downward spiral, with no exit strategy in sight. Given that this may happen for you at some point, you can prepare for that moment now, so that when it happens then, you'll have a clearer path back to the anchored inner peace you've come to know.

One way is to write a letter to yourself—a letter about the truth, a letter of support and love, a letter that brings you back to a place of inner clarity, no matter what is happening in your life. The intention is that this letter will help you interrupt any negative cycle you get caught within, at a time when you may feel unable to help yourself.

Below is a letter template, which can be personalized by editing or adding to it as you wish. To download the template, please visit: www.PinchMeLiving.com/Unleash-Your-Life-Free-Resources

Alternatively, you can write your own letter to yourself from scratch. Trust your intuition—whatever comes out is what needs to be written.

Keep the letter in a journal or in a safe place where you will easily find it if it is needed. Alternatively, give the letter to a loved one you are likely to turn to in difficult times, and tell this individual that if you are ever distressed or stuck, that is the time to receive the letter back. See the letter as a powerful tool to help you stop your spin and regain perspective and empowerment.

*Dear [insert your name here],*

*It's me here. I'm writing to support you, because right now I know you are experiencing some form of challenge, difficulty, pain, frustration, hurt or sadness. It is quite possible that you are mentally and emotionally off-center; as a result, you may be unable to see your own true nature or the truths about life.*

*You wrote this letter to yourself, to read specifically at times like this. You knew that at some point, because of your inherent human nature and your soul journey evolving, that you might stumble in a way that caused you to get into a spin, which you felt you couldn't get out of on your own. You wrote this letter while in full balance, in full clarity and with full power, to remind you now of how wondrous you are and how life is one continuous flowing unfolding ... to remind you that sometimes unfolding looks like challenges and feels like pain. Remember that from every breakdown comes a breakthrough. Never forget that bright shining diamonds are forged under great pressure.*

*Remember that reaching out for support is one of the bravest and smartest things you can do. Read this letter, talk to loved ones, remind yourself of the truths, and feed yourself positive messages that will uplift you and return you to a state of inner peace.*

*Check in with yourself. Is your present life built around your life anchors? Or, have other priorities taken over? Now is the time to return to those life anchors—those uplifting rituals that you know make a big difference to your perspective and how you feel.*

*There is nothing wrong, with you or with your life. Stumbling is never regression. You are progressing whether you realize it or not. No matter how many times you stumble in life, you are always falling forward into your own continuing unfolding, and into the evolution of learning and contribution that your soul came for.*

*While you may not be happy right now, remember that no matter what you face in life, you can be at peace. Peace is a perspective. That perspective is available to you in any moment. It is available to you right now. Forget about the memories of past moments. Forget about future projections. Today, please allow yourself permission to do nothing more than simply be and breathe. Right now that is all that you are asked to do. It is all you need to do.*

*Just breathe.*

*You are infinitely connected to the source of all creation. You are beheld as the unique, magical individual you are. You are loved beyond measure. You are never alone.*

*With love,*

*[Insert your name here]*

## Soul Language Mantra

*I am living my life purpose by being the full expression of who I already am—without inhibition, without apology, without judgment.*

*I am here to learn and to contribute while doing so.*

*I give life to all of my passions.*

*I act upon all of my inspirations.*

*I follow my intuition.*

*I step forward into all opportunities.*

*This is all I need to focus on.*

*The rest of my life unfolds magically when I am a clear channel for my soul language to flow through me.*

To download a free audio of this mantra, which you can listen to as a ritual to support your soul-led life, please visit: www.PinchMeLiving.com/Unleash-Your-Life-Free-Resources

## Speak to Your Soul

To download a guided meditation audio that supports you consciously tuning into and speaking with the soul aspect of yourself through a relaxing visualization process, please visit: www.PinchMeLiving.com/Unleash-Your-Life-Free-Resources

## Uplift Your Thoughts and Feelings

You can utilize your own new belief statements that you created in Part II, in written or audio format, as affirmations to uplift your thoughts and feelings. You can read them or listen to them consistently and repetitively during times when you feel low. This will help to reorient your perspective.

You may also wish to utilize the free affirmation audios available at www.PinchMeLiving.com/Unleash-Your-Life-Free-Resources. Let these tools lift you up at times when you feel unable to help yourself.

## Reminding Yourself of the 166 Truths

You can review the written summary of the one hundred and sixty six truths in this book at any time, or download and listen to the truths audio at: www.PinchMeLiving.com/Unleash-Your-Life-Free-Resources

Doing so will counter old perspectives and habits, support the clearing of any fog you may still be experiencing and uplift you back into your creative and blossoming mode.

## Continue to Let Go of Any Newly Discovered Blocks

As you create and blossom, you may discover that your forward momentum brings to the surface other, yet undiscovered blocks within you. There is absolutely nothing wrong with this. You haven't missed anything. Sometimes it is actually the process of expansion that glaringly shows you remaining points of contraction. Sometimes it is your light that allows you to see new shadows. It is like peeling back the layers of an onion—you can only see what lies below, once you truly remove the layer above.

As you create and blossom, if you do feel like you are holding onto something you do not need or want in your life, please revisit the exercises in Part II to clear any remaining fog, to let go of what no longer serves you.

## Revisit Your Life Map to Realign

You might find that while your new paradigm is embedding and your beliefs, thoughts and feelings are predominantly working in your favor, you may not be taking the optimal types of actions, or be in action to the extent you need to be.

If you notice slippage on your journey, you can revisit your Life Map at any time to reflect on whether your current actions are reflective of the actual action plan you set for each of the eight areas in your Life Map.

You can then realign your actions to bring about the change you desire.

# CONCLUSION

At the core of who you are rests the entire universe. Every part of your physical and nonphysical self reflects the wisdom of highest consciousness, the divinity of all creation.

This is who you are. Nothing will ever change that. Everything else is noise. Tune it out and tune into the miracle of your very being.

You were born with exactly what you need to fulfill your highest possibilities. There is nothing you are missing.

You are a leader. The leader of your life. You have the courage to walk through all challenges. You have the wisdom within you to face all problems with peace. You have the light within you to guide the way out of darkness; not only for yourself but also for all those people you love in your life.

Nothing and no one can stop you from living your fullest life, now that you have consciously awoken. You chose to clear the fog and you are now a channel for your passions, inspirations and intuition to flow freely into this world.

Your unique expression is a blessing to this planet. The world needs you. The universe loves you dearly. The hour of your greatness is now.

# About the Author

Bernadette is an author, transformational coach, retreat leader and speaker. She works with clients internationally helping them to unleash their inner peace, freedom and success, both personally and professionally, using her exclusive 3-step *Unleash Your Life* method for achieving peak performance in life.

To connect with Bernadette, and for more information on private coaching, retreats, live events, as well as free resources, please visit www.PinchMeLiving.com.

### Also by the Author:

*Pinch Me–How Following the Signals Changed My Life*

*Going Out on a Limb–How Signals Led Me Beyond My Limits & Into Truth*

Made in the USA
Columbia, SC
17 August 2019